About the Author

Aged twenty-five, and after three years of active service in Burma, Richard Causton returned to England in 1945 with the realization that the world of his early youth had gone forever. The principles and beliefs on which he had been brought up, even the very existence of a loving and all-merciful God – all were in doubt.

In 1958 he seized the chance of early retirement from the army, where, in his last post in the War Office, he was compelled to face for the first time the use of nuclear weapons and their appalling potential. At thirty-eight he began a fresh career in business.

In the 1960s, his business travels took him back to the Far East, where he encountered Nichiren Shoshu Buddhism in Japan. He describes it as an electrifying experience. All that he heard and read seemed exactly to match the beliefs and conclusions towards which he had already been moving. He began to practise and in 1971, aged fifty-one, he made his final commitment to Nichiren Shoshu Buddhism.

In 1974 he returned to England to join the two hundred or so pioneer members practising here at that time. Three years later he gave up business to become the first permanent staff member of Nichiren Shoshu of the United Kingdom (NSUK). He has been Chairman and General Director of NSUK since 1975 and is Vice President of the Nichiren Shoshu European Institute, and Vice President of the international lay society known as Soka Gakkai International.

'the Buddha is life itself . . .'
Daisaku Ikeda

NICHIREN SHOSHU BUDDHISM

— AN INTRODUCTION —

Richard Causton

RIDER
LONDON SYDNEY AUCKLAND JOHANNESBURG

Rider
An imprint of Random Century Group Ltd
20 Vauxhall Bridge Road,
London SW1V 2SA

Random Century Australia (Pty) Ltd
20 Alfred Street, Milsons Point, Sydney NSW 2061,
Australia

Random Century New Zealand Ltd
18 Poland Road, Glenfield, Auckland 10,
New Zealand

Random Century South Africa (Pty) Ltd
PO Box 337, Bergvlei 2012, South Africa

First Published 1988
Reprinted 1989 (twice)
This edition 1991

British Library Cataloguing in Publication Data
Causton, Richard, *1920–*
Nichiren Shoshu.
1. Nichiren Shoshu Buddhism
I. Title
294.3'928

ISBN 0–7126–2269–1

Set in Linotron Baskerville by Deltatype, Ellesmere Port
Printed and bound in Great Britain by
The Guernsey Press Co. Ltd, Guernsey, Channel Islands.

This book is printed on recycled paper.

Contents

Acknowledgements

Due to my rather hectic schedule and frequent travels, I asked one of my fellow Buddhists, Edward Canfor-Dumas, if he would be willing to undertake writing the first draft manuscript of this book. As a professional writer, this might have been difficult for him, but he readily accepted, carrying out his task whole-heartedly, although it must sometimes have been irksome for him to have to accept the corrections and changes which I made. I thank him with all my heart for his patience, for without him this book could never have been completed in the time available.

I also wish to record my thanks to Pat Allwright, editor of NSUK's monthly publication, the *UK Express*, and to Barbara Cahill, for their invaluable comments on the manuscript, as well as to Oliver Caldecott of Century Hutchinson for his unfailing enthusiasm and warm encouragement.

Most important of all, I express deepest gratitude to Daisaku Ikeda, president of our worldwide lay society, Soka Gakkai International, who is my master/teacher in life and from whom I have learned *everything*.

Richard Causton

REFERENCES

The author gratefully acknowledges permission to quote from the following works:

Major Writings of Nichiren Daishonin, Vols. 1–4, Nichiren Shoshu International Center (NSIC), Tokyo, 1979/81/85/86.

By Daisaku Ikeda:

A Lasting Peace, Wetherhill, New York, 1981.

Before It Is Too Late (with Aurelio Peccei), Macdonald, London, 1984.

Buddhism and the Cosmos (with Masayoshi Kiguchi & Eiichi Shimura), Macdonald, London, 1985.

Buddhism in Action, Vols. 1–2, NSIC, Tokyo, 1984/85.

Human Values in a Changing World (with Bryan Wilson), Lyle Stuart, Seacaucus, 1984.

Life, An Enigma, a Precious Jewel, Kodansha, Tokyo, 1982.

Man Himself Must Choose (with Arnold Toynbee), Kodansha, Tokyo, 1976.

Selected Lectures on the Gosho, Vol. 1, NSIC, Tokyo, 1979.

Alexander Borbély (trans. Deborah Schneider), *The Secrets of Sleep*, Longman Scientific and Technical, London, 1987.

Jacob Bronowski, *The Ascent of Man*, BBC Enterprises, London, 1973.

Ronald W. Clark, *The Life of Bertrand Russell*, Jonathan Cape and Weidenfeld & Nicolson, London, 1975.

Paul Davies, *God and the New Physics*, Pelican, London, 1984.

Satoru Izumi, *Guidelines of Faith*, NSIC, Tokyo, 1980.

By Yasuji Kirimura:

Buddhism and the Nichiren Shoshu Tradition, NSIC, Tokyo, 1986.

Fundamentals of Buddhism, NSIC, Tokyo, 1977.

Outline of Buddhism (ed.), NSIC, Tokyo, 1981.

'The Three Calamities and Seven Disasters', *Seikyo Times* Special Issue, World Tribune Press, Santa Monica, 1986.

Primo Levi, *If This Is A Man/The Truce*, Abacus, London, 1987.

By Bertrand Russell:

A History of Western Philosophy, George Allen & Unwin, London, 1946.

Why I Am Not A Christian (ed. Paul Edwards), George Allen & Unwin, London, 1957.

Tom Wolfe, *The Right Stuff*, Jonathan Cape, London, 1979.

Preface

Despite all the advances made by science and technology during the past hundred years, we live in a world where human suffering has never been greater. It is estimated that, every day, some 40,000 children die of hunger or hunger-related diseases; that more than 750 million people in the world lack the nourishment to sustain a healthy life; that over seventy-two million people have been killed in armed conflicts this century, more than in all previous centuries put together; and that, since the end of the Second World War, there have been at least 212 armed conflicts, internal and international, of which at least forty are still being fought. Even in the wealthiest, most advanced countries, millions are unemployed, poverty and crime are increasing, and though more people are materially better off than ever before, the symptoms of inner suffering – divorce, drug and alcohol abuse, depression and suicide – are all escalating at an alarming rate.

Not only is there no clear solution in sight to this suffering but, in most areas, it seems destined to get worse. To take just one example, it has been calculated that, at the present rate of destruction, the world's tropical rain forests will have all but disappeared in, at most, fifty years' time, with all that that means for the delicate balance of the global climate and ecosystem.

One result of the increase in the scale of human suffering has been the increasing feeling of helplessness experienced by those who are at all concerned about the problems facing mankind. 'It's terrible, but what can *I* do?' is the reaction of many as news of yet another disaster reaches them. And, in truth, other than giving money to a variety of causes and appeals there does not seem much that ordinary people can do in the face of such enormous and complex problems as world starvation, environmental pollution or the threat of nuclear war. As a consequence they pin their hopes on politicians or special-interest groups to work for change on their behalf for, no matter how strongly people may feel about these issues, realistically only a very small minority can afford to devote themselves wholly to working for their solution. The vast majority have families to look after, jobs to do and bills to pay. Not only are these the immediate necessities, but they also take up most of the attention of most people, most of the time. The time, energy or money available for larger issues is, therefore, usually minimal. Add to this the fact that many of the world's problems seem to be somewhat remote, either in terms of distance or time, and one has a recipe for a downward spiral of decay. All in all, it is hard to disagree with Aurelio Peccei, late president of the Club of Rome, when he says:

> In spite of being miserable and afraid because of the non-peace we experience within ourselves and in our connections with almost everything around us, we seem unable to cease acting in ways that constantly aggravate our situation. Indeed, at no time in history has our globe been so gravely riven with endemic warfare, military and civil violence, widespread torture and terrorism, overt or incipient destruction and scientific preparation for still further havoc.

Strange as it may seem, the world's current predicament was foreseen some 3000 years ago by the Buddha, Shakyamuni. In contrast to the apocalyptic prophecies of some other religions, however, Shakyamuni also predicted that, out of the very confusion of this time, which he termed 'the beginning of the Latter Day of the Law', a great teaching would appear, based upon his own highest teaching, the Lotus Sutra. This teaching would enable ordinary people to develop the qualities necessary to combat the enormous problems that they would encounter. The essence of this teaching was later defined as *Nam-myoho-renge-kyo* by a thirteenth-century Japanese priest called Nichiren Daishonin ('Daishonin' meaning 'Great Sage'), and has been carried down unaltered through more than 700 years by Nichiren Shoshu, the orthodox school of Nichiren Daishonin's Buddhism.

Now, it may seem esoteric in the extreme to look to Buddhism as the answer to pressing and practical human difficulties, especially to a western mind brought up against a background of science and materialism. This would, however, be to misunderstand the true nature of Buddhist teachings for, as more and more people around the world are discovering, and as the experiences related in this book testify, the practice of Nichiren Shoshu Buddhism has a profound and revolutionary impact on ordinary, daily life; an impact which enables one to fully realize one's own unique potential and to develop the ability to create the greatest possible value in any situation. It is probably the down-to-earth nature of these teachings and their practical value in overcoming human problems in daily life that has caused this Buddhism to grow so steadily and strongly in more than a hundred countries in recent times.

For it is a basic premise of Nichiren Shoshu Buddhism that, just as human beings have tied the knot which is their current predicament, so they can untie it through developing the 'qualities of the Buddha': wisdom, courage, compassion and life-force. Buddhism teaches that these great qualities are latent in *everyone* and that the more ordinary people are able to develop them amid the, at times, harsh realities of their everyday lives, the greater the problems that they will be able to tackle – and eventually overcome.

It all begins with individuals deciding to take responsibility for their own individual lives, reforming first themselves and their immediate surroundings and relations, and then gradually extending their own wisdom, courage, compassion and life-force into a wider sphere.

Daisaku Ikeda, the president of Soka Gakkai International, the worldwide lay society of the Nichiren Shoshu Buddhist movement for peace, education and culture ('Soka Gakkai' means 'value creating society'), and to whose writings it is hoped this work will serve, in part, as an introduction, makes the following statement in the foreword to his book, *The Human Revolution*:

> A great revolution of character in just a single man will help achieve a change in the destiny of a nation and, further, will cause a change in the destiny of all mankind.

The practice of Nichiren Shoshu Buddhism involves the determination to undertake this transformation of your own character and to see it through to the very end, not only for your sake, but for the sake of your family, your society and, ultimately, your world. Just how you can begin on this great journey is the subject of this book.

Introduction

The basic practice of Nichiren Shoshu Buddhism consists of chanting the phrase *Nam-myoho-renge-kyo* to the Gohonzon, a scroll inscribed with many Chinese and two Sanskrit characters. This is supported by the daily practice of morning and evening *gongyo*, the recitation of two key chapters of the Lotus Sutra, followed by chanting *Nam-myoho-renge-kyo* 'to your heart's content'. If you do this, study and teach others the Buddhist view of life to the best of your ability, you will develop a state of life in which your desires are completely fulfilled, which creates the maximum value and good fortune for yourself and your society, and which is powered by unshakeable happiness and confidence, no matter what problems you may be facing. Nichiren Daishonin, the founder of this Buddhism, states: 'A law this easy to embrace and this easy to practise was taught for the sake of all mankind in this evil Latter Day of the Law.'

This may sound incredible – not only in the sense of being too good to be true but, literally, unbelievable. How can chanting a phrase one does not even understand, over and over again to a piece of paper, possibly have such an effect? What does *Nam-myoho-renge-kyo* mean, anyway, and what is so special about this scroll, the Gohonzon? These are good questions, just a few of the many that will doubtless arise, and hopefully be answered, in the course of reading this book. For now, suffice it to say that perhaps the most challenging aspect of Nichiren Shoshu Buddhism is the way that it forces one to re-examine fundamental assumptions about the nature of life in general, and our own lives in particular. These assumptions are probably so deeply rooted that you may not even be aware you hold them. For example, consider the problem of suffering.

No one wants to suffer. But much as we would all like to live a totally happy life, suffering is an inescapable fact of our human existence. The observation that 'Man is born unto trouble, as sparks fly upward' may not have been much consolation to Job but, nevertheless, remains an uncomfortable truth. Generally speaking, sufferings arise through our encounter with problems and difficulties; this is why much of our time is spent trying to avoid them, even though they are inherent in life. In trying to avoid problems, however, we are often simply putting off the inevitable to a future date, by which time the trouble has usually grown much more difficult to resolve. Personal relationships are a good example of this. The failure to tackle a problem between two people – a clash of desires, for instance – usually for fear of not knowing what the consequences will be, or perhaps simply because of a dislike of conflict, can very easily lead to a build-up of resentments which, when finally expressed, can be immensely destructive. The story of the 'mild-mannered' civil servant who, in 1987, was jailed for strangling his wife after twenty-six years of marriage, ostensibly because she simply moved his favourite mustard from its usual place at the dinner table, is an extreme, but true, example of this.

One of the natural consequences of the close link between problems and suffering is that people tend to confuse the one with the other. For example, if you are unemployed, it is very probable that you are also unhappy; you will probably think you are unhappy because you are unemployed. While it might very well be true that you would probably be happier in work than out of it (though this is debatable, in view of the number of people who complain about their jobs), strictly speaking your unhappiness is not because you are unemployed but, rather, because you feel helpless in being unable to find a job. In other words, it is not so much our problems which cause us to suffer as our inability to overcome them.

This may seem like splitting hairs but, in reality, the difference is fundamental. Problems that we feel confident we can solve, even if only after a great deal of time and effort, we label very differently as 'challenges'. In short, whether our problems are sources of suffering or sources of growth depends entirely on our attitude, both to the problem and to ourselves.

This point was once made in a graphic way to a member of Nichiren Shoshu of the United Kingdom (NSUK) who, soon after starting to practise this Buddhism, found himself in Japan. He decided to ask for guidance from a vice-president of the Soka Gakkai (Japan's equivalent of NSUK). As he walked into the vice-president's office, he was immediately ordered to lift a large table standing near the door. Somewhat surprised at this greeting he nevertheless tried to oblige. As the table was made of solid brass with thick marble legs, after two or three attempts he shook his head apologetically. 'I'm sorry, I can't,' he said. 'It's too heavy.' 'No,' the vice-president corrected him. 'It's not too heavy – you're too weak. The table's weight is the table's problem. The fact that you can't lift it is yours.' In other words, the vice-president wanted to make the point, straightaway, that, whatever the NSUK member had come to see him about, it is important to remember that our natural tendency as human beings is always to find reasons outside ourselves, in our environment, to excuse what are really our own shortcomings.

Nichiren Shoshu Buddhism teaches that it is our fundamental attitude to problems and the suffering which usually accompanies them that determines the extent to which we win or lose in creating a happy life. The Chinese, for example, write the word 'crisis' using two characters, one of which means 'danger', the other 'opportunity'. The crucial issue, then, is whether or not we can recognize the opportunity amidst the danger. Daisaku Ikeda writes:

> Society is complex and harsh, demanding that you struggle hard to survive. No one can make you happy. Everything depends on you as to whether or not you attain happiness . . . A human being is destined to a life of great suffering if he is weak and vulnerable to his external surroundings.

Of course, this is not to deny the gravity and scale of some of the problems facing mankind today. Starvation in the Third World, the threat of nuclear war, the escalating pace of the destruction of the natural environment – these are not going to disappear overnight simply because people start to think about them in a different way. Neither is it possible to deny the real physical suffering of someone with a painful illness. Even so, the nature of any problem relates directly to our own strength: when we are weak, our problems seem large, even insuperable; when we are strong, they appear to be small.

The real question, then, is how to make ourselves stronger. The answer that Nichiren Shoshu Buddhism gives is that, when we chant about our problems, we can use the very sufferings we are trying to overcome to help us grow. This may sound strange but, from the viewpoint of this Buddhism, sufferings – whether personal, social or those facing mankind as a whole – are not just inevitable: they are *essential*. In other words, problems are the very means by which people can develop their full potential as human beings. As Nichiren Daishonin says, 'Only by defeating a powerful enemy can one prove his real strength.'

This idea will be explained more fully in the following chapters but, to put it simply, the highest teachings of Buddhism show how the desire to overcome suffering can be one of the greatest incentives for progress. The development of medical science is perhaps the most obvious example of this, but one can also point to the principle at work in the development of whole countries: the suffering caused by periodic famines in India, for example, forced the nation's agronomists to tackle the basic problems of food production; they have solved this to the extent that India is now not only self-sufficient in food but also a net exporter.

When it comes to personal suffering the principle works in a more particularized way, one which responds to the individual's unique circumstances. Stewart Anderson, for instance, first encountered Nichiren Daishonin's Buddhism in 1980 in a pub: 'I was intrigued by this man's attitude to life and his insight and wisdom about situations. His life was such a mess but there was a calmness. He seemed to be in control of it and that was what inspired me about the practice. I chanted for about six months before I decided to receive the Gohonzon.'

It was two years later, during an NSUK summer study course, that Stewart first developed symptoms of AIDS. 'On that course I began to see my tendencies to escape, to be irresponsible, and on the third day I couldn't get out of bed. The course doctor said I should return to London. That was when I got the first insight into how cared for and protected we are in this organization. I felt everything would be all right because I had the organization of which I was proud to be part.'

At first no one could discover what was wrong with him. In the early eighties AIDS was known simply as the 'gay syndrome' and, apart from NSUK and his Buddhist practice, Stewart had nowhere and nothing to turn to for support as his energy began to fade, his glands became swollen and spots broke out all over his body. One thing he discovered, though, was that the progress of the then mystery disease seemed to be directly related to the strength of his practice – the less he did, the worse it became. About a year after his sickness became manifest, a senior NSUK leader wrote to give him some strict but necessary guidance about his lack of constancy:

> I feel concerned about your tendency to slip every so often so far as your practice is concerned. There is no room for this if you are to have a happy life in the future. Day in and day out you must never give in or allow the negative forces [in your life] to take over. If you attack your sickness in this unrelenting way you will win a victory . . . Attack! Attack! Attack! That should be your motto until your life is totally transformed . . . Then you are a true disciple of Nichiren Daishonin.

The significance of this letter was not clear to Stewart in those early days of his illness: 'I didn't realize this guidance was going to save my life. I still wasn't aware of the fragility of life. I was still trying to avoid my karma, the destiny I had created for myself, and was still trying to defy the law of cause and effect. This was my escapist nature.'

The Buddhist concept of karma will be discussed in more detail later but, put simply, it teaches that the effects we experience in the present are the inevitable results of causes we have made in the past, either in this lifetime or over many previous lifetimes. Similarly, the causes we make now will determine the nature of the future we will either enjoy or suffer. In Stewart's case it was not until AIDS was finally diagnosed in 1985, after the appearance of the first spots of Kaposi's sarcoma, a rare form of skin cancer, that he finally began to change his attitude to his own karma and, with it, his life. Surprising as it may seem, what could have been taken as very bad news had the opposite effect, as he explains: 'This official diagnosis was the biggest benefit I have had from this practice. It wasn't enough to be told that I had AIDS through a blood test – I had to see the physical manifestations. I felt I could identify the karma. I needed something like that to take my life seriously. It made me aware of the spiritual aspect and power of my life. At times I was disillusioned but I always felt gratitude to be alive. I just had to keep going. I had never felt gratitude before. Now I say thank you every morning for being able to change my karma. It was a distinct turning-point because before I was just trying to get away from life.'

But having finally taken the decision to join battle with his disease Stewart then had to take the necessary action – which was far from easy: 'I had to get in tune with myself – and the truth hurts. I realized I was scared of winning, of succeeding, of taking a gamble. I never thought of death as a problem but I was scared to demand the cancer out of my life *now*. In 1986 it got to the point where living with cancer was settling with second-best. It was eating my life-force and I felt sometimes that I would rather be dead. I was not interacting with society. I had a self-centred practice and I didn't feel that I was living. I was going wrong somewhere. I set myself a challenge: to chant for seven hours for seven days. I needed to prove that if I set my mind on something I could do it. I had read great experiences about other members in the NSUK magazine, the *UK Express*, but I didn't believe that I, personally, had Buddha nature, the supreme state of life.

'Until this chanting session I had been following a macrobiotic diet and swimming, trying to get a balanced life. But more cancer was appearing. Then I realized I had been looking outside myself for my happiness and security. Now I felt sure that the way forward lay in the spiritual side of my life. I distributed a hundred notices of this chanting session, inviting people to support me, and during it I chanted for good health and happiness so that I could work for a peaceful world based on this Buddhism, rather that just to cure myself of AIDS, which had become the focus of my life. And I treated this chanting session as life and death: if I couldn't complete it, I thought, I might as well be dead.'

Throughout the seven days of chanting Stewart was ill and exhausted. 'But spiritually I was so alive! I couldn't go to hospital because people were coming over to chant with me. On the last day I led *gongyo* with forty people. It was so dynamic, and during the last half-hour of chanting I knew I had the universe behind me. Since that activity I have never looked back. I had complete conviction that I was drawing on everything in the universe. The real question was whether I dared ask for it.'

His biggest battle was with the pneumonia he contracted over the Christmas of 1986. Pneumonia is the largest single killer of AIDS sufferers and, when it struck, Stewart spent three days entirely alone, too weak to move, until his father found him and rushed him to hospital. 'It was there that I had to let go. I didn't know what was happening. I just had to trust. When I was in hospital another senior member of NSUK came to see me. He brought a big bunch of flowers and was beaming. Everyone else seemed scared, as if I was going to die. I was physically sick, but spiritually I was very much alive and well. I felt I had to get out of that bed: I had articles to do for the *Observer* and the *UK Express*. And I had to go to Japan to apologize for my past causes and express my gratitude in front of the Dai-Gohonzon [the original Gohonzon inscribed by Nichiren Daishonin]. I had a mission and a purpose and that was why I survived. There was simply no time to die. I had always felt tremendous pressure to cure AIDS, to change my karma and the karma of AIDS sufferers everywhere. I feel proud to have such a purpose. The doctors at the hospital notice this and ask me what I do. I tell them I chant. The Buddhist attitude is noticed because I am taking control of my life.

'It's easy to give up with AIDS because your body is failing you. I do understand why people give up. You can easily develop your own sense of isolation, a sense of being a victim. I want to cure this disease so I can go on to my next life. I want to break my bad karma and die with peace and dignity, with all this behind me.'

Sadly, after a courageous battle with his illness, Stewart did die, in September 1987. One might be forgiven for thinking that, because he did not overcome his disease, he was ultimately defeated, but, as we shall see later in the section on the Buddhist view of life and death, this is to regard death from too narrow a perspective. Even if one does not believe in the eternity of life, it is an undeniable fact that, through his practice of this Buddhism, Stewart was able to both prolong and improve the quality of his life. A passage from a letter Nichiren Daishonin wrote in 1279 on this very subject inspired Stewart through much of his struggle. It reads:

A single life is worth more than the universe. You still have many years ahead of you and, moreover, you have found the Lotus Sutra. If you live even one day longer, you can accumulate that much more good fortune. How precious life is!

Stewart's comment on this passage is revealing: 'This letter is about living one day at a time, with gratitude. By chanting today I am making the causes to chant tomorrow: therefore, what great joy to be chanting! When I came out of hospital on New Year's Eve I was very, very weak. I couldn't stand up for three minutes at a time. This changes your attitude to life. Each breath is precious.'

Moreover, as one of the UK's longest-surviving AIDS patients, Stewart felt a special responsibility to try to instill hope into the millions of people who doctors predict will die before a cure to this disease is found. Through being featured in a single article in the *Observer*, he had many offers to transmit this hope through books, documentaries and the radio. These words, culled from the article he wrote for the *UK Express* not long before he died, serve as a fitting testimony to his fighting spirit:

You see people suffering and they don't have to. Suffering is not the real issue. People forget that we have this choice, that life really is in our hands. When you struggle it's important to remember that you've chosen your karma, that you've created it. Through challenging AIDS I have been able to take responsibility for my life. When I die it will be a celebration of how precious my life is.

Stewart Anderson's experience is an example of the principle known in Buddhism as 'turning poison into elixir': in other words, taking what to all appearances is a terrible situation and making the best of it – literally; not just in the sense of cheerful and stoic endurance but, through the practice of this Buddhism, using the situation to progress far beyond our original starting-point, so that we end up much happier and more fulfilled – in every way – than when we began. It is also an example which strikingly illustrates the Chinese concept of 'crisis' mentioned earlier: that opportunity exists even in the midst of danger.

To many it may seem startling that there exists a form of Buddhism which, though based on a teaching thousands of years old, nevertheless has a direct and practical application to such a modern problem as AIDS. The fact that such a form of Buddhism does exist probably means that a number of ideas about this religion held in the West will have to be revised. It is not difficult, however, to see how these ideas have grown up, so it is worthwhile pausing for a moment to examine them.

Buddhism has not been clearly understood in the West for three main reasons: the history of the spread of Buddhist teachings to the West; the inherent difficulty posed by many of those teachings; and the difficulties posed by their sheer number.

To start with history, the Buddhism first encountered by travellers from Europe was the type called Hinayana.* This form of Buddhism, once dominant in India and still the main religion of Sri Lanka and south-east Asia, follows the earlier teachings of Shakyamuni, Buddhism's historical founder, and places great emphasis on a strict and highly detailed code of personal conduct. So strict is Hinayana in its pure form that it is impossible to follow while living in the everyday world. For example, some Hinayana priests rigorously observe 250 commandments for each of the four acts of walking, standing, sitting and lying, totalling 1000 commandments in all. As one might expect, therefore, Hinayana Buddhism has a marked tendency towards monasticism, as monks are the only people who can afford the time and effort to wholly devote themselves to it.

As many statues of the Buddha and countless bodhisattvas originally found in Hinayana temples now fill our museums, Hinayana is probably the form of Buddhism best known in the West; for some people it has even created the impression that Buddhism involves the worship of idols. Moreover, since the application of Hinayana Buddhism to daily life is limited, its appeal to date has been mainly as a subject for academic study. This has naturally tended to reinforce the idea, already inherent in the Hinayana form, that Buddhism is primarily concerned

*Literally, the 'lesser vehicle', 'vehicle' indicating a teaching or means to 'carry' people to enlightenment. About a century after Shakyamuni's death schisms began to form within the community of monks that he had established; these subsequently divided into two schools. The conservative Theravada school, later termed Hinayana by Mahayana Buddhists, held strictly to doctrine and practice as originally formulated.

with intellectual abstraction, a means of escaping from the material side of life into 'a higher reality' through various forms of physical and mental discipline.

The other main stream of Buddhist thought, called Mahayana,* flowed northwards from India through Tibet and China to Korea and Japan. This stresses the need for Buddhism to be a religion of the common people, capable of helping them tackle the day-to-day realities of living; it is much less well known and understood in the West. The little that is known relates to what has been termed 'provisional' Mahayana Buddhism which, in some sutras, resembles certain aspects of Christianity, teaching as it does of mythical 'pure lands' in the eastern or western parts of the universe and salvation through the offices of legendary Buddhas and bodhisattvas. Of true Mahayana Buddhism (so called because Shakyamuni told his disciples to discard all his previous teachings, the essence of which are contained in the one supreme teaching of the Lotus Sutra), very little is known at all. In addition, the attention that yoga, transcendental meditation, the Hari Krishna and Japanese Zen sect have all attracted in Europe and America in recent times has further confused the picture, to the extent that many people now have vague notions that these disciplines are virtually interchangeable and, since they are all originally from the Orient, are all 'something to do with Buddhism'.

This confusion as to the true nature of Buddhism has been further compounded by the fact that, theoretically, its doctrines are often very difficult to understand. It would probably be fair to say that the overriding popular image of Buddhism is that of an abstruse, complex and mystical teaching of 'the meaning of life', one which is studied in monkish isolation, practised in silent meditation and whose goal is 'inner peace' as an end in itself. In short, most people believe that Buddhism, being ineffably profound, can be understood fully only by highly dedicated intellectuals.

Even leaving aside the emphasis laid for historical reasons on the Hinayana form of Buddhism, it is easy to see why this image of Buddhism should have arisen in the West. In simple terms, Buddhism is a philosophy which explains how life works and how

*Literally, the 'greater vehicle'. The Mahayana teachings are so called because they are not only concerned with individual salvation but stress the importance of leading *all* people to enlightenment.

one can live it happily and creatively. Since life itself is anything but simple, and as the teachings of Buddhism have evolved gradually over the past 3000 years or so, they naturally mirror this complexity, at times even saying things which seem to be completely contradictory. Especially challenging is the teaching of the Lotus Sutra in which Shakyamuni describes what it means to be enlightened. Before he does so, though, he warns that what he is about to explain will not be easy: 'Among all the sutras I have preached, now preach, and will preach, this Lotus Sutra is the most difficult to believe and the most difficult to understand.' In fact, it would be fair to say that the difficulties posed by many Buddhist teachings have meant either that they have been largely ignored, as in the case of the Lotus Sutra, or that gradually the focus of attention has tended to move further and further from the true intention of the teaching to a wholly intellectual examination of doctrinal theory.

Indeed, there is a story about Shakyamuni which, although apocryphal, aptly highlights the awareness within Buddhism itself of the pitfalls of mere intellectualizing. While walking one day in the Deer Park at Benares, Shakyamuni comes across a deer lying on the ground, a hunter's arrow in its side. Clearly dying, the deer is being watched by two Brahmans who are discussing the exact moment at which life leaves the body and speculating on the nature of life after death. Seeing Shakyamuni, and knowing him to be a man of wisdom, they ask his opinion. Shakyamuni immediately crosses to the deer and pulls the arrow out.

In other words, the true spirit of Buddhism has always been more concerned with providing fundamental and *practical* solutions to the problems of suffering than with debating points of philosophy. In this sense, the whole theoretical framework of Buddhist doctrine is simply a by-product of the basic desire to relieve human misery, despair and confusion. This is not to say that the philosophical framework is superfluous – far from it – but simply to emphasize that compassionate action is the prime point of all Buddhist teachings. In the study of Buddhism, then, it is vital to remember that theory is important only as the basis for action – action taken for the sake of oneself and for the sake of others.

The story of Shakyamuni's own enlightenment underlines this

point. According to the traditional version of the beginnings of Buddhism, Shakyamuni lived roughly 3000 years ago in northern India. Born a prince of the Shakya caste and originally called Siddhartha Gautama, Shakyamuni grew up in regal luxury. It had been prophesied before his birth, however, that he would never inherit the throne but, rather, was destined to become a man of great wisdom. His father, Shuddhodana, therefore saw to it that the young prince would never be tempted to leave by coming into contact with the world outside the palace walls. One day, however, Shakyamuni found himself at one of the four gates to the palace and happened to see a man bent by old age. He said nothing but next day, at another gate, came across a cripple; the next day, at the third gate, he saw a corpse; and on the fourth day, at the last gate, he met a religious ascetic. Greatly disturbed by these four encounters Shakyamuni determined to leave the palace to search for the solution to what he had come to realize were the four inescapable sufferings of life: birth (into this troubled world), old age, sickness and death.

At first he sought out the foremost spiritual teachers of his day and practised the extreme forms of asceticism they advocated as the means to realize the ultimate reality of life. After following their teachings for a number of years, and on the point of death from fasting, Shakyamuni realized that their path to enlightenment was useless. Instead, after regaining his health and strength, he sat down under a pipal tree, entered a state of profound meditation and finally attained enlightenment. Thereafter, he began at once to teach to anyone who would listen.

As the depth of his understanding far surpassed that of even the most learned men of his day, however, he had to prepare his listeners by first teaching them more easily understandable doctrines, often using parables and everyday analogies in the process. In this way Shakyamuni was gradually able to elevate the life-condition of those he taught, while always holding to his ultimate aim (achieved towards the end of his life when he preached the Lotus Sutra) of showing to all people that they themselves – without exception – inherently possessed Buddhahood, the highest state of life, and so could develop the qualities needed to conquer their sufferings. As he says in the Lotus Sutra:

> This is my constant thought:
> how I can cause all living beings
> to gain entry to the highest way
> and quickly attain Buddhahood.

In Buddhism, this spirit of universal and impartial compassion is called *jihi,* comparable in some ways to the function of love in Christianity. Literally, *ji* means to remove suffering and *hi* means to give fundamental happiness. Implicit in the concept of *jihi,* then, is an emphasis upon action.

Shakyamuni wanted to discover the solution to the problems of birth, old age, sickness and death, and so took the necessary action to reach the understanding of life he sought. Once he had attained enlightenment he spent the rest of his life among the people, actively passing on what he had learnt and ensuring that his teachings would be transmitted to posterity. In this light, the idea that Buddhism is something that is the special preserve of wise men meditating on mountain tops begins to look a little misplaced.

In view of the enormous number and diversity of Buddhist teachings currently extant, it is perhaps scarcely surprising that such erroneous ideas have developed. Indeed, confusion as to the true nature of Buddhism has even reigned at various times in the Orient itself. In some ways, the situation in which the West finds itself today is similar to that of the Chinese in the second and third centuries AD, when first faced with a vast body of different Buddhist sutras and treatises. To solve the problem, the leading minds of the time set to work comparing and systematizing the various teachings; eventually, a priest called Chih-i (later named the Great Teacher T'ien-t'ai) developed a definitive standard, known as the Five Periods and Eight Teachings, by which to judge them.

This standard classified Shakyamuni's teachings according to the chronological order in which he expounded them, the nature of the particular doctrine taught in each sutra and the method of its exposition. By comparing the various sutras in this way T'ien-t'ai came to realize that not only did Shakyamuni's teachings expound doctrines of different levels of profundity according to the nature, intellectual capacity and circumstances of his audience, but that all the sutras were a means of preparing his followers for what Shakyamuni himself declared was his highest teaching, the Lotus Sutra. This sutra, which he taught for the final eight years of his life, is the only one which teaches that *all* people – be they good or evil, men or women, intellectuals or simple peasants – have the inherent potential for enlightenment and can become Buddhas in their present lifetimes. As Nichiren Daishonin says, 'In Buddhism, that teaching is judged supreme which enables all people, good or evil, to become Buddhas. So reasonable a standard can surely be grasped by anyone.' Needless to say, the principles and theories discussed in this book have all been developed on the basis of the Lotus Sutra, by great masters of Buddhist thought, most particularly by T'ien-t'ai (538-97) and Nichiren Daishonin (1222-82).

Indeed, it was Nichiren Daishonin who took the final all-important step to transform profound theory into practical action and, thereby, enable ordinary people, within their own lifetime, to reveal their highest state of life in the midst of day-to-day reality. His realization of the nature of the Buddhist practice which would achieve this is the reason why he is known as the 'true' or 'original' Buddha, whose mission it was to reveal this ultimate truth to the people when the right time had come. According to the Lotus Sutra, that time is now and will last for 'ten thousand years and more', on into eternity. In other words, this means that Nichiren Daishonin is the Buddha for our present age, for whom Shakyamuni and T'ien-t'ai prepared the way.

Bearing these points in mind, and before we go on to discuss in more detail the Buddhist view of life, it is important to mention a central feature of Buddhism which sets it apart from a religion such as Christianity (with which most people in the West have at least a passing familiarity), namely, its atheism.

At heart, the difference between the two religions lies in their respective explanations of the nature of the primary force of the universe and how we, as human beings, relate to it. Christianity teaches the existence of an all-powerful and all-seeing God. In contrast, Buddhism asserts the existence of a universal Law of life, expressed as *Nam-myoho-renge-kyo*. Of course, it must be admitted that the Christian idea of God has evolved considerably from the Yahweh of the ancient tribes of Israel and that, to some Christians today, God is not a being in any real sense but, rather, an abstract force with certain similarities to the Buddhist concept of the universal Law. Even so, the implications of this basic difference between the two religions are far-reaching.

Fundamentally, Christianity teaches that there is an unbridgeable gulf between humanity and God for, even if one is taken into His grace, a human being can never actually become God or his equal. In contrast, Buddhism teaches that all people have the inherent potential to attain the supreme life-condition of Buddhahood in this lifetime and, indeed, that the prime purpose of a Buddha is to awaken ordinary people to, and then teach them how to bring forth, their Buddha nature. In the Lotus Sutra, for example, Shakyamuni states, 'At the start I pledged to make all people perfectly equal to me, without any distinction between us,' and, throughout his writings, Nichiren Daishonin is at pains to convince his followers that Buddhahood is not the exclusive possession of the Shakyamuni who died over 2000 years before, but that they all have it too. He says, 'We common mortals can see neither our own eyebrows, which are so close, nor heaven in the distance. Likewise, we do not see that the Buddha exists in our own hearts.'

Buddhism explicitly denies the existence of a force external to human life. As Nichiren Daishonin states in *On Attaining Buddhahood*, one of his most famous writings:

> You must never seek any of Shakyamuni's teachings or the Buddhas and bodhisattvas of the universe outside yourself. Your mastery of the Buddhist teachings will not relieve you of mortal sufferings in the least unless you perceive the nature of your own life. If you seek enlightenment outside yourself, any discipline or good deed will be meaningless. For example, a poor man cannot earn a penny just by counting his neighbour's wealth, even if he does so night and day.

The implication of this denial is that, ultimately, human beings are totally responsible for their own destinies. The ramifications of this throw into sharp relief the differences between the teachings of Christianity, centred on God, and those of Buddhism, centred on the human being.

For example, while both doctrines stress the importance of prayer as a means of relating to either God or the universal Law, the attitude behind the prayer differs markedly. In Christianity, prayer is essentially an act of humility: one tries to discover and carry out God's will here on earth and asks for His help, inspiration or forgiveness in the face of the problems and sufferings one might encounter.

In Nichiren Daishonin's Buddhism, prayer takes the form of chanting *Nam-myoho-renge-kyo*, which reveals one's inherent Buddhahood, the highest state of one's life. In other words, rather than asking for help from without, whilst chanting you summon up courage and wisdom from within your own life in order to confront and overcome any problem you may be facing. In addition to this, by chanting *Nam-myoho-renge-kyo* you reveal the Law in your own life, thereby putting yourself in harmony, or rhythm, with the universal Law. To explain further, Buddhism teaches that everything in the universe is an expression of this Law and acts in accordance with it. 'Law' here is used in the scientific rather than the legal sense, in that we 'obey' the Law of *Nam-myoho-renge-kyo* in the same way that we 'obey' the law of gravity. If we act contrary to the law of gravity – by walking off a tall building, say – we usually suffer grave consequences. Similarly, if we go against the Law of life – for example, by denying cause and effect, a central aspect of this Law – eventually, and inevitably, we will end up suffering.

To pursue the analogy a little further, although the law of gravity may seem to be obvious, young children clearly have very little idea of it, which is why they sometimes wander perilously close to the edge of danger, totally unafraid, while their parents suffer fits of consternation. A child's understanding of, and respect for, this basic physical law only comes as it grows older and its consciousness develops. In a similar way, without a clear understanding of the Law of *Nam-myoho-renge-kyo*, people wander perilously close to the edge of suffering – and, as often as not, fall into it. This is one reason why it is so important that we should learn of the existence of this Law, because even if we do not understand theoretically what it means, or how it works, we can put ourselves in rhythm with it simply through chanting *Nam-myoho-renge-kyo*. In this way, and quite naturally, we can begin to use this universal Law to create value for ourselves and others, and gradually come to understand it. As Daisaku Ikeda explains:

Birds fly about high in the sky. Yet it does not happen that two birds collide with one another. Again, many fish live in the sea. Yet it is unheard of for two fish to bump into each other. In the immense breadth of the sky and sea, birds and fish live and move about freely because of their instinctive knowledge of the routes of the sky and the sea as well as the principles that govern the processes of flight and swimming.

In the same way, when living in accordance with the Law in the depths of life, human beings will not uselessly collide with one another. They will not come into conflict with each other on account of minor negative feelings such as jealousy, hatred and arrogance, thus creating unhappiness and misfortune for themselves. Therefore, when we chant *Nam-myoho-renge-kyo* with deep faith, we call forth the power to be able to develop a noble life-condition and to respect and cherish one another with a mind as vast as the sky and the sea.

But if we do not need to understand *Nam-myoho-renge-kyo* to benefit from chanting it, Buddhism does not teach the necessity of blind faith. On the contrary, a theoretical understanding is vital if we are to get the most from our practice. In the same way, we do not need to understand how a motor car works to be able to benefit from driving it: all we need to know is how to drive it properly. Nevertheless, if we do know what happens under the bonnet, when we run into problems we can easily get going again. It is all the more important to have this understanding when the 'car' that we are driving happens to be our own life.

Nichiren Daishonin explains that there are actually three different ways in which one can understand, evaluate and judge any religious or philosophical teaching; these are termed the Three Proofs. The first of these is 'documentary proof', referring to the actual written evidence of the teaching. The documentary proof of Christianity, for example, is the Bible, that of Islam the Koran, that of Buddhism the sutras, and so on.

The second is called 'theoretical proof', and means the extent to which the doctrine in question adequately explains the reality of life as it is generally understood at that point in time. Thus, for a long while, Christianity explained in Genesis how God had created the universe in six days and that Adam and Eve were the forebears of the human race, cast out of the Garden of Eden for disobedience to God. Right up to the time of Darwin's theory of evolution, the cosmogony of Genesis was taken in the West as the 'Gospel truth' – literally – and indeed there are still some fundamentalist Christians who prefer the Bible's explanation to that of science. The important point about theoretical proof, however, is that it should offer a coherent and consistent explanation of the subject in question.

Most religions and philisophies stop at these two proofs, but Nichiren Daishonin adds a third – 'actual proof'. In terms of religion, this means examining what the actual effect is of putting into practice the theoretical doctrine. In other words, does it work? Many religions demand 'faith' from their adherents to plug the gaps in doctrinal explanations that cannot be demonstrated – for example, that when we die we will go to heaven or hell – so that 'faith' in an afterlife, say, equates to a profound belief or trust in something essentially unprovable. In Nichiren Shoshu Buddhism, however, to have faith means to take action – that is, to practise; profound belief in the theory comes only as a result of seeing actual proof or benefit, the effects of practice. To give an analogy, say someone you know recommends a film, which you decide to see. Essentially, going to see the film is an act of faith in your friend's judgement. If it is as good as your friend said it was, your faith in her will be deepened. On the other hand, if the film is terrible you are less likely to trust her judgement the next time she recommends a film. Either way, your actual experience of the film is what affects your future action.

Of the three proofs, then, Nichiren Daishonin states that the third is by far the most important for, no matter how wonderful a theory one expounds, unless it can enable those practising it to overcome their sufferings, in reality it is little better than useless. To return to our analogy of the motor car, documentary proof might correspond to a salesman's brochure describing the latest model; theoretical proof could be the salesman explaining how the widget in the engine has improved the performance of this car over every car that has ever been known; and actual proof would be seeing what happens when you turn the key in the ignition. If nothing happens, nothing the salesman says will convince you that the car is not a dud. Significantly, it is this emphasis on actual proof that brings Nichiren Shoshu Buddhism very close to scientific method: all three proofs are automatically applied to all scientific theories but, in the end, it is demonstrable proof that determines which are valid and which are not.

Even so, understanding the theory of the Buddhist view of life underpins the practice of chanting *Nam-myoho-renge-kyo*. As Nichiren Daishonin says: 'Exert yourself in the two ways of practice and study. Without practice and study, there can be no Buddhism.' With that thought in mind, let us examine some of the basic principles of Buddhism, principles which have been distilled from the experience of mankind over a period of some 3000 years and which, thanks to their perfect clarification by Nichiren Daishonin, can be directly applied to the everyday reality of ordinary people living now.

Part One
The Buddhist View of Life

'Buddhism is reason.'
Nichiren Daishonin

1

The Ten Worlds

Imagine it is Monday morning. The alarm has just gone off, waking you from a deep and peaceful sleep. With a groan you drag yourself out of bed and pull the curtains. It is raining. You get dressed and go into the kitchen where you put the kettle on, feed the cat, then settle down to your own breakfast. You note with interest from the back of the cereal packet that your bowl of corn flakes provides at least a quarter of an average adult's recommended daily intake of vitamins niacin, B_1, B_2, B_6, B_{12} and D and, just then, hear the flap of the letterbox rattle. There are two letters – one from the electricity board, the other from the tax office. Fearing the worst, you decide to open the electricity bill first. It is enormous. In fact, it is outrageous. Deciding that those stupid bureaucrats at the electricity board must have made a mistake, you resolve to write them a stiff letter the minute you get to work. But then, it was a very cold winter and you did leave the heating on most of the night, most of the time. Your heart sinks. They might be right after all. And if they are, there goes your summer holiday. Feeling very depressed, you open the ominous brown envelope from the Inland Revenue and – a tax rebate! More than enough to pay the electricity bill, right or wrong, and have plenty left over for the holiday. You whoop for joy and go off to work, oblivious of the pouring rain . . .

Apart from the tax rebate, perhaps, the passage above could be said to describe a perfectly ordinary, average morning, one experienced (with variations) by millions of people every day throughout the country. In the course of this short vignette, however, you have experienced nine of the Ten Worlds.

The Ten Worlds, or Ten States of Life, an absolutely fundamental principle of Buddhism, teaches that everybody possesses ten basic inner states of being which we all experience from moment to moment. Briefly, these Ten Worlds are Hell, Hunger, Animality, Anger, Tranquillity, Rapture, Learning, Realization, Bodhisattva and Buddhahood. To explain a little further, Hell is the state of suffering; Hunger is the state of being under the sway of desires; Animality is the state of instinctive behaviour; and Anger is the state of constant competition or conflict, in which one tries arrogantly to surpass others. The first three are called the Three Evil Paths and, together with Anger, comprise the Four Evil Paths – varying conditions of unhappiness. Tranquillity is the neutral state of peace and calm, and Rapture is the state of being temporarily overjoyed at the gratification of a desire. The six states from Hell to Rapture are called the Six Paths and arise spontaneously in our lives when prompted by external factors. In contrast, the four remaining worlds, called the Four Noble Paths, are characterized by the inner effort it takes to manifest them.

The state of Learning is that in which we learn something from the teachings of others, while the state of Realization is that in which we come to some partial understanding of life, however great or small, through our own efforts and observations. Bodhisattva is the state of altruism – of finding joy through helping others; and, finally, the state of Buddhahood is defined as absolute happiness and is attained only as the result of the actions we take when in the state of Bodhisattva.

It might seem simplistic to reduce the whole range of human experience to just ten states but, as Daisaku Ikeda explains:

> The Ten States are abstract in the sense that they are generalities drawn from human experience. Having taken into account all the various conditions in which the self might exist, Buddhist philosophers concluded that there are ten basic life conditions. The number is not accidental, nor was it chosen because ten is the basis of the decimal system, or some such thing as that. It was chosen so as to be all-inclusive on the one hand, and on the other to find the smallest number of catagories. Eight categories would

have meant combining two essentially different states; twelve
would have meant dividing what are essentially two single states
to make four. I assure you the whole thing has been well thought
out.

Bearing these brief explanations of the Ten Worlds in mind, let us
look again at the description of the start of an average day.

Firstly, while asleep, you are in the state of Tranquillity. Sleep
does not automatically mean Tranquillity. If you were having a
nightmare, for instance, you would be in the state of Hell, and if
you were dreaming of your lover you might well be in the state of
Rapture – or not, as the case may be. Then the alarm goes. You
wake up because the state of Animality is momentarily activated:
in this case, manifesting itself as the instinct of fear. As soon as
you are awake and realize you are not being attacked, the
knowledge that you have to get out of your warm and comfortable
bed to face once more the rigours of the world plunges you, even
though only momentarily, straight into Hell. Seeing that it is
raining keeps you there. As you get dressed, however, Animality
reasserts itself as you start to feel hungry. You might logically
think that feeling hungry means you are in the state of Hunger
but, as Daisaku Ikeda further explains, 'there is a difference
between the hunger whose source is voraciousness and the
hunger that comes from normal instinct, and this is the difference
between those in the state of Hunger and those in the mindless
state of Animality'.

Driven by Animality into the kitchen, you start to prepare
breakfast. Once again, though, your state changes when the cat
meows and you realize, after a moment's thought, that she is
probably feeling hungry too. That realization, indeed all the
realizations you have had since waking up, are very minor instances
of the world of Realization in your life. Deciding to feed the cat is an
example of Bodhisattva nature at work; while reading the back of
the corn flakes' packet finds you in the state of Learning.

Then the letters arrive. Fear at the sight of letters that could
contain bad news is another example of Animality, and your
assumption that the electricity bill is wrong is an example of the
state of Anger. It is important to note that one does not
necessarily have to be angry to be in the state of Anger. Anger
here is characterized by a contentious and arrogant attitude to
others – 'those stupid bureaucrats' at the electricity board, in this

instance. It does not matter that the bill might very well be wrong: Anger shows itself in your automatic reaction that you are in the right. A moment later, as you think back to the winter, Anger passes away and Hell reappears. Your dream of a summer holiday, a true manifestation of the state of Hunger, the world of desires, seems impossible. And then, as you discover you have got a generous tax rebate, the world of Rapture explodes into your life. In fact, so strong is it that it completely changes your attitude towards the day. The things that before were prompting the state of Hell to manifest itself, like the weather and the thought of going to work, now appear to be not so bad after all. But *they* have not changed – *you* have, at least a dozen times since waking up.

This is a gross underestimation of our real changeability; it is theoretically possible to analyse in even more minute detail the myriad changes we experience within ourselves from moment to moment. As Daisaku Ikeda says, 'In Buddhism it is taught that one's mind fluctuates 840 million times a day. The alterations in one's life are, in other words, infinite. One's life is a succession of momentary instances of hot, cold, doubt, delight, sadness and other conditions.'

The idea that all life is in a constant state of flux is by no means exclusive to Buddhism; indeed, it is one which is shared with most eastern philosophies and religions and which also has found expression at various times in western ones: the Greek philosopher Heraclitus, for example, who lived before Socrates and Plato, was said to have summed up his belief in universal change in the phrase 'all things are flowing'. Buddhism differs, however, in its detailed explanation of exactly how life changes from moment to moment, and yet follows a discernible pattern according to the universal Law of *Nam-myoho-renge-kyo*. As the British historian, the late Arnold Toynbee, says: 'The Buddhist analysis of the dynamics of life . . . is more detailed and subtle than any modern Western analysis that I know of.'

As this analysis starts with the subjective life of the human being and then works outwards through society and the physical environment to, ultimately, the entire universe, it is worthwhile examining each of the Ten Worlds in greater depth, as they are central to Buddhist thought.

HELL

In February 1944 Primo Levi, then a young Jewish chemist, was transported with 650 others from a detention camp in Italy to the labour camp of Monowitz-Buna, near Auschwitz. On arrival, most of the old men, women and children went straight to the gas-chamber. The hundred or so left were loaded onto lorries and taken to the camp. Levi has said:

> The journey did not last more than twenty minutes. Then the lorry stopped, and we saw a large door, and above it a sign, brightly illuminated (its memory still stikes me in my dreams): *Arbeit Macht Frei*, work gives freedom.
>
> We climb down, they make us enter an enormous room that is poorly heated. We have a terrible thirst. The weak gurgle of the water in the radiators makes us ferocious; we have had nothing to drink for four days. But there is also a tap – and above it a card which says that it is forbidden to drink as the water is dirty. Nonsense. It seems obvious that the card is a joke, 'they' know we are dying of thirst and they put us in a room, and there is a tap, and *Wassertrinken Verboten*. I drink and I incite my companions to do likewise, but I have to spit it out, the water is tepid and sweetish, with the smell of a swamp.
>
> This is Hell. Today, in our times, hell must be like this. A huge, empty room: we are tired, standing on our feet, with a tap which drips while we cannot drink the water, and we wait for something which will certainly be terrible, and nothing happens and nothing continues to happen. What can one think about? One cannot think any more, it is like being already dead. Someone sits down on the ground. The time passes drop by drop.

This description is very close to the Buddhist concept of Hell. For many years, people were taught to think of hell as a distinct place, usually an unbearably hot region, far underground, where people were tormented throughout eternity for their wrong-doings here on earth, usually by devils who delighted in the suffering they were inflicting. A version of this idea of hell was strong in thirteenth-century Japan, and was one which Nichiren Daishonin was concerned to rectify: 'First of all, as to the question of where exactly hell and the Buddha exist, one sutra states that hell exists underground and another sutra says that the Buddha is in the west. However, closer examination reveals that both exist in our five-foot body.'

According to Buddhism, Hell is not confined to any particular place but, rather, is a state of indescribable suffering which one projects onto the external environment. It is a state in which your whole life seems to contract and becomes concentrated on the cause of your agony. To give a simple example, if you have a bad toothache, your whole being is occupied by the pain of your tooth, no matter how idyllic your surroundings may be. In the case of Primo Levi and his fellow Jews, his surroundings were neutral – 'a huge, empty room'; it is their agonizing thirst, concentrated on the tap dripping water they cannot drink, coupled with their terrible sense of foreboding, which makes this room 'hell'. Even time seems to slow almost to a standstill, measured in the drips of the tap, so that the agony appears interminable.

The Japanese word for Hell is *jigoku*, written with two characters meaning 'the lowest' and 'to be bound or imprisoned'. Undoubtedly, one of the characteristic aspects of the state of Hell is the lack of ability to act or think freely, a result of the dramatic reduction of one's life-force, the vital energy of life itself, which is expressed both physically in one's bodily mechanisms and functions, and spiritually in one's thoughts, hopes and emotions. In this state, it is 'like being already dead', as Levi says. The awareness of this lack of freedom in itself can drive one deeper into suffering. Significantly, the chapter in Levi's book, *If This is a Man*, from which this passage is taken, is entitled 'On the Bottom', reflecting Levi's profound understanding of the true nature of Hell. Later in the same chapter he says:

> In a moment, with almost prophetic intuition, the reality was revealed to us: we had reached the bottom. It is not possible to sink lower than this; no human condition is more miserable than this, nor could it conceivably be so. Nothing belongs to us any more; they have taken away our clothes, our shoes, even our hair; if we speak they will not listen to us, and if they listen they will not understand. They will even take away our name . . . Imagine now a man who is deprived of everyone he loves, and at the same time of his house, his habits, his clothes, in short, of everything he possesses: he will be a hollow man, reduced to suffering and needs, forgetful of dignity and restraint, for he who loses all often easily loses himself. He will be a man whose life or death can be lightly decided with no sense of human affinity, in the most fortunate of cases, on the basis of a pure judgement of utility. It is in this way

that one can understand the double sense of the term 'extermin-
ation camp', and it is now clear what we seek to express with the
phrase: 'to lie on the bottom'.

Fortunately, most of us will never have to suffer the sort of
agony which Levi and other death-camp victims went through
(though it is shameful to think that in some parts of the world
Hells like these are still being created). But that is not to say that
the Hell of other individuals cannot be as intense. The grief of
losing a loved one, the fear of one's own death, the prisons of
poverty and illness – the variety of Hell is matched only by that of
human beings themselves. And even though we may be unable to
understand an individual's particular Hell – if they are claustro-
phobic, for instance – or may perhaps think the cause of it
insignificant, for that person it is real and undeniable.

Nichiren Daishonin states, 'Rage is the world of Hell.' In this
case, the rage is not that of the world of Anger, in which it is
directed towards others in an attempt to prove one's superiority
(or in which one's inferiority has been revealed) but is essentially
directed towards oneself. It is the rage of frustration and even
self-destruction, often including the desire to destroy one's
surroundings, seeing in them some sort of responsibility for one's
suffering. Youths on bleak, high-rise council estates may express
their rage through vandalism, while people in the deep despair of
an incurable illness may express their rage at their helplessness
by committing suicide.

It should be clear from what has been said that the world of
Hell has a very strong psychological component, one, indeed,
which could be said to be deeper and more difficult to alleviate
than that of the body. People crippled with severe physical
disabilities, for example, may not be in any physical pain, yet can
be suffering endless torment inwardly at their lack of mobility
and independence. Often, this psychological suffering has no
obvious external cause at all. Depression, a condition all too
common in our society, exhibits all the symptoms of the state of
Hell, yet seems to come and go of its own volition. The low life-
force of Hell shows itself in the first instance, perhaps, in an
unwillingness to get out of bed, and then by the growing failure to
be motivated by anything or anyone in one's surroundings; time
seems to slow down and all the individual is aware of is that, for
some reason, he or she feels terrible.

Worry is also a manifestation in the mind of the world of Hell, a particularly cruel and subtle one. Worry consists of imagining the worst possible outcome of some event, suffering as if that imagined consequence had actually happened and then compounding the suffering by realizing that, in any case, we are usually unable to affect the outcome one way or the other. Even if people tell us not to worry, that it can do no good, and we know rationally that they are right, our tendency is to indulge our pessimistic fantasy until such time as it is proved right or wrong by the event itself.

One further aspect of the world of Hell that needs to be mentioned is the lack of hope one feels in this state. It is often said that where there is life there is hope, but as Primo Levi's description of Monowitz-Buna testifies, it would be more correct to say that, on the contrary, where there is hope there is life:

> Their life is short, but their number is endless; they, the *Muselmänner*, the drowned, form the backbone of the camp, an anonymous mass, continually renewed and always identical, of non-men who march and labour in silence, the divine spark dead within them, already too empty to really suffer. One hesitates to call them living: one hesitates to call their death death, in the face of which they have no fear, as they are too tired to understand.

If that 'divine spark' could be identified as hope, then these *Muselmänner* are truly no-hopers – both in the sense of those with no hope and, thus, those for whom there is no hope. It might not be too fanciful to see *muselmänner* in our own society too – those people deprived of hope for the future by unemployment, say, or the fear of nuclear war; deprived of that 'divine spark' which motivates and sustains creative action and which enables men and women to enjoy a vision of how they can shape their own lives.

To all intents and purposes, the state of Hell really is the lowest of the ten worlds. Part of the greatness of Buddhism, however, lies in the teaching that all the nine worlds, from Hell to Bodhisattva, have both a positive and a negative aspect (Buddhahood alone being wholly creative), and that all are necessary to life. It might be thought that there can be absolutely no redeeming features in the world of Hell, but actually there are. Firstly, and quite simply, without Hell we could never know happiness. Then again, the desire to keep out the world of Hell is a powerful motivation for action: if we did not suffer the pain of hunger, we would never know when to eat, for instance. Similarly, suffering can be a form of protection: if fire did not hurt, we could seriously injure ourselves without being aware of it. Perhaps most importantly, though, if we never suffered ourselves, we would never be able to identify and sympathize with the suffering of others, or be moved to help them. In other words, in Buddhism the world of Hell leads directly to the world of Bodhisattva.

HUNGER

The world of Hunger is one in which our desires are dominant. Human beings have many different desires, from the instinctive desires for food, warmth, sleep and sex, to higher, more complex spiritual desires like those for love, social justice and self-improvement. The most fundamental desire, and the one which sustains and underpins all the others, is the simple desire to continue living.

Desires are the main driving force of life. For example, generally speaking, we work because we want to earn money, first to buy the things we need for our survival, then perhaps so that we can afford to raise a family and, probably, to make our lives as comfortable as possible. Ideally, if we enjoy it, we also work because it fulfils to some extent a more abstract, more 'spiritual' desire in us – the desire to feel needed, perhaps, or to make a contribution of some kind to a wider society than just our family. Without desires we would never be motivated to do anything; apathetic people achieve very little.

Although desires are essential to life, however, it is also essential that we control them. A person who cannot control his or her desires is actually their slave and, because it is the very nature of desire to want something, can never be satisfied for any length of time. Individuals who are always changing their jobs, where they live, their cars, their lifestyles or their partners are more likely than not to be in this state of Hunger, a state of almost permanent dissatisfaction with what they actually have; they are driven by the thought that their happiness lies in possessing or experiencing something currently out of their reach – be it money, fame, power, a relationship – or more of the same. In its extreme form it is a state in which no sooner has one got something desired than its attraction palls and one realizes it is not enough. In this sense, then, hunger is a kind of psychological condition characterized by a constant inner restlessness, an intense yearning for happiness and fulfilment which fixes upon various things in the environment in the vain hope that they will finally satisfy this all-consuming desire.

Fyodor Dostoyevsky's short novel, *The Gambler*, set against the background of the then fashionable gaming-rooms of mid-nineteenth-century Germany, paints a vivid picture of a society in the clutches of hunger:

> After ten o'clock at night those left around the tables are the genuine, desperate gamblers, for whom nothing exists in any health resort but roulette, who have come for nothing else, who hardly notice what is going on around them and take no interest in anything else all the season, only play from morning till night and would perhaps be ready to play all through the night as well, if it were possible. They are always annoyed at having to disperse when the roulette tables close at midnight. And when, about twelve o'clock, before closing the tables, the head croupier announces 'Les trois derniers coups, messieurs!' [The last three bets, gentlemen!], they are sometimes prepared to stake on those last three turns everything they have in their pockets, and actually do lose the biggest amounts of all at those times.

As this passage shows, inherent in the world of Hunger lies the extreme of obsession in which desire is so strong, so dominant, that it can completely distort one's perspective on reality. The need to satisfy an obsessive desire obliterates all other considerations so that one's capacity to make sound judgements is severely restricted. It is possible to argue that in the grip of such extreme hunger one cannot be said to exercise real judgement of any kind, so impelled is one by strong desire. Passionate love often falls into this category as the age-old saying that 'love is blind' suggests.

Nichiren Daishonin says simply that 'greed is [the world] of Hunger' and, much as we would prefer to ignore this unpleasant fact, it is the sum total of the apparently innocent desires of ordinary individuals that lies at the root of some of the gravest problems we face today. Individually, we may not consider ourselves 'greedy' in wanting, say, a new car or a washing-machine, but that is only because our lowest expectations are already set so high by the society in which we live. If we consider what we possess, above and beyond that which is strictly necessary for our survival, and how much more we probably want, or even feel we need, our 'greed' might become more apparent. For example, Nichiren Daishonin says, 'Man has two kinds of treasure: clothing and food . . . Man's life is sustained by what he eats. That is why food is his treasure.' The fact that it is unlikely many people outside the Third World would look on such basic commodities as food and clothing as 'treasures', even though they may know from a theoretical viewpoint how essential they are, is in itself an indication of how distorted our lives have become by the world of Hunger.

Fundamentally, it is greed which has led to the destruction of so much of our natural environment. The desire for an ever-increasing standard of material well-being has, until very recently, blinded us to the inevitable consequences of short-term profiteering from the earth's natural resources. The fact that mankind is still indulging in this rape of the natural world, while continuing to ignore its effects, shows just how strongly the world of Hunger can affect us, collectively, as a society.

Indeed, it is even questionable whether, in some areas, our higher material standard of living means we are better off. For example, just over a hundred years ago, a Parliamentary inquiry set out in a horse and carriage to drive the forty or so miles across London, from west to east, to determine the state of the roads and the traffic. Their average speed was 14 mph. A hundred years later, when another inquiry team travelled the same route by car, their average speed was only 12 mph. A 2 mph drop in average speed plus a huge increase in carbon monoxide and lead pollution is not much to show for a century of 'progress'. As Aurelio Peccei observes: 'The myth that growth – growth of any kind whatsoever – is good in itself has polluted our minds for a long time and is a misconception that still retains some power to tantalize.' In this sense, we are perhaps not so far from the obsessed gamblers of Dostoyevsky's portrait.

Hunger does have a positive aspect, however, for the restless dissatisfaction that can cause such suffering to an individual can also be the very energy he or she needs to achieve something great. It was Hunger (literally in some cases) which prompted so many people to flock to the United States of America at the turn of the last century, and Hunger which then spurred them on to rebuild their lives in a foreign land; in the course of this they contributed significantly to making the United States the world's leading economic power. Similarly, it is an almost physical hunger which drives some people to work relentlessly in their all-consuming desire to alleviate poverty and injustice in the Third World, for example, or to see peace across the globe.

In striking contrast to some earlier forms of Buddhism, Nichiren Shoshu Buddhism teaches that it is impossible to eradicate desires without eradicating life itself, and that repressing them only leads to them appearing in other guises as various forms of neurosis – guilt, for example. The real challenge, therefore, lies in sublimating our desires and reorientating them towards creative and valuable ends. Inevitably, this means recognizing that, although we can get a certain amount of short-term satisfaction from fulfilling our own selfish wants, ultimately our greatest happiness is inextricably bound up with the desire to work in some way, however apparently insignificant, for the happiness of our fellow men and women.

ANIMALITY

As its name suggests, the world of Animality is that in which we behave like animals. *Homo sapiens* evolved over millions of years to form a distinct and powerful group of that branch of the animal kingdom known as primates, and so it is hardly surprising that we still possess many animal characteristics.

Whereas desires dominate us all in the world of Hunger, in Animality we are under the control of our instincts. In common with animals, our instincts are essentially a means of enabling us to adapt to, and take advantage of, our environment, thus ensuring our survival, both individually and as a species. The instinct of fear warns us of danger, the instinct for sleep is vital to refresh energy, the sex instinct is vital to perpetuate the species, and so on. Although these instincts express themselves as desires (so that, for example, when we are tired we *want* to sleep), they are distinguished from the desires of the world of Hunger by the absolute necessity that they be satisfied for us to continue living. We feel hungry, we eat, our hunger abates as we feel fuller and so we stop eating – until such time as our hunger instinct tells us that we must eat again. If we eat when we are not hungry then, paradoxical as it may sound, we are actually back in the world of Hunger, the world of greed and unsatisfied desires. In this case, the reasons for eating are purely psychological – the need for consolation, maybe, as perhaps somewhere deep in our subconscious we associate being fed with our parents' affection; or perhaps our strong desire for a particular taste simply overrides all other considerations.

A number of the animal instincts we have retained are, however, of more questionable value. For example, as Nichiren Daishonin says, 'It is the nature of beasts to threaten the weak and fear the strong.' According to this standard, any society or organization in which the 'pecking-order' is paramount, in which one kowtows to those higher than oneself while lording it over those who are lower, has Animality as its basis, no matter how apparently civilized it or its members may appear to be. This form of Animality is perhaps most obvious in highly structured and strongly hierarchical organizations like the armed forces and the police but, in reality, it is pervasive throughout society, in business, administration, the professions – even in political and some religious organizations which preach human equality and the brotherhood of man.

The exercise of power for selfish and partisan ends is another manifestation of the world of Animality and what is most often meant by 'the law of the jungle'. Aggressiveness and territoriality amongst animals are clearly means of self-protection – ensuring a food supply, for instance, or guarding one's family or mate – as well as fixing a place in the group hierarchy; by and large they fulfil this function in human society too. For example, on an individual level, there has only to be a suggestion of a shortage of a basic commodity – bread, say – to see the Animality latent in people spring to the surface as they rush to the shops and strip the shelves. And, indeed, anyone who has had the misfortune to work in a large store at sale time knows only too well what human Animality can be like. The Animality of organizations can be seen when they use their power simply to benefit their members at the expense of a wider community: as sometimes when a union uses its muscle to force up wages, without caring that prices will then usually rise as a result; or when a business cartel or monopoly forces up prices simply to increase profits. Animality crosses all political and social divides and, in its negative form, is always ugly. Without a doubt, it was the world of Animality in human beings which prompted Thomas Hobbes to describe the life of man as 'solitary, poor, nasty, brutish and short', and which he considered man's natural condition.

Above all, Animality is characterized by what Nichiren Daishonin calls 'foolishness'. Even though we are clearly part of the animal world, we are distinguished from other animals by the possession of faculties by which we make judgements about our environment and our relationship to it. It is when we do not exercise these faculties that we can truly be said to be in the world of Animality.

For example, animals appear to have no sense of the passage of time. They recognize night and day by the appearance of light and dark, and they certainly respond to the passage of the seasons – migrating animals possess a mysterious sense of the right time to move to their winter or summer homes, for instance – but time in the sense of events either remembered or foreseen appears to be totally absent in all but the highest primates. To all intents and purposes, animals live happily immersed in the present, simply responding to the stimuli of their environments and their instincts.

In contrast, human beings have an innate temporal sense, from which it follows that we are able to learn from events in the past and also to plan events in the future, sometimes very far in the future – *Homo sapiens* is the only animal to date who has established pension schemes, for instance. But when we, too, become 'immersed' in the present and act solely according to our instincts, without regard to the consequences of our actions, we slip once again into the world of Animality, of 'foolishness'. For example, a man who drinks too much at a party, happily absorbed in his pleasure, but who knows he will later have to drive home, is putting his life (and others) at risk simply for momentary satisfaction. 'Foolish' is one word that justly describes this condition – 'thoughtless' and 'mindless' are others. As Daisaku Ikeda notes, 'to act solely on instinct is to invite disaster, and those who can do no more than follow their instincts have no control over their fate.'

This lack of control, particularly self-control, is highlighted when those dominated by instinctive behaviour meet a higher intelligence. Nichiren Daishonin comments, 'Fish want to survive; they deplore their pond's shallowness and dig holes to hide in, yet tricked by bait, they take the hook. Birds in a tree fear that they are too low and perch in the top branches, yet bewitched by bait, they too are caught in snares. Human beings are equally vulnerable.' If men have tamed and subjugated such a large extent of the animal world through intelligence rather than force, it is precisely because instinctive behaviour is, to a high degree, predictable behaviour. As Nichiren Daishonin's last sentence suggests, to live dominated by instincts is to be highly susceptible to manipulation by others. This is well known by politicians (not by accident did George Orwell choose to set his famous satire on dictatorship in *Animal Farm*) and also by advertising men who will use bikini-clad models to sell almost everything – including, sometimes, bikinis.

But perhaps the ultimate 'foolishness' of the world of Animality is its inherent tendency to destroy the basis of its own existence. In the animal world the strong devour the weak but, on the other hand, are totally dependent upon the weak being able to reproduce fast enough to keep them fed. If the weak cannot do this for any reason – because of sickness, say – the strong are doomed to eat themselves into extinction; unable to realize the consequences of their action, programmed by their instincts, they cannot stop nor find any alternative, and will continue to devour the weak until catastrophe strikes. The crisis of Third World debt is a very good example of this animalistic tendency at work even amongst the sophisticated, computerized world of high finance. And on an even larger scale, one cannot help but wonder how much longer as a race we will be able to afford the immense sums we spend each year on arms while, across the globe, the poor struggle for survival. If we want evidence that the world of Animality is still a powerful factor in human behaviour we need look no further than this supreme folly.

The three worlds of Hell, Hunger and Animality are called the Three Evil Paths because they tend to lead so easily from one to the other, trapping people in the vicious circle of very low life-conditions. Say you have got very little money, perhaps just enough to keep yourself alive, but no more, and let us say there are things you want but cannot afford. Your desire for these things comes from your Hunger state and the frustration of your desire puts you into the state of Hell, the state of suffering. If you then become so desperate with frustration that you decide to steal from someone else to get what you want, you will move into the state of Animality. If you are then caught and sent to prison you will probably find yourself back in Hell. To take another example, say you have an unhappy, hellish relationship with your partner. You hunger for the affection and intimacy that is no longer there and so seek consolation in an affair with someone else. For a time you can indulge this affair and avoid having to think about the future, but then you start to feel deceitful and guilty, your new relationship suffers and, before long, you find yourself even unhappier than before. These are simple (though not uncommon) examples, but this pattern of moving between the Three Evil Paths is repeated in a myriad subtle combinations by many people all the time.

ANGER

In a sense, the Three Evil Paths are all states of blindness: the blind, destructive rage of Hell, the blind, all-consuming desire of Hunger and the blind, urgent instinct of Animality and, as such, all have the tendency to make one stumble around in suffering. Anger, the fourth of the Ten Worlds, although definitely still one of the lower life-states (and often grouped with the first three to make the Four Evil Paths), differs from Hell, Hunger and Animality in that it possesses a degree of self-awareness. In terms of the Ten Worlds, Anger is identified with the workings of the ego, that part of the consciousness in which the self is aware of its own uniqueness and its apparent separation from the rest of the universe. As Arnold Toynbee comments:

> A living being is partially detached from the rest of the universe and partially attached to it. This relation gives a human being a choice of attitudes and behaviour. Man may try to dominate the rest of the universe and exploit it; that is, to make himself the

whole universe's centre and *raison d'être*. Insofar as a human
being follows this greedy desire, his conduct will be evil.

Nichiren Daishonin describes the chief characteristic of Anger
as 'perversity', alluding to the fundamental distortion of perspective that occurs when the ego places itself at the centre of the
universe. The desire to dominate in the state of Anger is different
from that in Animality because of the element of self-knowledge
involved. The lion may be called the 'king of beasts', but there is
no sense in which he is aware of this fact; he kills when hungry,
not to prove a point. In other words, in Animality you win or lose
according to your strength; in Anger you feel you deserve to win
regardless of your strength.

Anger, then, is not to be confused with simply being angry, for
the world of Anger does not appear just when you lose your
temper. Rather, Anger is the state of supreme self-centredness in
which we believe that we are fundamentally better than other
people and in which we delight in displaying this supposed
superiority to the world. In one of his major writings T'ien-t'ai
describes Anger as follows:

> The person in the Realm of Anger has an irresistible urge to win
> out over everyone else. Like the hawk flying high in the sky in
> search of prey, he looks down upon others and respects only
> himself. He makes a superficial show of benevolence, righteous-
> ness, propriety, wisdom, and faith, and he may even display a
> primitive form of moral integrity, but inside he is a monstrous
> egotist.

Interestingly, parts of the following passage from Tom Wolfe's
chronicle of the first astronauts, *The Right Stuff*, bear a striking
resemblence to T'ien-t'ai's description:

> To take off in an F-100 at dawn and cut in the afterburner and
> hurtle twenty-five thousand feet up into the sky so suddenly that
> you felt not like a bird but like a trajectory, yet with full control,
> full control of *five tons* of thrust, all of which flowed from your will
> and through your fingertips . . . to describe it, even to wife, child,
> near ones and dear ones, seemed impossible. So the pilot kept it to
> himself, along with an even more indescribable, an even more
> sinfully inconfessable, feeling of superiority, appropriate to him
> and his kind, lone bearers of the right stuff.

From *up here* at dawn the pilot looked down upon poor hopeless Las Vegas (or Yuma, Corpus Christi, Meridian, San Bernadino or Dayton) and began to wonder: how can all of them down there, those poor souls who will soon be waking up and trudging out of their minute rectangles and inching along their little noodle highways toward whatever slots and grooves make up their everyday lives – how could they live like that, with such earnestness, if they had the faintest idea of what it was like up here in this righteous zone?

But of course! Not only the washed-out, grounded and dead pilots had been left behind – but also all of those millions of sleepwalking souls who never attempted the great gamble. The entire world . . . *left behind*. Only at this point can one begin to understand just how big, how titanic, the ego of the military pilot could be. The world was used to enormous egos in artists, actors, entertainers of all sorts, in politicians, sports figures, and even journalists, because they had such familiar and convenient ways to show them off. But that slim young man over there in uniform, with the enormous watch on his wrist, that young officer who is so shy he can't even open his mouth unless the subject is flying – that young pilot – well, my friends, his ego is even *bigger*! – so big, it's *breathtaking*!

The person in the state of Anger cannot bear to lose. Quite simply, he must be the best. He must have the best job, the highest salary, the prettiest wife, in short, anything and everything which will separate him from, and place him above, the common herd of humanity. Arrogance, conceit, contempt for others (often in the form of patronizing pity), a highly critical streak and a powerful competitive urge (leading to conflict with others) are all aspects of Anger. The desire for fame is also a quintessential manifestation of this state, for there is nothing more reassuring to the ego than having lots of people look up to you; many highly successful people are indeed driven by Anger, which is one reason why they have been able to do so well. Anger is not restricted, however, to the rich and famous. Even in the humblest of situations such as an ordinary office, say, the world of Anger may appear – as vindictive gossiping about a fellow worker, for example.

The curious fact about people in the world of Anger, though, is that hidden deep within their lives is usually a large amount of anxiety about themselves, an anxiety which is covered up and compensated for by the assertion of their superiority. Often this sense of inferiority is hidden so deeply that a person in Anger may not be consciously aware of it, which is one reason why he may be so hard in his criticism of weaknesses in others: subconsciously he recognizes the failings as his own and, in the harshness of his criticism (to which he may well not give voice), he tries to deny what his subconscious mind admits. On the other hand, if you are not fooled by the external image of the person in Anger but see through to the hidden anxiety, he will probably feel dislike and animosity towards you for unmasking him – not so much to others as to himself – and will probably avoid you as a result. The ego must be protected at all costs, even if it means running away. As Nichiren Daishonin says, 'An arrogant man will be overcome with fear when he meets a strong enemy.'

On a larger scale, Anger expresses itself as nationalism, racism, sexism, and religious and political intolerance for, as Dr Bryan Wilson, one of the world's leading authorities on the social effects of religion, has pointed out, 'intense group loyalty is almost always associated with strong disparagement of other groups.' In other words, any form of discrimination which sees the multifarious differences between people as evidence of supposed inferiority or superiority is a manifestation of the 'perversity' which Nichiren Daishonin identifies as central to Anger.

However, just as the Three Evil Paths have a positive function, so does Anger, as a source of the energy needed to fight injustice and inequality. It is Anger, the awareness of the self, which enables us to assert the inherent dignity of our own individual lives, as well as that of others, and to challenge those who would seek to dominate, repress or manipulate. Anger in this sense is thus often the passionate driving force for personal and social reform and can, therefore, be as creative as it is usually destructive.

TRANQUILLITY

As its name suggests Tranquillity, the fifth of the Ten Worlds, is the state of being at peace or at rest; one of the major functions of

Tranquillity is to restore energy. This state is not confined to simply putting your feet up after a hard day at work, say, but rather describes what Buddhism teaches is the basic life-condition of human beings. This state is thus also called the world of Humanity.

It may seem strange to assert that Tranquillity is the basic state of humanity as, in everyday life, people are often energetic in an argumentative and aggressive way. The reason can perhaps be best understood by substituting 'humaneness' for Humanity and remembering that, when people are in conflict with one another, they are displaying not their 'humaneness' but, rather their Anger and Animality. In other words, the world of Tranquillity is also the world of Humanity because when people are truly humane they are also at peace with themselves.

Nichiren Daishonin states that 'Calmness is [the world] of Humanity', while another Buddhist text lists eight qualities of this state: intelligence, excellence, acute consciousness, sound judgement, superior wisdom, the ability to distinguish between truth and falsehood, the ability to attain enlightenment, and good karma from the past (that has enabled one to be born as a human being). As we saw in our consideration of Animality, what distinguishes humans from animals is, essentially, the possession of highly developed faculties, such as these, with which they can relate to their environment in a more considered way. This is not to say, however, that human beings always do, of course. Broadly speaking, when people act according to their instincts, without considering the effects of their actions, they are in Animality; when they do think of what they are doing, they are in the state of Humanity.

Tranquillity is a fundamentally neutral state, the state you find yourself in when nothing in your environment has either upset or excited you and thus called forth one of the other states of being. In this state you are generally in control of your lower life-conditions and are therefore not easily roused to anger or passion. You are considerate to others, rational rather than emotional, and do not seek or enjoy conflict.

For example, imagine yourself in a busy shopping street, full of people. In that great mass of people there will be a wide variety of life-conditions but, whatever their inner state, as long as the shoppers go about their business peacefully, they will be predominantly in the state of Tranquillity. But suppose you bump into someone. He swears angrily and berates you for your stupidity while you, seeing that the collision was a simple accident and that no one has been hurt, simply apologize. The person you bumped into has a strong tendency towards Anger in his life and so his Humanity disappears at the slightest upset; by contrast, you are able to exercise superior judgement and self-control and so, keeping calm, remain in the world of Humanity or Tranquillity.

One problem with this state, though, is that, being essentially neutral, it is vulnerable to all sorts of influences and so is difficult to sustain. Thus, if a person persists in being offensive, it is quite likely that you will quickly move from the state of Humanity and into that of Anger as well. Many arguments follow this pattern and everyone knows the tremendous effort it sometimes takes not to lose one's temper in the face of provocation. This is because the state of Humanity can be seen as a somewhat unstable point of balance and, as such, often does not possess enough life-force to counteract the surges of energy that come from the worlds of Hunger, Animality and Anger.

In an extreme form, Tranquillity can be wholly negative. Laziness, the unwillingness to make effort, is an example of this state; so is the desire not to 'rock the boat', the unwillingness to tackle problems and difficulties because of the upheaval such a course of action will mean to one's life, even though it may be absolutely necessary. Negligence is thus another of the manifestations of this state, as is apathy, the condition of simply not caring enough to make any effort to improve one's self or one's environment. Indeed, a society that, while acutely aware of the problems facing it, as a whole sits and passively watches television for many hours a day, might very well be described as being in an extreme state of Tranquillity.

Indeed the trend towards Tranquillity in western society is growing as the mechanization and computerization of work increases and more and more people find themselves without a job or simply with more time on their hands. The propaganda for Tranquillity has increased, too, despite the fact that there are so many problems needing urgent attention. 'Leisure' has become a commodity to be bought, sold and consumed as something desirable in itself, rather than as a means of restoring one's energy and preparing oneself for further efforts. In reality, though, the satisfaction inherent in Tranquillity is extremely limited and without the counterbalance of those life-states involving effort soon becomes enervating and Hellish, as anyone who has been unemployed for any length of time can testify. This is nothing to do with the work ethic but is rather a recognition of the natural function of the state of Tranquillity.

To give an analogy, although different people feel they need different amounts of sleep and, generally speaking, enjoy the amount they consider right for them, nobody can sleep all the time and very few people would enjoy lying in bed all day and night. The most satisfying sleep always comes after one has made a great effort and achieved something worthwhile. Then again, after a satisfying sleep, quite naturally one wants to be active again. Buddhism teaches that this is part of the fundamental rhythm of life and that, if we are living fully and creatively, the state of Tranquillity is one in which it is impossible to remain for any longer than is necessary for us to restore ourselves in order to function effectively.

RAPTURE

The world of Rapture is what we experience when our desires are fulfilled. It is an intense and exhilarating state in which we feel glad to be alive and in which everything is bathed in the glow of our own well-being. When in Rapture we truly feel ourselves to be living to the full; we have more energy and zest for life than normal, our senses seem to be heightened, everyday events appear fresh and stimulating and time seems to rush by as we feel our days to be rich and crammed with experience. Nichiren Daishonin sums up this state when he says 'Joy is [the world] of Rapture.'

In Buddhism, though, Rapture is the state of relative rather than true happiness because, wonderful as it is, Rapture can never last for long. It needs only the passage of time, or even simply a slight change of circumstances, for Rapture to disappear and one of the other states to reassert itself. For example, taking the first mouthful of delicious food when you are very hungry can be a moment of intense Rapture. It is unlikely, though, that the second mouthful will cause as intense a feeling, even less likely that the third and subsequent mouthfuls will do so and, by the time that you have finished eating, you may already be moving into the torpor of Tranquillity; undoubtedly, as time passes, your feeling of Rapture at satisfying your hunger will disappear completely. Alternatively, if, when savouring that first delicious mouthful, you discover a fly in your soup, your Rapture would vanish immediately, most likely to be replaced by the world of Hell or Anger.

While it is true that, to a large extent, happiness is a result of fulfilling our desires, it is actually the nature of those desires which determine the degree to which we might be called happy. For example, an alcoholic desires a drink and might be overjoyed when he gets one but there is no way that his condition can be described as a happy one. By contrast, a scientist might desire to find a cure for cancer and, even though he has not yet achieved his goal, could experience great joy simply in the challenge of his work.

Buddhism identifies three distinct levels of happiness, or Rapture. The first level, called the world of Desires, corresponds to the desires inherent in the six lower worlds, such as the delight we feel at satisfying our instinctive urges, at achieving social recognition, at overcoming our suffering, and so on. The second level, the world of Form, might be called 'rapture of the body', for this is the surge of well-being we feel when we are fit, healthy and full of life. It is the sort of rapture you experience after an early morning swim, say, when you feel refreshed, wide awake and 'raring to go', or in the exercise of your natural talents. The third level of happiness, the world of Formlessness, could be called 'rapture of the spirit', the happiness you feel when living fully and creatively, and when you experience your life expanding and becoming richer. Buddhism teaches that this is the most satisfying and enduring sort of Rapture possible; it is the kind of Rapture the cancer research scientist may feel but the alcoholic almost certainly does not.

Ideally, of course, one should aim for happiness at all three levels, though this is extremely difficult to achieve. Nevertheless, Nichiren Shoshu Buddhism teaches that it is possible to establish indestructible happiness at the third level, in the world of Formlessness, through the development of our highest state of life, our Buddhahood. Buddhahood will be discussed more fully a little later. For now, suffice it to say that the life-force and wisdom generated in the world of Formlessness by revealing our Buddhahood, spills over into the world of Form, enabling us to live more healthily, while, at the first level, in the world of Desires, the solidity of happiness we feel at the core of our being can help us to counteract behaviour which may cause suffering for ourselves and others. This is not to say that Buddhism believes that suffering can be eliminated from life – it does not – but that, with such a secure foundation in the world of Formlessness, all suffering can be contained and absorbed in a larger happiness. This is how Stewart Anderson was able to say, with complete sincerity, that he felt great joy despite his illness – the joy of Buddhahood.*

Many people in modern industrialized society, however, seem to think that the rapture of the world of Desires *is* happiness, and yearn for an existence in which this essentially unstable sort of happiness can somehow be made permanent, even though the difficulty of sustaining this kind of rapture amid the realities of everyday life has long been recognized in a number of different cultures. One result of this yearning for the unstable to be stable is the idea that permanent happiness (a permanent state of Rapture, in other words) exists somewhere other than here in the real world – in short, in Heaven or paradise.

For instance, for those favoured by Allah ('those on the right' in the following passage), the paradise of Islam is, in Buddhist terms, quite explicitly the world of Desires made permanent:

> They shall recline on jewelled couches face to face, and there shall wait on them immortal youths with bowls and ewers and a cup of purest wine (that will neither pain their heads nor take away their reason); with fruits of their own choice and flesh of fowls that they relish. And theirs shall be the dark-eyed houris, chaste as hidden pearls: a guerdon for their deeds. There they shall hear no idle talk, no sinful speech, but only the greeting, 'Peace! Peace!' Those on the right hand – happy shall be those on the right hand! They shall recline on couches raised on high in the shade of thornless sidrahs and clusters of talh;† amidst gushing waters and abundant fruits, unforbidden, never-ending.

*See Introduction
†Unknown, though possibly the banana fruit.

While the Heaven of Christianity is not pictured quite as concretely as this, it is, nevertheless, traditionally a place where human souls, the incorporeal forms of men and women liberated from the demands of the flesh and the vagaries of earthly existence, dwell with God in eternal bliss.

By contrast, Heaven in Buddhism is nowhere else but in this world and is simply another name for the world of Rapture. From this perspective, then, one can say that, for hundreds of years in one form or another, western society has aspired to the world of Rapture as the highest possible state for human existence. Nowadays, with Christianity exerting less influence than it once did, this aspiration is not so often expressed directly as a desire for religious salvation, but indirectly, as two of the main currents in contemporary society.

The first of these is romantic love. Love, Rapture and Heaven have long been conflated in the West. Certainly, from the Renaissance onwards, poetry, and then popular music, have driven deep into our cultural consciousness the synthesis of these ideas so that it is almost impossible to express one without reference to the other. For one example from among many, consider Irving Berlin's 'Dancing Cheek to Cheek'.

In the first verse Berlin sings of being 'in heaven' and finding happiness when out dancing 'cheek to cheek' with his partner. But substitute 'love' or 'rapture' for 'heaven' in the first line, and any one of the three for 'happiness' in the third line, and the song would still be perfectly intelligible (if no longer a hit). The desire for romantic love is so strong in our society that it could be seen as having displaced religion as the main source of 'spiritual' fulfilment and, indeed, almost displaced it as the means to personal salvation. 'Saved by the love of a good woman' may be a cliché but, in many instances, it is only the love of another person, man or woman, that gives some people a sense of worth or any meaning to their lives. This way of thinking, however, also leads to the expectation that one's partner will – nay, *should* – make one truly happy. This puts an intolerable strain on many relationships as it is unrealistic to demand that one's partner provides a continuous supply of Rapture when permanence and stability are the very qualities the world of Rapture simply does not possess. Perhaps this is one reason why so many marriages break down these days.

The second of the ways that Rapture is expressed in contemporary society is in consumerism, founded on the idea that happiness lies in the possession or consumption of something, material or abstract. With regard to the former Daisaku Ikeda observes:

> Material culture which encourages the proliferation of desires has as its aims the creation of the state of Rapture. Certainly, many people, though perhaps unconsciously, regard the state of Rapture, represented by material affluence, as an ideal condition. To carry on the analogy, the aim of Western materialistic culture appears to have been to employ all the means of science and all the resources of the earth to build palaces for this state of Rapture.

Perhaps the ultimate expression of this drive to build 'palaces of Rapture' is the 'theme park', springing up all over the industrialized world, even as the natural environment is being further degraded by pollution and other associated evils.

Consumerism, however, is not limited to material things. 'Experience' is also now something to be consumed. For example, more people travel now, and more widely, than they ever have done before. While this is a reflection of the speed with which we can now be transported to 'foreign parts' and of the growth in affluence of much of the world, and though travel in itself is neither good nor bad, much travel is motivated by the unconscious belief that, fundamentally, happiness lies in a place other than where we are at the moment, a special place different from everyday reality. Thus, going to work can never constitute 'real' happiness, but going on holiday to the sun can. Indeed, it would be interesting to discover just how many people now think of paradise, not as some place above the clouds, but as a tropical island.

Essentially, Buddhism teaches that the greatest of joys comes from producing rather than consuming, from creating value and happiness for one's fellow human beings rather than enjoying short-term pleasure, however often repeated. When people learn this, they will also discover that happiness is something that can be experienced here and now, no matter where you are or what your circumstances. As Milton's Satan was moved to say:

The mind is its own place, and in itself
Can make a Heaven of Hell, a Hell of Heaven.

The six worlds from Hell to Rapture are known collectively as the
Six Paths; those who live dominated by these lower worlds are as
if on a constant merry-go-round, trapped by the demands of their
desires and the influence of their immediate external environment. The Six Paths are intimately bound up with each other so
that the individual can slip very easily from one to another: from
Rapture into Anger, for example, if first extravagantly praised
then harshly criticized; or from Tranquillity into Hell if, when
sitting in the warm watching television, you suddenly remember
you have to face the bank manager about your overdraft in the
morning. It is fair to say that moving like this among the Six
Paths describes the reality of life for most people. Buddhism
teaches, however, that these six lower worlds do not constitute
the entirety of life, for when we raise our eyes from the immediate
exigencies of day-to-day living and make an effort to improve our
understanding of ourselves and the world at large, we enter the
Four Noble Paths of Learning, Realization, Bodhisattva and
Buddhahood. In so doing, we are starting on the process of
developing our true potential as human beings.

LEARNING AND REALIZATION

The two worlds of Learning and Realization share many of the
same characteristics and are usually considered together. In
Japanese they are known as *nijo*, meaning 'two vehicles', the two
kinds of teaching expounded by the Buddha to 'carry' one to a
greater life-condition. Both Learning and Realization, therefore,
have self-betterment as their goal, the main difference between
them lying in how this is achieved.

In Japanese, the world of Learning is designated by the word
shomon, which literally means 'voice-hearers', as the *shomon*, or
men of Learning, were originally those who heard the 'voice' of
Shakyamuni Buddha when he was preaching. Strictly speaking,
then, the world of Learning applies to the Buddha's disciples,

those who try to attain enlightenment by following his teachings. In a more general sense, however, it applies to that aspect of our consciousness which can learn from the realizations of others and apply what we have thus learnt to our own lives. In this sense, the world of Learning might be said to correspond to intelligence and to be concerned with existing knowledge.

The world of Realization, on the other hand, might be said to correspond to wisdom or insight, the state which enables us to come to an understanding directly from our own observations, experience and reflection. This understanding may be as grand as the workings of the universe, or as humble as how to wire a plug. What matters in the world of Realization is that we come to that undertanding largely through our own efforts. The Japanese word for this state, *engaku*, refers to those who try to reach enlightenment without encountering a Buddha or his teachings, and whose enlightenment is therefore partial or incomplete.

The distinction between these two states is often not as sharp as this. For example, one could say that a person studying arithmetic is in the state of Learning while he is sincerely trying to understand why two plus two makes four, but enters the world of Realization when he does understand, even though his knowledge has been imparted to him by a teacher. Similarly, the state of Realization is also often called Absorption, although this term could equally be said to be characteristic of the state of Learning. Clearly, however you draw the line, the worlds of Learning and Realization are closely related for, just as those in Learning receive the fruits of the efforts of those in Realization, so great efforts in the world of Learning can often lead to new realizations, as Bertrand Russell vividly describes:

> Every one who has done any kind of creative work has experienced, in a greater or lesser degree, the state of mind in which, after long labour, truth or beauty appears, or seems to appear, in sudden glory – it may be only about some small matter, or it may be about the universe. The experience is, at the moment, very convincing; doubt may come later, but at the time there is utter certainty. I think most of the best creative work, in art, in science, in literature, and in philosophy, has been the result of such a moment. Whether it comes to others as to me, I cannot say. For my part, I have found that, when I wish to write a book on some

subject, I must first soak myself in detail, until all the separate
parts of the subject matter are familiar; then, some day, if I am
fortunate, I perceive the whole, with all its parts duly interrelated.
After that, I only have to write down what I have seen. The
nearest analogy is first walking all over a mountain in a mist, until
every path and ridge and valley is separately familiar, and then,
from a distance, seeing the mountain whole and in bright
sunshine.

Using Russell's analogy, the 'long labour' of 'walking all over a
mountain' of existing knowledge on a particular subject, could be
said to be the cause, Learning, while 'seeing the mountain whole
and in bright sunshine' is the effect, Realization. Again, one
might point to knowing the parts separately and then seeing their
interrelation as another characteristic distinction between
Learning and Realization. One of the main differences between
the state of Realization, or partial enlightenment, and Buddhahood is that, in Buddhahood, one's awareness of the interrelation
of all phenomena is complete rather than partial.

Russell's mention of creative work in the fields of art, science,
literature and philosophy is also significant for, though not
confined to these fields, the worlds of Learning and Realization
are dominant in these areas and. particularly in the realm of
science, totally interdependent.

For instance, as a young man Copernicus (1473–1543) learnt
the then prevalent Ptolemaic view of the universe which, stated
simply, asserted that the sun, the stars and the other planets
revolved around the earth in a series of concentric circles. From
his own observations Copernicus came to the realization that,
broadly speaking, the opposite was true. Copernicus's theory was
later studied and developed by Kepler (1571–1630) who concluded that planetary motion was elliptical rather than circular.
Galileo (1564–1642), while adopting Kepler's theories, confirming and extending their application through the use of the
telescope (which he had also adopted and improved), came to
some important realizations of his own, particularly as a result of
independent experiments in the field of dynamics, the science of
motion. The realizations of these three men were in turn
absorbed by Newton (1642–1727) who synthesized them into his
famous three Laws of Motion. These provided the basis for all
astronomy, indeed for all physical science, until Einstein (1879–

1955) put forward his theory of relativity in 1905 and undercut the Newtonian view of the universe as completely as Copernicus had the Ptolemaic almost 400 years earlier.

In respect of science, one can see how the repeated pattern of Learning leading to Realization has resulted in an upward curve of staggering technological achievement and material progress. Applied to the non-scientific world, however, the picture is anything but progressive. For example, in the centuries since his death there has been no dramatist in the English language who can compare with Shakespeare, either poetically or in terms of the depth of his understanding of human nature. In music, the achievements of Mozart and Beethoven are still unsurpassed, if not unmatched, and the giants in the world of religion all lived hundreds, if not thousands, of years ago. Modern philosophy may or may not have added significantly to our understanding of the human condition but, generally speaking, in the non-scientific world we can discern no mirror image of the worlds of Learning and Realization leading to an ever-increasing under-standing of life. One needs to ask why this is so.

The answer that Buddhism gives points up the inherent limitations of Learning and Realization, an awareness of which prompted Shakyamuni, before he taught the Lotus Sutra, to specifically deny the ability of any men of 'the two vehicles' to attain enlightenment.

The first limitation is that these two worlds are basically self-centred. Although their goal is self-betterment and, ultimately perhaps, even enlightenment, it is self-betterment purely for one's own sake. As such Learning and Realization have a strong tendency to deteriorate into the world of Anger, of separating oneself from other people and looking down on them. This tendency is marked in many students and tutors in centres of academic excellence, for example, and in professions which demand a high level of intellectual training. Even in the world of medicine, which is meant to be based upon the desire to care for others, doctors can display a contempt for their patients (and each other) which belies their supposed superiority.

This self-centredness might equally well manifest itself as a state of such absorption in the subject at hand that everything else is obliterated from view. To a certain extent this is unavoidable as concentration is necessary to the successful completion of any task, and may result in nothing more harmless than the absent-minded professor, so bound up in his work that he forgets to tie up his shoes or put on matching socks in the morning. Such self-centred absorption can be more damaging, however, when it appears as the husband who consistently ignores his wife at breakfast by reading the newspaper or who is so wrapped up in his hobbies and interests that he neglects his family; and it can be fatal when it appears in a group of specialists so wholly concerned with the technical problems their research presents that they do not stop to consider the larger implications of what they are doing. The men who developed the first atomic weapons would fall into this category.

The second limitation, closely allied to the first, is that those who have attained a high level of achievement in their field often find it extremely difficult to accept that the conclusions they have come to by themselves may not be wholly correct. In science this bar to progress is not insuperable, as the validity of any hypothesis has to be proved either experimentally or theoretic-ally. This means that, ultimately, differences of opinion can be settled by reference to agreed and accepted norms (even if the hypothesis overturns those norms, as in the case of Einstein's theory of relativity). In the non-scientific world, however, there is a lack of agreement on the framework of reference itself. A communist and a capitalist, or an atheist and a Moslem, have immense difficulty even in recognizing each other's vision of the world, no matter how learned or erudite they might be. One characteristic of the truly wise man is that he can recognize the wisdom in others and is more concerned in discovering the truth of any situation than in simply defending his own opinion. By contrast, those in Learning and Realization tend, as time goes on, to place faith in their judgement and their judgement alone. In this light, the reaction of the German mathematician, Gotlob Frege, to a letter from Russell in 1902 pointing out a basic mistake in his theories, appears quite extraordinary. Russell later explained:

> As I think about acts of integrity and grace, I realize that there is nothing in my knowledge to compare with Frege's dedication to truth. His entire life's work was on the verge of completion, much of his work had been ignored to the benefit of men infinitely less

capable, his second volume was about to be published, and upon finding that his fundamental assumption was in error, he responded with intellectual pleasure clearly submerging any feelings of personal disappointment. It was almost superhuman, a telling indication of that which men are capable if their dedication is to creative work and knowledge instead of cruder efforts to dominate and be known.

As Russell implies, Frege's magnanimity was almost unbelieveable simply because it so goes against the grain of the academic world that they both inhabited.

The tendency of those in Learning and Realization to have such an overweening confidence in their own abilities and judgement would not be so important were it not for the fact that people in whom these worlds are dominant tend to have a great deal of influence, if not actual power, over the lives of others. Their undoubted superiority in factual knowledge and skill in argument usually lends them a degree of persuasiveness that is hard to combat. Politicians and civil servants are the most obvious examples here, but, as often as not, they too are dependent on the 'expert' advice of specialists to help form their judgements. It is extremely dangerous, however, to rely too heavily on the narrow expertise of others. Aurelio Peccei puts it succinctly when he notes:

> Experience has vividly shown that, if we leave the world to those who actually wield power – politicians, developers, technocrats, bureaucrats and businessmen – we walk straight into trouble, leading with our chin, because these are the very people who give insufficient consideration to the indirect or delayed effects of their acts on our sensitive ecological and social environments. Engineers too, who in their own field can do splendid things, must be restrained.

To give just one contemporary example, 'experts' calculated that the chance of a nuclear reactor exploding were so infinitesimally remote as to be non-existent, especially when weighed against the various sophisticated safety devices that would stop any accident getting out of hand, and yet first Three Mile Island, then Chernobyl, proved them wrong. Ultimately, both accidents were the result of human error, so one is forced to conclude that until that can be eliminated, the operation of advanced and potentially dangerous technology such as one finds in nuclear power stations can never be truly safe.

Nowadays, thanks to the dominance of science and technology in our culture, we have fallen into the habit of thinking that the narrow rationality that has produced the undoubted material achievements which surround us can be applied with equal success to all the problems which confront us. When the 'experts' disagree, however, and men and women who clearly are highly educated and highly rational come to completely opposite opinions as to the best way to produce a thriving economy, say, then such rationality is shown to be wanting. In essence, this is because the worlds of Learning and Realization are very like the advanced computers that they have produced. In other words, what you get out depends entirely upon what you put in. Someone in whom Anger is strong, for example, will 'process' this state through Learning and Realization, possibly to attain a position which will prove his superiority to others; someone in whom Hunger is powerful may study hard simply to get the qualifications necessary for a high-paying job; and someone who is dominated by Animality may use the highest sort of intelligence to devise what may appear to be clever and sophisticated but is, in truth, just another means of dominating others. It has been estimated, for example, that 90 per cent of all the scientists who have ever lived are alive today, and that almost half of them are engaged in weapons' research.

The idea that we can 'think' ourselves out of trouble is one that is very strong in our personal lives; but 'thinking' is not effective if the way we think is actually a large part of the trouble. Thus, when faced with a problem in a close relationship, many people sit and analyze all aspects of the problem in the finest detail, discussing it with friends, family or even professional counsellors of one sort or another. In this way, they can often come to a very good theoretical understanding of their situation and may even have a clear view of their own strengths and weaknesses and what they have to do if they want things to change. Simply knowing what is wrong does not, however, necessarily give you the strength to take the necessary action. Laziness, for instance, can sometimes be overcome by the simple exertion of willpower, but then, if you are lazy, in all probability you lack the very willpower you need to make more effort. Similarly, a woman who is continually beaten up by her husband or lover but who keeps going back to him is in the grip of forces more powerful than her rational judgement can control, be they economic or emotional.

Clearly, even though they belong to the Four Noble Paths, the worlds of Learning and Realization are very much double-sided in nature. At best, when based on the desire to improve the human condition, they can lead to discoveries which are of immense benefit; at worst, as when based on the desire to extort more profit for profit's sake, they can lead to the degradation of the natural environment and, ultimately, to the destruction of life itself.

In the final analysis, the pattern of coming to certain conclusions about the world and one's place in it, through learning knowledge of the past and melding it with one's own experience, should not be confined to science alone nor, indeed, to the creative arts or philosophy, but, rather, should constitute the basis of all human existence. As Daisaku Ikeda says, 'The *raison d'être* of all humans lies in crystallizing and utilizing the past for the sake of the future.' Only as more and more ordinary people come to understand both this and that their own unique wisdom can make a vital contribution to solving the problems which beset us, will the worlds of Learning and Realization cease to be the exclusive preserve of specialists and begin to work consistently for the betterment of all mankind. To see how this can come about, we need to consider the two highest states of being, those of Bodhisattva and Buddhahood.

BODHISATTVA

The world of Bodhisattva is characterized by the spirit of *jihi* which, as we saw earlier, is the desire to replace suffering in others with happiness. Like all the Ten Worlds, Buddhism teaches that the Bodhisattva nature exists as a potential in everyone which, in view of 'man's inhumanity to man', we may sometimes find hard to believe. But, as Nichiren Daishonin says, 'Even a heartless villain loves his wife and children. He too has a portion of the Bodhisattva world within him.' Of course, as Nichiren Daishonin implies, the degree to which this Bodhisattva nature has been revealed and developed varies greatly from individual to individual. That of the 'heartless villain' extends only as far as his immediate family while, for some people, it may be even more restricted: the bitter misanthrope, for example, who hates all mankind but loves and cares for a favourite cat or dog.

At the other extreme to the misanthrope stands the person whose life is dominated by the world of Bodhisattva. Those in this state gain the greatest possible joy and satisfaction from devotion to the happiness of others, often at the expense of their own comfort or even, sometimes, their lives. Nurses are a very good example of this world, which is doubtless what prompted the journalist, the late James Cameron, while in hospital fighting the illness that was eventually to kill him, to remark that his profession probably ranked only slightly higher than that of the lawyer, but definitely way below that of the nurse. Those in whom Bodhisattva is dominant are not motivated by fame or fortune and, often as not, pass their whole lives without any great wealth and in relative obscurity. Living and working among the people, they challenge the reality of suffering day by day, inspired by a concern for others which largely obliterates their own personal desires.

A mother's pure love for her child is perhaps the best analogy of the compassion inherent in the world of Bodhisattva, a compassion that is total and unconditional, concerned wholly with the well-being, growth and fulfilment of those other than oneself. Paradoxically, though, Buddhism teaches that this altruistic concern for the happiness and growth of others is the very way the Bodhisattva, too, becomes happy and fulfilled. The problem is that, while we tend to see it as natural that this sort of compassion exists in parents for their children (even if we know that it is by no means always the case), we think it less natural to offer such compassion to strangers.

This is because parents are able to see their children as a direct extension of themselves. The biological link is so close and so strong, particularly for the mother, that it is possible to have an almost complete empathy with one's offspring, at least when they are very young. The less direct the relationship, however, the more difficult this feeling of identification with, and thus compassion for, another person becomes. Even the compassion felt by man and wife for each other is usually much less than that of parent for child, being more subject to selfish desires and various forms of egotism; as our relationships gradually become more tenuous and impersonal, so our compassion for others tends to dry up altogether. There is definitely also an element of self-protection here for, to identify with another's suffering, however remote, is also to admit both one's instinctive desire to alleviate it and the limits of one's ability to do so.

Thus, it is usual for each of us to construct an unconscious hierarchy of compassion. Seen as a pyramid, at the top we might put our children, for example, then our spouse, our parents, our friends and wider family, then, maybe, our country and, finally, the unknown, anonymous rest of mankind. Somewhere in the pyramid we place ourselves. From time to time our Bodhisattva nature may be stirred by television pictures of disasters and suffering in faraway parts of the world, and we may give money to a variety of charities, but it takes an enormous amount of life-force to sustain a concern for other people on anything but the most immediate scale.

And yet, as the problems confronting us become larger and more interconnected, so that the growth of Third World debt begins to undermine the western economies, for example, or warfare in one area of the globe leads to instability in another, concern for the welfare of strangers is becoming no longer simply an ideal, but an absolute necessity. As Nichiren Daishonin says in one of his most important writings, *Rissho Ankoku Ron (On Securing the Peace of the Land through the Propagation of True Buddhism)*, 'If you care anything about your personal security, you should first of all pray for order and tranquillity throughout the four quarters of the land, should you not?' The 'land' referred to here is thirteenth-century Japan, then suffering a seemingly unending series of calamities and disasters, but the principles expounded in this treatise have an urgent relevance to the whole world, now. For what sense is there in having children, for whom we will feel the utmost tenderness and the greatest hope, if by the time they have grown to adulthood the state of the world has so degenerated that they cannot get a job, live in peace, or even breathe fresh air? We might say, then, that one of the greatest challenges confronting us is how to extend our individual Bodhisattva nature, that loving compassion of the mother for her child that dwells in each of us, so that it can embrace the whole of mankind.

In the West this challenge has, for many hundreds of years, been embodied in the great Christian doctrine of loving one's enemies and one's neighbour as oneself. Unfortunately, Christ taught this as an ideal only and did not leave a practical method that would enable ordinary people to develop the high state of life in which this is possible. Of course, there have been exceptional men and women in history who, inspired by Christian doctrine, have been able to manifest their Bodhisattva natures to an extremely high degree – Florence Nightingale and Martin Luther King are but two of the more recent; generally speaking, though, despite aspiring to the loftiness of the ideal, Christians have often found it is extremely difficult, if not impossible, to love even other Christians, let alone those who follow different teachings.

Until the appearance of Nichiren Daishonin, in Buddhism too the highest states of life – Bodhisattva and Buddhahood – were taught as being far above the level of ordinary people. One could become a Buddha only after countless aeons of 'good works' as a bodhisattva, but the descriptions and images of the bodhisattvas themselves were so fantastic that they bore very little relation to everyday life and it was not at all clear how one could become one. Bodhisattva Kannon, for example, is supposed to be able to assume thirty-three different forms and appear anywhere in order to save people, while Bodhisattva Yakuo can cure all spiritual and physical illnesses, and the infinitely wise Bodhisattva Kokuzo 'dwells in space'. To all intents and purposes, then, these beings are no different from gods, embodying supernatural qualities no common mortal could emulate.

It was Nichiren Daishonin who explained that the qualities all these great Bodhisattvas actually represent the magnitude of compassion lying dormant in ordinary individuals and the various forms which this inherent compassion can take. Thus Bodhisattva Kannon represents the many ways that the quality of mercy can be displayed; Yakuo stands for medicine; and various other bodhisattvas represent wisdom, learning, music and the arts, and so on. Their one common feature is that their various skills or qualities are directed towards the happiness of others. In this sense, then, Florence Nighingale might be said to be an embodiment of Bodhisattva Yakuo, working as she did to relieve the suffering of sickness throughout her life.

The fact that ordinary people possess these great qualities as a potential in their lives does not necessarily mean that they will actually reveal them. It took the Crimean War to bring about the revolution in Florence Nightingale's attitude which led her to dedicate the rest of her life to establishing the basic standards for nursing which we still know today. Similarly, it often takes an equally profound experience in our own lives for us to decide to work for the welfare and happiness of others, and so manifest the qualities of one or more of these bodhisattvas.

The rock musician Bob Geldof is an interesting example of this. Like many people he was deeply shocked by what he saw of the famine in Ethiopia on television in 1984 but, unlike many others, he realized he was in a position where he could do something to help on a very large scale. By raising money for those starving, first with the Band Aid record at Christmas of that year and then through the transatlantic Live Aid concerts in 1985, he acted, albeit briefly, as the embodiment of Bodhisattva Myo'on, who relieves suffering through music and the arts. Although we may not act in as spectacular a way, we too can behave as embodiments of these great bodhisattvas when we decide to use our own unique skills and talents to help others.

This is an extremely important point to remember, for it helps to explain some of the more esoteric and puzzling aspects of Buddhism. For example, the Lotus Sutra describes a moment when Shakyamuni Buddha, having finished preaching the Law to an enormous assembly, including such great bodhisattvas as Yakuo and Miroku, repeatedly urges them to protect and propagate the Law after his death. Naturally, they all shout their assent to this command but, suddenly, Shakyamuni says, 'Desist, men of devout faith! There is no need for you to protect this sutra,' whereupon the ground splits open and there appears a host of magnificent bodhisattvas, more numerous than the sands of 60,000 Ganges rivers, whom no one in the assembly has ever seen before. These are the Bodhisattvas of the Earth, led by four bodhisattvas even more magnificent than the others – Jogyo, Muhengyo, Jyogyo and Anryugyo. It is to them, and specifically to Jogyo, that Shakyamuni entrusts the task of expounding the Lotus Sutra in the distant future, the 'Latter day of the Law'.

Now, this is clearly a metaphorical event, but what does it mean? There are a number of important implications to be drawn from it, of which for now three deserve discussion. The first is that the Bodhisattvas of the Earth are greater than 'provisional' bodhisattvas like Yakuo and Miroku. This is because while provisional bodhisattvas are able to help people by applying their specific skills to suffering, the Bodhisattvas of the Earth are able to give the key to indestructible happiness by teaching the Law whereby people can become Buddhas. Thus, for example, a doctor may be able to cure his patient, which is wonderful, but that will not enable the patient to attain enlightenment, which would be better still.

Secondly, the appearance of the four leaders of the Bodhisattvas of the Earth represents the inherent potential human beings possess of developing qualities even greater than those embodied in the provisional bodhisattvas. As Nichiren Daishonin explains, 'Jogyo represents the self; Muhengyo represents eternity; Jyogyo represents purity; Anryugyo represents happiness.' Daisaku Ikeda examines this statement in some depth:

> In my interpretation, the virtue of self means the strengthening of the self to the point where it can withstand challenges from without and turn difficulties into opportunities for growth. Eternity means a firm belief in eternal life, together with an effort, founded thereon, to press forward ceaselessly towards the goal. The sense of eternity strengthens one's confidence that through compassionate action one can change one's neighbours, one's surroundings, one's country, or even the whole world.
>
> Purity means a clean and brilliant life, in which evil or egoistic instincts are powerless to sway one. A life devoted to helping others, rather than pursuing one's own advantage, sheds the light of true wisdom and intelligence. Happiness means the joy of living on an unshakeable foundation rooted in the life-force of the cosmos.

Thirdly, and most importantly, it follows from this that just as we ordinary human beings can act as the embodiments of provisional bodhisattvas by displaying the compassionate qualities they represent, so we can act as Bodhisattvas of the Earth by dedicating ourselves to teaching others the Law. In effect, this means that by sincerely propagating the Buddhism which teaches others how to reveal their inherent Buddhahood, we quite naturally develop the qualities of the four leaders of the Bodhisattvas of the Earth who are themselves manifestations of the world of Buddhahood. In this way, we ordinary human beings are able to display the greatest possible compassion and thus gain the greatest possible joy.

For all its great qualities, however, even the noble world of Bodhisattva possesses negative aspects. One of these is the tendency to feel superior and condescending towards those you are helping, offering them pity or charity rather than true compassion; another is the danger of begrudging the time and effort one devotes to the happiness of another. Those looking after elderly relatives at home are often prey to this emotion, for example, though it is in fact common to many areas where people serve each other, especially at work. In fact, to discover a state of being which is wholly positive, in that it always expresses itself by creating value, regardless of the situation, one has finally to turn to the highest of the Ten Worlds, that of Buddhahood itself.

BUDDHAHOOD

From the moment of Shakyamuni's enlightenment under the pipal, or Bodhi, tree in India some 3000 years ago, there have always been three basic questions and one basic problem involved in any discussion of the world of Buddhahood, the supreme state of human life. The questions can be summed up as: 'What? Me? How?'; in other words, 'What is the nature of Buddhahood?' 'Do I really possess it?' and 'How can I see it?' The problem is that the answer to each of these three questions is, as Shakyamuni warned, both 'difficult to believe and difficult to understand'. Ultimately, just as you have to eat a strawberry to know what it tastes like, so Buddhahood must be experienced to be understood. Even so, a theoretical explanation can be a good starting-point.

So, first of all, what is Buddhahood? Perhaps it would be easier to begin by saying what it is not. Buddhahood is not a supernatural quality which enables you to perform superhuman or magical feats like levitation; neither is it a transcendental state, divorced from the everyday reality of this world, in which you experience mental bliss and peace. Buddahood exists and can only be manifested, here and now, through the actions of real people in this real world. Nichiren Daishonin says, 'The real meaning of the Lord Shakyamuni Buddha's appearance in this world lay in his behaviour as a human being. How profound!' In other words, Shakyamuni was not a god but a man, and Buddhahood, although the highest state of life, is one that is attainable by all people. Thus, there is no fundamental difference between a Buddha and an ordinary person: a Buddha is simply an ordinary person 'awakened' to the true nature of life. As Nichiren Daishonin further explains, 'While deluded, one is called a common mortal, but once enlightened, he is called a Buddha.'

If you refer back to the introduction to this section on the Ten Worlds, however, you will notice that the start to a typical day mentions only nine of the Ten Worlds, from Hell to Bodhisattva. This is because although everybody possesses the tenth world, Buddhahood, until they learn of its existence, realize they must possess it too, and then discover how to manifest it, their Buddhahood lies dormant in their lives. For example, Daisaku Ikeda describes Buddhahood like this:

> [It] is the joy of joys . . . Birth, old age, illness and death are no longer suffering, but part of the joy of living. The light of wisdom illuminates the entire universe, destroying the innate benighted nature of man. The life-space of the Buddha becomes united and fused with the universe. The self becomes the cosmos, and in a single instant the life-flow stretches out to encompass all that is past and all that is future. In each moment of the present, the eternal life-force of the cosmos gushes forth as a gigantic fountain of energy.

Clearly, there are few of us who can honestly claim to experience life like this. Possibly, from time to time, we may feel moments of intense Rapture which briefly correspond to parts of the description here, but those moments are essentially transient. The joy of Buddhahood is different from that of Rapture, not least because it is a joy that cannot be destroyed by suffering but, rather, can absorb it, and is a joy enriched by a deep understanding of how life works from moment to moment. Wisdom, courage, compassion, life-force – these too are qualities of the world of Buddhahood which are lacking in the world of Rapture.

From this description it can be seen that Buddhahood does not manifest itself as a special 'extra' state of life but, rather, is that quality which, when dominant in an individual, enriches every moment of his or her daily life, making even the supposedly mundane or problematic aspects of existence a source of happiness. It follows from this that, once we begin to reveal our Buddhahood, we do not have to try to suppress or deny any of our lower states of life, as our Buddhahood quite naturally enables us to reveal the positive aspects of our other nine worlds, from Hell to Bodhisattva, and so continually create value for ourselves and others. This is why in Nichiren Shoshu Buddhism there are no commandments, no rules to regulate human conduct. Instead, the emphasis is wholly upon learning more and more about our own Buddhahood, and about how to reveal and make it dominant in our lives. How you actually live – for example, whether you smoke, drink or eat meat – is thus entirely up to you. When you start to practise this Buddhism, though, and begin to experience the wisdom and compassion of your own Buddha nature working in your life, you will quickly come to see which of your actions create true value for yourself and others and which cause suffering, though whatever course you decide to take remains wholly up to you.

Once he had attained enlightenment, Shakyamuni too had the initial problem of explaining to the people of his day exactly what it meant to experience enlightenment or Buddhahood. Perhaps the best analogy for the task facing him would be to liken it to Einstein trying to explain relativity to nursery-school children. In the Lotus Sutra, therefore, Shakyamuni described the nature of his enlightenment, that is, his subjective experience of Buddhahood, by describing the appearance of the Treasure Tower. This was an enormous stupa, covered in rare and precious gems, which rose out of the earth until it reached a height equal to half the earth's diameter. Obviously, such an event never happened, but is rather an analogy employed by Shakyamuni to express the richness and magnitude of his supreme state of life, a vivid and powerful image that could be understood by the people of early India, used as they were to fantastic tales of god and goddesses, devils and demons.

In contrast, T'ien-t'ai, faced with the problem many hundreds of years later of explaining Buddhahood to the more sophisticated and logical Chinese, employed the theory known as *ichinen sanzen*; this literally means 'three thousand worlds in a single moment of life'. This theory, however (of which the Ten Worlds is a part and which will be explained more fully later in this book), even though very precise, is still extremely difficult to understand intellectually. As a result, many people believed that one had to be some sort of genius to become enlightened.

For Nichiren Daishonin the problem was slightly different as, by the time he appeared in thirteenth-century Japan, everybody thought they knew what Buddhahood was – namely, the state of life that Shakyamuni Buddha alone had achieved, so that by then both he and Buddhahood were regarded as virtually divine. Playing devil's advocate in one of his writings, Nichiren Daishonin sums up the attitude toward Shakyamuni and Buddhahood then current (and, incidentally, still prevalent in many parts of the East):

> Shakyamuni, the lord of doctrine, is the Buddha who has destroyed all the three illusions. He is the sovereign of all sentient beings in the entire universe – kings, bodhisattvas, people of the two vehicles, common mortals and heavenly beings . . . How could such a great Buddha dwell in the hearts of us common mortals?

This brings us to the second question: 'Do I, the person reading this book, possess Buddhahood?' The answer is 'Yes'. The problem is that, never having experienced it, you probably cannot believe that such a wonderful state of life is possible, let alone that it exists in your life. Of course, this is a natural reaction and one anticipated by Nichiren Daishonin: 'Buddhahood is the most difficult state to demonstrate. But since you possess the other nine worlds, you should believe that you have Buddhahood as well. Do not permit yourself to have doubts.' One way of interpreting this statement might be to say that if you can see that the theory of the nine worlds from Hell to Bodhisattva accurately describes the reality of life as you know it, so you should have confidence that the tenth world, Buddhahood, also exists.

This brings us to the third question: 'How can I see this Buddhahood?' Nichiren Daishonin is unequivocal. To give in full a passage quoted earlier, he says:

> While deluded, one is called a common mortal, but once enlightened he is called a Buddha. Even a tarnished mirror will shine like a jewel if it is polished. A mind which is presently

clouded by illusions originating from the innate darkness of life is like a tarnished mirror, but once it is polished it will become clear, reflecting the enlightenment of immutable truth. Arouse deep faith and polish your mirror night and day. How should you polish it? Only by chanting *Nam-myoho-renge-kyo.*

Once again, the real problem here is whether you can believe this for, although on one level this third question appears to be simply about method, fundamentally it is a demand for the actual proof discussed earlier and, as such, is absolutely crucial.

In the final analysis, the only way to test the validity of Nichiren Daishonin's assertion that you, too, possess this supreme state of life called Buddhahood, is to do as he suggests: chant *Nam-myoho-renge-kyo* and see for yourself. In this sense, practising Nichiren Daishonin's Buddhism is just like going to the doctor: if the diagnosis is right, the medicine will work; which is another way of saying that if the medicine works, then the diagnosis must be right.

MUTUAL POSSESSION

Before we go on to look at some experiences of people who did decide to put theory to the test, there are three further aspects of the principle of the Ten Worlds that need some explanation.

The first of these is that, although everybody possesses all the Ten Worlds, in different people different worlds are stronger and weaker and, in most people, one world tends to dominate. So, for example, the test pilot in Tom Wolfe's *The Right Stuff* is dominated by Anger; Alexei, the hero of Dostoyevsky's *The Gambler*, is dominated by Hunger; Florence Nightingale was dominated by her Bodhisattva nature, and so on. This is very important, because whichever state is dominant in your life also affects all the other nine. Thus, although a person in whom the state of Anger is very strong also possesses the state of Bodhisattva, for example, any compassionate action he takes will probably be accompanied by feelings of superiority towards those whom he is helping. By contrast, the Anger possessed by the person in whom the Bodhisattva nature is dominant will almost invariably be expressed on behalf of those for whom he or she is caring. Indeed, Florence Nightingale's battles against the hierarchy of the British Army during the Crimean War are a classic example of this.

This brings us to the second point. The fact that any one of the Ten Worlds can affect all the others is explained in a principle called the *mutual possession* of the Ten Worlds. The pre-Lotus Sutra teachings described the Ten Worlds as if they were actual physical locations into which a person was born according to the causes that he had made in his previous existences and in which particular world that person was destined to stay for a lifetime. Thus, beings in Hell existed underground, those in Animality in the sea, on the land and in the air, those in Humanity on the earth, and so on.

In contrast, the Lotus Sutra teaches that the Ten Worlds are ways of describing the subjective experience of individuals, and, furthermore, that each of the Ten Worlds 'possesses' or 'contains' all the others. This means that each of the Ten Worlds gives the others its own particular 'flavour'; for example, the Hunger of a person dominated by Tranquillity may appear as a longing for something but without any action taken to achieve it, while the Hunger of someone in the grip of Animality can be seen in, say, the desperate, grasping desire of one of those sale-time shoppers mentioned earlier. Similarly, the Tranquillity of someone dominated by Animality could well appear in one of those same shoppers sitting contentedly on the bus home, highly satisfied with the bargain he or she has managed to grab before anyone else, while the Tranquillity of someone who lives in the state of Hell could be a complete resignation or apathy in the face of suffering. In effect, then, the mutual possession of the Ten Worlds multiplies these ten basic states of being, making them more subtle and complex. As T'ien-tai states, 'Life at each moment is endowed with the Ten Worlds. At the same time, each of the Ten Worlds is endowed with all the others, so that an entity of life actually possesses one hundred worlds.'

The mutual possession of the Ten Worlds is also the theoretical basis for explaining the possibility of moving from one state to another, from moment to moment. If the world of Rapture, for example, did not 'contain' the world of Hell, it would be impossible to feel over the moon at one moment and then, thanks to some bad news, down in the dumps the next. Similarly, if the world of Hell did not 'contain' the world of Rapture, no piece of good news could ever cheer us up, however momentarily. Thus, according to this principle of mutual possession, at any moment we have the possibility, at the next moment, of either remaining in our present life-state or moving into any of the other nine. This not only accounts for people's changeability, but also explains how we can sometimes act in ways which we know to be contradictory, irrational or even harmful. To take an example, the psychiatrist who gets terribly depressed even though he knows everything there is to know about clinical depression and successfully treats it in others, can become so only because Hell also exists in the worlds of Realization and Bodhisattva: to put it another way, his capacity for suffering cannot be eradicated by his knowledge.

A question arises from the idea of the mutual possession of the Ten Worlds: when we are in Hell, say, then where exactly is our Rapture and all the other nine worlds from Hunger to Buddhahood? Where do the other nine worlds 'go' when we are in the tenth? This brings us to our third point, as the answer that Buddhism gives is that they are in a state of latency, called *ku*.

The concept of *ku** has caused a great deal of difficulty for people trying to understand Buddhism through the ages because it refers to a state that is 'neither existence nor non-existence'. To most western minds this statement will probably appear to be nonsensical: either something exists or it does not. The concept of *ku*, however, explains that there are a number of phenomena which do not fit into this rigid duality. For example, we all know that we can get angry from time to time, but we also know that it normally takes something quite specific for us to lose our temper – an insult, a personal injustice, whatever. When we do lose our temper the outwards signs are very obvious: a fierce expression, direct stare, raised voice, harsh tone and so on. When our temper has cooled, however, these signs disappear. We know that we still possess a temper but, right now, we can point to no evidence that it exists within us. At that moment, our anger is in the state of *ku*: it exists and yet it does not; we know that our temper is 'somewhere' within our life and, at the same time, there is absolutely no way to confirm this except by becoming angry again.

Take another example: a tape cassette of music. The music

*Skt *sunya* or *sunyatta*, meaning 'Void'.

stored on the cassette is in a state of *ku* until the cassette is actually played. Strictly speaking, one can say that the tape exists and that the tape is covered with a series of magnetic impulses but the music itself exists only when a number of external conditions are met; in this case, when the tape in the cassette is passing over the play head at the right speed, and when those magnetic impulses are then translated and boosted through an amplifier and finally broadcast as sounds through a speaker. The absence of any one of these factors will mean the music stays in *ku*.

To put it simply, one might say that *ku* is applicable to those matters which we know to have a certain continuity but which only appear when the conditions are right. To all intents and purposes, the rest of the time they do not seem to exist at all. Memories are another good example of this, as we only know we have them when they pop into our conscious mind; the rest of the time they exist in the unconscious, unknown to us, in *ku*.

Nichiren Daishonin was well aware of the problems posed by the concepts of *ku* and the mutual possession of the Ten Worlds. He says, 'The mutual possession of the Ten Worlds is as difficult to believe as fire existing in a stone or flowers within a tree. Yet under the right conditions such phenomena occur and can be believed.' We may take it for granted that coal can be burnt, for example, and that a cherry tree blossoms in spring, because we have probably all had some direct experience of these events. Imagining for a moment that we have had no such experience, if we encountered a cherry tree in winter we would most likely think it dead, as that is what the evidence of our senses tells us; if, having been convinced that it was alive, we then decided to dissect and analyze it, we would find nothing to suggest that it would be covered in flowers in spring: those flowers at that moment do not exist. And yet they do, in *ku*, waiting for the right time and conditions to appear.

The reason these two related concepts are so important is that they help to explain, theoretically, why it is possible for anyone, in any condition of life, to reveal his or her Buddhahood. Even if you have never actually experienced your Buddhahood, it exists, at this very moment, in the state of *ku*, and, just like the flowers in the cherry tree, is simply waiting for the right conditions in order to appear. Following on from the passage quoted above, Nichiren Daishonin says:

Since you now believe that Humanity contains the other eight worlds from Hell to Bodhisattva, why are you still unable to include Buddhahood? The Chinese sage-kings Yao and Shun were impartial towards all people. They perceived one aspect of Buddhahood within Humanity. Bodhisattva Fukyo* saw the Buddha in everyone he met, and Prince Siddartha [Shakyamuni] was a man who became a Buddha. These examples should help you to believe.

In addition to this, the mutual possession of the Ten Worlds also explains that the world of Hell contains Buddhahood; this means that no matter how much you are suffering at this moment, at the very next you can reveal the highest condition of life. Similarly, even the world of Buddhahood contains the world of Hell; in other words, even those who have attained this great life-condition are still human beings and, as such, can still suffer. The difference is that in Buddhahood one's suffering is fundamentally for the sake of others, to prove by example that chanting *Nam-myoho-renge-kyo* can overcome that suffering and thus inspire others to chant themselves. More important still, the fact that Buddhahood exists in each of the other nine worlds underlines the point that a Buddha is not superhuman but an ordinary human being – albeit, an enlightened one.

But again, this may be an idea which is difficult to accept and will be dealt with more fully later. For now, let us turn for a moment from theory to practice and look at the experience of three people who, through applying the practice of Nichiren Shoshu Buddhism to their daily lives, were able to challenge and overcome specific areas of suffering.

THREE EXPERIENCES

Although one can chant *Nam-myoho-renge-kyo* anywhere and at any time that is convenient, a real commitment to practising this Buddhism comes only when one decides to receive the Gohonzon, the scroll described briefly in the Introduction. With a fundamental problem facing her, Angela Bolger decided to receive her

*An imaginary bodhisattva who appears in the Lotus Sutra and shows respect to everyone for their innate Buddha nature, despite being ridiculed and attacked with sticks and stones.

Gohonzon in June 1984. As she explains, 'Four years before I had become epileptic. My attacks were so severe that I would have to go into hospital afterwards and it would take a week to recover. Once it was established that the attacks would recur, lengthy tests and investigations were carried out to discover the best treatment. In the end I was offered drugs which would have to be taken daily and could make me dizzy, drowsy or lose my memory. I decided not to take the drugs and began to look for alternative therapies. I also met this practice.

'Quite quickly I found I could avert an epileptic attack by chanting but, though I was grateful for this, I felt I could not be completely well until I understood the cause of the illness. This was largely because I was aware that there was something wrong with my whole life for, however hard I tried to be good or do "the right thing", I always seemed to be defeated in some way. This became more easy to understand when I learned more about Buddhist philosophy which teaches that human suffering is the result of the three poisons of greed, anger and stupidity arising from the lower states of life. At the end of the lecture where this point was explained to me for the first time, the speaker suggested we should chant to challenge the particular poison which dominated each of our lives.

'Straight afterwards I went home to take up this challenge through chanting. Within a few minutes I was beside myself with rage. I was extremely shocked by this as I had always considered myself to be a reasonably even-tempered person. Still, as I told myself, at least I knew what I was up against now. Nonetheless, I was so horrified by my discovery that I wanted to hide in a dark corner. It was as if I was suddenly transparent and everyone would be able to see the horrible oozing pus of anger inside me, or they would hear it in my voice if I spoke. At first, I chanted for it to go away as I couldn't bear to live with it. Still, the more I chanted the angrier I became and I realized that it simply would not just evaporate. The only way out was to meet this thing face to face, in front of the Gohonzon, experience the anger for what it was and somehow win through.

'So the challenge was on. During the months that I fought with it I was amazed that my anger only manifested itself when I was alone. When I was with others it just did not appear. I regarded this as a form of "protection" from my practice to the Gohonzon.

What's more, as I continued to chant about it, I realized that *all* my sufferings were the result of my anger, for anger is not just stamping and shouting, it is also resentment, critical attitudes, begrudging time and effort, as well as lack of gratitude, respect and sincerity. I could see all those things in my own life, in my dissatisfaction, my problems at work and my failed relationships.

'In the end I knew that my anger was so great that I had pushed it deep down inside me because it was too awful to reveal. I came to understand that my epilepsy was nothing other than a safety-valve which went off whenever my system could not take the pressure of this accumulated anger one second longer. In other words, my illness, though clinically defined as epilepsy, was in reality just another symptom of profound anger.'

There is a principle in Nichiren Shoshu Buddhism which states that one of the quickest ways of changing any personal problem is to make great efforts for the fundamental happiness of others. This may sound paradoxical, but the idea behind this principle is that, by concerning yourself with the happiness of others, you can expand your own life so that you are no longer dominated by an introspective and suffocating concentration on your own problems. A drop of ink in a cup of water, for example, will turn the water blue; the same drop of ink in the ocean will completely disappear. By gradually expanding your life through efforts for others, therefore, not only is your suffering lessened but you also develop strengths of wisdom, courage and compassion which you can then use to solve your own troubles.

Bearing this in mind, then, and having come to the realization that her illness lay rooted in her anger, Angela set herself what might seem an unrealistic target: she determined to break the back of her problem by the middle of March 1985, then only a few weeks off. That was when she would be heavily involved in helping run a major NSUK event and she felt that, by doing her utmost for others, she could change the anger that was poisoning her life. Above all, she wanted to see positive proof of this change through an improvement in her work situation and her relationships with other people, particularly her family. Now that her goal was clear, her chanting brought her to another important realization. 'I came to regard my anger as a wonderfully positive thing,' she says. 'Anger generates tremendous energy which can be harnessed to create real value. It could be my most precious weapon in the fight to change my whole life towards working for peace.'

As the NSUK event approached, though, her anger became worse and worse but, on the day itself, she was too busy to spend any time thinking about herself. That came later. 'The next Monday I woke up and felt that after all my effort, nothing had changed. Consequently I grew angrier than ever and chanted and chanted and chanted to truly change my life. I had never been so sincere about anything.

'Then, quite naturally, the change occurred and I felt its effects. I found new ways to solve old problems at work and encompass new ones; I began to relate to people far more easily and as my compassion grows stronger I am finding it easier to tell other people that they too can become happy through practising this Buddhism. Not least, I have become much closer to my family. Medically, I am considered to be free from epilepsy. As a result, I have been able to introduce several medical practitioners to Nichiren Shoshu Buddhism, and also contribute to a greater understanding of the causes for this illness and help encourage other victims in their fight.

'Best of all, I find the energy that once appeared as anger becoming more and more a passion to achieve happiness for myself and others. The experience has given me the conviction that, whatever happens to me, I can win with the Gohonzon. I consider my anger a valued companion on the path to a peaceful, creative world based on this Buddhism, and am proud and grateful to have so precious a gift and to be able to appreciate it for what it is.'

If Angela Bolger's problems stemmed from the dominance of her Anger, Graham Warwick's suffering was rooted in Hunger, a Hunger that became obsessive. Graham started drinking when he was sixteen and, by the time he began to chant, had been a heavy drinker for over twenty years. 'In the early years,' he says, 'it didn't take much to produce that beguiling sense of freedom, apparent wit, wisdom and pseudo-sophistication within the boundaries set by my social peers. As we all know, this is a very vulnerable time in life, an ideal opportunity for the three poisons of greed, anger and stupidity to predominate. Although my drinking was still at the puppyish stage, those three poisons were hard at work. Within two years much of my leisure time was spent in a pub or at weekend parties where I could get manfully drunk and, for my age, skilfully slander those with a less glib tongue than mine.'

For some time Graham still took an interest in a variety of things but gradually all his activities began to be governed by alcohol. 'If I was going somewhere, what most concerned me was whether I could get a drink there, or later at the nearest pub. I was convinced that no real enjoyment was possible unless alcohol was part of the proceedings at some point. This continued for some time until I met a girl who aroused quite different feelings in me.'

At that stage of Graham's life everything seemed to be wonderful. He had honestly never felt so happy or alive and his girlfriend seemed to enjoy social drinking as much as he did, although she did not share his attitude of drink being the central pivot of life and drinking companions the only companions worth having. But as Graham explains, 'I was too happy to pay attention to that, as yet, small difference. The relationship blossomed despite a certain amount of outside opposition, various warnings in the shape of disharmony between us from time to time, and one disastrous period just before we decided to live together. However, I still found it easier to blame every setback on circumstances, other people (including her) and anything else that came to hand. Because of my inflated ego I had not even an inkling that *I* could be in any way fundamentally responsible for the negativity in my life. Nonetheless, for most of the time, things were very good between us. We lived together for over eight years but our relationship followed the classic cycle of rapture, bewilderment when things began progressively to deteriorate and, finally, disillusionment.' Eventually they decided to split up, although they have kept in touch and remain very fond of each other.

At the time, though, the failure of this relationship hit Graham hard. 'Much of the responsibility for its breakdown was due to my ever-increasing dependence on drinking, instead of facing problems. Nearly all our friends drank. I spent most of my time either drinking at the pub or with friends I had invited back so that I could carry on drinking at home. Despite some major attempts at improving the situation, none of them initiated by me, this continued and I started drinking at home whether friends were available for an alibi or not. I became aggressive, morose and often unapproachable. From time to time alcoholic-ally stimulated remorse would allow me to see what I had allowed to happen to my life, but another drinking bout soon cured that. When the break-up finally came I dived into a well of booze and self-pity.' Things improved after a time, though, and then Graham met his present wife. Needless to say, the cycle began to repeat itself. 'It says a lot for her that we are still – and happily – together,' he now admits.

There followed years of violence within the marriage which Graham explains as 'vicious recrimination directed outward for things I should have realized were products of my own negativity. Things went from the pits to worse until about six months before meeting this practice we both made genuine attempts to repair the damage. As always, booze thwarted any headway that was made. When I met the practice at first I dismissed it as rubbish, despite several brushes with it. My wife proved to be more receptive and, since we were introduced to it by very old friends we had known independently before we were married, I eventu-ally began to chant. However, I still drank heavily, missed days from work and allowed all the negativity in me to surface without really challenging it. I still wouldn't finally accept how I was using alcohol to generate more and more bad causes in my life.'

Then, one Saturday, an NSUK leader phoned to ask if he would help look after the NSUK centre in Richmond, Surrey, the next day. On the occasions Graham had done this before he had really enjoyed it, but this time he was a bit put out by the request. He was definitely an Indian, not a chief; nonetheless, he agreed. He continues, 'Needless to say, I had been in the pub that lunchtime and had been busily working my way through a quantity of wine when he called. The result was that I forgot all about it. The next day, Sunday, I had a call from Richmond asking me where I was; I denied all knowledge of the commit-ment, although I felt a very uncomfortable warning pang. I'd been to the pub again that lunchtime and dismissed the unease I felt, but phoned the leader who had originally asked me to find out what was going on, still not allowing myself to believe I'd forgotten. He recommended that I chant about it, which I did. There was no way that I could keep up the illusion in front of the Gohonzon, despite the lunchtime drinking session, but still I wouldn't see the warning I'd been given.

'The following week I drank so much that most of the weekend was lost to me; nothing unusual, but I refused to heed that warning too. After all, when I checked up I found I hadn't done anything outrageous. I did the same thing the next weekend but, this time, accidentally injured a friend because I couldn't stay on my feet; this prompted my wife to give up on me for the day, walk off and leave me to it. At this I insisted on going back to the pub where I threatened to assault a fellow NSUK member who'd come to look for me to suggest I went home to sleep it off.

'The next day, Monday, I suffered from an almost suicidal bout of remorse. I panicked at the thought of seeing anyone I knew. I couldn't face the Gohonzon. The only person I could bear to see was my wife. In fact, the person I'd threatened came round that evening to see how I was, but I hid, refusing to open the door and pretending that no one was home. This went on for two days and then I pulled myself together enough to face the Gohonzon again, with the determination to challenge my drinking and win. I had finally realized after all these years how I had allowed – in fact, how I had engineered – all the suffering in my life, and that the greatest suffering had always been as a result of the drink I had so willingly poured down my throat.'

For the next three months Graham continued to chant to overcome his addiction. He also drank nothing alcoholic, forcing himself to visit the local pub or go where others would be drinking, simply to reinforce his determination. 'I was amazed how easy it proved to be after so many years of hard drinking, after all the lies I had told myself about my need for a drink before I could gain genuine pleasure in people's company.'

Then, in the December, several people he knew received the Gohonzon and he attended one particular celebration where food and wine was served. 'When a toast was suggested I realized that, through the power of the Gohonzon, I had conquered my greed for alcohol and accepted half a glass of wine so that I could add my own congratulations to those of the other members. I then happily went back to drinking lemonade.' When Christmas Day arrived he had a drink at the pub and, later, at a friend's house to celebrate the season. When, on Boxing Day, he and his wife had lunch with some friends, he says, 'Again I felt confidence in my ability to drink with the same wisdom and pleasure as anyone else. Finally, at a party my wife and I threw on New Year's Eve, I knew that I'd got it licked: I could drink at the appropriate times and confound the "devils" when they sought to tempt me back to my old, negative ways. I now know that I'm totally free of one of the deadliest prisons to which a human being can consign him or herself.'

What Graham feels he has learnt from his experience is perfectly clear. 'I've received actual proof that nothing in this world, no problem, no matter what its nature, can withstand sincere chanting to the Gohonzon. To say that I found (and still find) great difficulty in practising this Buddhism would be no more than the literal truth, but I will be eternally grateful to my wife and those two people who first introduced me to *Nam-myoho-renge-kyo.*'

Both Angela Bolger and Graham Warwick were fortunate in being able to identify and overcome the central problem in their lives within a relatively short time of starting to practise. For others, this process can take longer, as it may not be at all obvious where the true cause of their suffering lies. Jiggy Bhore is a case in point for, as she says, 'During three years of practice I had never really dared consider my own stupidity. I have had many, many benefits from the practice, but there had come a time when I began to suffer from jealousy and feelings of inferiority. Talking with a fellow member one evening she happened to mention that she thought her dominant poison was ignorance. I had an awful sense of recognition, as I knew then that my own ignorance of my Buddha nature was what was causing me such suffering. I determined to challenge this poison.'

This was easier said than done, though, as Jiggy soon discovered. 'It was very, very difficult. It happened that I was not working just then and so, in theory, I had plenty of time to chant. I found it hard because the feelings that came up were so strong and so negative. The more I chanted the worse I felt. This was the complete reverse of anything I had ever experienced. Over a period of about two weeks I saw my stupidity very clearly indeed. I realized that I was frightened to chant for absolute happiness because I didn't think I could possibly attain it. I imagined that the best I could hope for was a sort of calm stoicism. I saw myself as a boring, lonely, middle-aged woman who filled her life with spurious "good works" of a vaguely religious nature, and felt that I was basically unlovable, that I must simply make do, keep a stiff upper lip and soldier on. Never before had I experienced the depth of my own negativity and slander of my own life. My misery and resentment could not be hidden.' This feeling that life was only to be endured at least kept her in front of the Gohonzon, however, even though she was sometimes doing more crying than chanting. 'And truly no prayer goes unanswered in this practice,' she says, 'for a busy senior leader managed to visit me one evening.'

Jiggy told her that she was sure that, when people looked at her life, they must think that practising Buddhism was just something to fill up the gap where a husband and family should be. But, as Jiggy explains, 'She told me that no one could judge my life and that, whether I was married or not, absolute happiness only comes from within, and that now was the time to totally trust the Gohonzon, which was only an outward manifestation of my own inner Buddhahood, and to commit myself to working for the establishment of world peace. I felt much better when she left, but was still full of self-doubt.' The next morning another senior leader came to do *gongyo* with her and, after an hour's chanting with her, Jiggy knew that she had somehow changed something fundamental in her life. 'I chanted for a couple of hours after she had left and cried again, but this time it was tears of wonder and gratitude.

'Nothing in the outward circumstances of my life had changed: I was still single, out of work and certainly no younger, but everything was different. It was as if a tough shell of false "good behaviour" had cracked open so that the new shoot of my limitless true self could emerge. I knew my own uniqueness; I felt free and light and very, very happy. I am determined to live the sentence from the Lotus Sutra which says, "Singlemindedly yearning to see the Buddha they do not begrudge their lives," so that as many other people as possible may enjoy the knowledge of their own Buddha nature.'

There are several aspects of these three experiences that deserve discussion, not least of which is that all three people would consider themselves to be perfectly 'ordinary' and yet they have all realized an extraordinary quality in their lives through chanting *Nam-myoho-renge-kyo*. It should be stressed, however, that although in each case a major source of suffering was challenged and overcome, chanting *Nam-myoho-renge-kyo* is not an

instantaneous miracle cure. Revealing one's Buddhahood and
learning how to apply it to daily life is not easy for, even if one
practises assiduously, it takes a deep and sincere desire to change
oneself within, coupled with great and consistent effort, to solve
any fundamental problem. Buddhism teaches that changing
oneself is the single most difficult feat in the entire universe, so we
should not be too surprised if it cannot be done overnight. As in
the examples of Jiggy and Graham, it might take some time and
much chanting simply to summon up the courage to face the fact
that a particular problem exists in our life. Indeed, Graham
continued to drink for some time after he started to chant; this
simply had the effect of exacerbating his problem, however, so
that he was no longer able to ignore the suffering he was creating
for himself and others. Only when he decided to *challenge* his
weakness was he able to overcome it.

Through their own efforts in applying the theory and practice
of this Buddhism to their own lives, then, all three discovered that
their suffering could be traced back to the dominance within
them of one of the lower worlds. In terms of the mutual possession
of the Ten Worlds one could say that, before challenging the
source of their suffering, Angela's life displayed the Hell inherent
in Anger, Graham's the Hell inherent in Hunger and Jiggy's the
Hell inherent in Animality. That Jiggy's dominant life-state was
Animality is not at first obvious (as it was not to her, either), until
we remember that stupidity, or ignorance, is a fundamental
characteristic of that world. In this instance it expressed itself in
Jiggy's ignorance of her own true worth; her suffering came from
her voluntary placement of herself on a rung well below other
people. All three experiences, however, demonstrate the close
interrelationship between the six lower worlds and, especially,
between the Three Evil Paths of Hell, Hunger and Animality.
This relationship is particularly apparent in Graham's experience. His obsessive Hunger for drink also brought out a
strong state of Animality as, when he drank, he became
completely immersed in the Rapture of the present moment and
was unable to consider the consequences of his actions – Hell, or
various forms of suffering – until it was too late.

It is very important that each of the three discovered that the
fundamental cause of their suffering lay nowhere else but *hidden*
deep within their own lives, below the level of their conscious

minds. The realization that both suffering and happiness come from within is central to practising this Buddhism. In Jiggy's case, to all outward appearances nothing had changed at all and yet, because her fundamental attitude had changed, her suffering disappeared. Yasuji Kirimura, a senior member of the SGI (Soka Gakkai) Study Department, explains this: 'People tend to think that their sufferings are caused by factors in the external world, but Buddhism maintains that the fundamental cause lies in negative impulses, delusion and ignorance inherent in one's own life.' One can certainly see these factors at work in the experiences outlined above: Graham's delusion that he could not gain genuine pleasure in other people's company unless he had had a drink; Jiggy's ignorance of her uniqueness, coupled with the delusion that she could not be happy without a husband and family; and the negative impulses generated by Angela's hidden anger. Indeed, Angela had repressed her anger to such an extent that she did not even think she had it. Nevertheless, it had to find expression and did so in the form of epilepsy.

This is significant as one of the major causes of suffering in the West is the attempt that is made, often at an unconscious level, to stifle or even destroy certain aspects of ourselves that, for one reason or another, we feel to be unattractive or unacceptable. Buddhism teaches, however, that *all* the Ten Worlds are inherent in life and that it is impossible to eradicate any of them. Thus, once she had discovered the nature of the problem, Angela then realized that, rather than chanting for it to disappear, the very anger that was causing her such suffering could be not just transformed into something creative, but could actually become her greatest strength. Similarly, Graham's insatiable Hunger for drink was not merely straitjacketed so that, deep down, it still burnt away hidden from sight, immediately to run amok again at the merest whiff of alcohol; instead, it has been genuinely purified so that he can drink in moderation like most people.

One of the truly great things about this practice, therefore, is that we do not have to feel guilty about our weaknesses or those aspects of our lives that we feel to be ugly and usually prefer not to see. Rather, through honestly chanting about them, they can become, in Angela's words, 'valued companions': in other words, we still have those impulses which Buddhism maintains are a fundamental cause of suffering but, rather than working negatively, they become positive. To express it in terms of the mutual possession of the Ten Worlds, Angela, Graham and Jiggy all discovered that, along with Hell, Buddhahood too exists in the worlds of Anger, Hunger and Animality, and that it can be revealed through chanting *Nam-myoho-renge-kyo*. Thus, the Buddhism of Nichiren Daishonin is not concerned with the suppression of negative impulses and tendencies which, like a tightly coiled spring, must eventually spring back into life again –but with their total transformation.

It may be difficult to understand how such low life-states as Hell and Anger can possess the supreme condition of Buddhahood. Nichiren Daishonin explains that Buddhahood can exist only *because* we have all the other nine worlds and those aspects of our nature which perhaps we would rather keep hidden away. This can be best explained using the analogy of the lotus flower: it is only because its roots are buried deep in the muck of a muddy swamp that it is able to produce such a beautiful blossom. In other words, it is only because we have the 'muck' of ordinary human desires and ordinary human problems in our lives, desires and problems that we cannot either satisfy or overcome in other ways, that we begin to chant *Nam-myoho-renge-kyo* and, in so doing, reveal the 'blossom' of our highest selves, our Buddhahood.

This totally interdependent relationship between Buddhahood and ordinary life is expounded only in the Lotus Sutra and is expressed in three important phrases: *bon'no soku bodai*, literally meaning 'the desires of ordinary life are at the same time enlightenment'; *shoji soku nehan*, literally meaning 'the sufferings of life and death are nirvana (or enlightenment)'; and *sokushin jobutsu*, literally meaning 'same body become Buddha' – in other words, one becomes a Buddha without changing one's basic nature as a human being. The key word common to all these phrases is *soku*. *Soku* is literally translated as 'the same thing', 'as it is' or 'equals', and yet, like may Chinese characters used to express Buddhist concepts, it has deeper levels of meaning.

Implied in the meaning of *soku* is the dynamic idea of transformation, the sort of transformation experienced by Angela, Graham and Jiggy. *Soku* does not mean that the desires of ordinary life are, in themselves, enlightenment, or that ordinary people are Buddhas just as they are, but that, theoretically, enlightenment is inherent in human suffering and human desires and that the world of Buddhahood is inherent in ordinary people. To put it another way, *soku* implies that, fundamentally, there is no distinction between the world of Buddahood and the other nine worlds from Hell to Bodhisattva. This may be difficult to understand but, basically, *soku* reinforces the point that Buddhahood is not an ethereal or 'other worldly' state, but a quality which finds expression in the behaviour of ordinary people and the practicalities of everyday life. In short, we do not practise this Buddhism to become saints or superhumans but to become great human beings, capable of solving every human problem.

Again, *soku* may be best illustrated through an analogy. Most people know that if you place an unripened green tomato on a sunny windowsill it will quickly ripen and turn red, just as it is. A ripe tomato and an unripe one are not the same and yet the change takes place within the same fruit. Although it is true that various external factors, such as the effect of sunlight, are involved in the change, the important point is that the tomato itself contains the inherent potential for this change to come about. In the same way, the life of an ordinary human being itself contains the inherent potential to become enlightened.

Although the Lotus Sutra teaches this as a theory, however, it is silent on the means by which ordinary people can reveal their Buddhahood, and so the concept of *soku*, inspiring as it is in the Lotus Sutra, is still just a concept. It was not until the appearance of Nichiren Daishonin that the theory of *soku* was translated into reality for, as he says, 'The single word *soku* is *Nam-myoho-renge-kyo*.' This is extremely important because it means that, when Nichiren Daishonin established *Nam-myoho-renge-kyo*, he made it possible for ordinary people to become aware of the existence of Buddhahood within themselves. In Nichiren Shoshu Buddhism, therefore, there is no need for the suppression of desire, the intellectual analyzing of problems, or the conscious effort to live by some demanding (and possibly outdated) moral code. Instead, by honestly expressing our desires and sufferings when we chant, we can be confident that we are allowing the process of transformation to take place within us, whether we are at first consciously aware of it or not. Nichiren Daishonin sums up the naturalness of this process in the following passage:

Attaining Buddhahood is nothing extraordinary. If you chant

Nam-myoho-renge-kyo with your whole heart, you will naturally become endowed with the Buddha's thirty-two features and eighty characteristics.* Shakyamuni stated, 'At the start I pledged to make all the people perfectly equal to me, without any distinction between us.' Therefore, it is not difficult to become a Buddha. A bird's egg contains nothing but liquid, yet by itself this develops into a beak, two eyes, and all the other parts which form a bird, and can fly into the sky. We, too, are like the egg, ignorant and base, but when nurtured by chanting *Nam-myoho-renge-kyo*, we develop the beak of the Buddha's thirty-two features and the feathers of his eighty characteristics and are free to soar into the skies of the ultimate reality.

By now, you cannot fail to have been impressed by the importance that Nichiren Shoshu Buddhism places on the fundamental practice of chanting *Nam-myoho-renge-kyo*. The time has come, therefore, to look a little more closely at what this phrase means and at how chanting this invocation to the Gohonzon can gradually improve your life by bringing out the highest state of being possible – your own Buddha nature.

---

*Unusual and awe-inspiring attributes of the Buddha described in the sutras taught before the Lotus Sutra as a means to encourage people to seek the Buddha and aspire to Buddhahood. They signify the Buddha's great wisdom, ability, mercy, etc.

2

The Meaning of Nam-Myoho-Renge-Kyo

Myoho-renge-kyo is the title of the Lotus Sutra. The Lotus Sutra was originally written in Sanskrit, the literary language of ancient India, the country in which it was first expounded. In Sanskrit the title is *Saddharmapundarikasutra*, literally meaning 'The Sutra of the Perfect Law of the Lotus'. When Buddhism was introduced into China, all the sutras were eventually translated into classical Chinese, the language of the court, the arts and administration, if not the ordinary people. *Miao-fa Lien-hua Ching* is the title of the Lotus Sutra as rendered into classical Chinese by Kumarajiva, a great Buddhist scholar and translator who lived between AD 344–413, that is some 200 years before T'ien-t'ai, and who translated a vast body of Buddhist writings. Kumarajiva's translation is not the only extant version of the Lotus Sutra in classical Chinese but it is generally considered to be the best because, to his great skills as a linguist, he was also able to add a deep understanding of the Buddhist teachings themselves.

The influence of China on its neighbour, Japan, has been enormous and, in time (according to traditional accounts during the sixth century AD), Buddhism was introduced to Japan via Korea. Although the Japanese had even adopted the Chinese alphabet, they did so only to write their own spoken language, so the title of the Lotus Sutra, while written with ancient, classical

Chinese characters as *Miao-fa Lien-hua Ching*, was pronounced in Japanese as 'Myoho-renge-kyo'. Similarly, the rest of the sutra, parts of which those who practise this Buddhism recite twice a day during *gongyo*, is written in classical Chinese and pronounced according to Japanese phonetics. This Japanese is not the language of modern Japan but, again, is a classical, literary and ancient form of Japanese, somewhat comparable to early or Chaucerian English, so even the Japanese have difficulty in understanding what it means, just as the Chinese have difficulty in understanding the meaning of *Miao-fa Lien-hua Ching*.

Myoho-renge-kyo literally means 'Mystic Law of the Lotus Sutra', a close translation of the Sanskrit title, *Saddharmapundarikasutra*. *Nam* is a verbal contraction of the written Sanskrit word *namu* or *namas* (in rather the same way that 'don't' is a verbal contraction of 'do not'), and literally means 'devotion'. This word was placed at the beginning of the title of the Lotus Sutra by Nichiren Daishonin, who says, 'People place the word *Nam* before the names of all deities and Buddhas in worshipping them. But what is the meaning of *Nam*? This word derives from Sanskrit, and means to devote one's life.' Thus, from one angle, *Nam-myoho-renge-kyo* could be said to mean, literally, 'I devote my life to the Mystic Law of the Lotus Sutra.'

Although on one level it might seem quite straightforward to say what *Nam-myoho-renge-kyo* means, to understand the depth of meaning in this phrase is actually extremely difficult. Since *Nam-myoho-renge-kyo* expresses, in words, the Law of life which all Buddhist teachings in one way or another seek to clarify, this is hardly surprising: as Nichiren Daishonin explains, 'To practise only the seven characters of *Nam-myoho-renge-kyo* may appear limited, yet since this Law is the master of all Buddhas of the past, present and future, the teacher of all bodhisattvas in the universe, and the guide that enables all human beings to attain Buddhahood, its practice is incomparably profound.' To begin to understand this it might be helpful to compare certain aspects of *Nam-myoho-renge-kyo* with Einstein's famous formula for the theory of relativity, $E=mc^2$.

$E=mc^2$ is written with five separate symbols, literally meaning 'Energy equals mass multiplied by the square of the speed of light'. Although a lay person may be able to understand the literal meaning of these words and may even, in a general sense, understand the theory of which these words or symbols are the expression, unless he or she has a great deal of knowledge and understanding of physics, particularly nuclear physics, the full depth of meaning will be lost. For the same reason, a lay person cannot truly appreciate the enormity of Einstein's achievement, not only in realizing this law but also in crystallizing it so precisely in just five symbols. Each of those symbols is, in itself, the crystallization of a profound concept of physics or mathematics which, though abstract, nevertheless relates directly to the events and objects of the real world. In formulating the theory of relativity as $E=mc^2$, therefore, Einstein was not making anything up, neither the symbols nor the ideas they express, but rather coming to a deeper understanding of the profound relationship between ideas that already existed about the basic phenomena of the universe: energy, matter, light and time.

Turning now to *Nam-myoho-renge-kyo*, each syllable of this 'formula' is written with a separate Chinese or Sanskrit character so that there are seven characters in all (remembering that *Nam* is a verbal contraction of the written form *Namu*). Leaving aside *Nam* for the moment, let us look a little more closely at the five characters of *Myoho-renge-kyo*.

As already explained, *Myoho-renge-kyo* is the title, or *daimoku* (invocation), of the Lotus Sutra. In Buddhism the title given to any sutra or treatise is extremely important as it encapsulates the entirety of the teaching that follows. Nichiren Daishonin explains this idea by reference to the name 'Japan':

> The spirit within one's body may appear in just his face, and the spirit within his face may appear in just his eyes. Included in the word 'Japan' is all that is within the country' sixty-six provinces: all of the people and animals, the rice paddies and other fields, those of high and low status, the nobles and commoners, the seven kinds of gems* and all other treasures. Similarly, included within the title, *Nam-myoho-renge-kyo*,† is the entire sutra consisting of all

*They differ slightly according to various sources. The eleventh chapter of the Lotus Sutra defines them as gold, silver, lapis lazuli, coral, agate, pearl and carnelian; in the same chapter they also indicate seven precepts, or rules, for attaining enlightenment.

†The title of the Lotus Sutra is *Myoho-renge-kyo* but the title of the Law or ultimate truth, as expounded by Nichiren Daishonin, is *Nam-myoho-renge-kyo*. Nichiren Daishonin is explaining that the title, *Nam-myoho-renge-kyo*, embraces within its meaning the entire Lotus Sutra.

eight volumes, twenty-eight chapters and 69,384 characters without exception. Concerning this, Po Chu-i* stated that the title is to the sutra as eyes are to the Buddha.

The importance of the title of the Lotus Sutra can be judged by the fact that the first of T'ien-t'ai's three major works, *The Profound Meaning of the Lotus Sutra (Hokke Gengi)*, is devoted entirely to explaining what the five charcters of *Myoho-renge-kyo* mean. Partly, this is because written Chinese is an extremely concise language in which each separate character can subtly convey a variety of different, though related, meanings. In addition to this, and in a way similar to the symbols used to express Einstein's theory of relativity, each of the five characters of *Myoho-renge-kyo* is in itself a profound expression of one aspect of life. Brought together, they express a relationship even more all-embracing than Einstein's $E=mc^2$: that between life itself and the entire universe. Nichiren Daishonin says:

> *Myoho-renge-kyo* is the king of sutras, flawless in both letter and principle. Its words are the reality of life, and the reality of life is the Mystic Law [*myoho*]. It is called the Mystic Law because it explains the mutually inclusive relationship of life and all phenomena. That is why this sutra is the wisdom of all Buddhas.

This is an enormous claim and, once again, one that is 'difficult to believe and difficult to understand'. When trying to evaluate it, though, we must feel very much like the lay person trying to judge whether $E=mc^2$ is, in fact, correct: at a loss, in other words. As the Lotus Sutra itself states, this Law 'can only be understood and shared between Buddhas', which is like saying that $E=mc^2$ can only be understood and shared between nuclear scientists. In effect, this would seem to mean that, as this Law can only be shared between the 'experts', the Buddhas, no one who is not already an 'expert' can even begin to understand it.

Nichiren Daishonin confidently asserts, however, that anyone *can* come to an understanding of this Mystic Law, though not, as with nuclear physics, through the application of a highly developed intellect. He says:

> If you wish to free yourself from the sufferings of birth and death you have endured through eternity and attain supreme enlighten-

*A noted Chinese poet (772–846).

ment in this lifetime, you must awaken to the mystic truth that has always been within your life. This truth is *Myoho-renge-kyo*. Chanting *Myoho-renge-kyo** will therefore enable you to grasp the mystic truth within you.

In this context it is important to understand that 'mystic' does not mean 'magic', or imply deliberate vagueness of thought, but rather that which, though absolutely real, defies narrow rationality or translation into words. We have already seen how the concept of *ku*, the state of neither existence nor non-existence, falls into this category, while in everyday life music is perhaps the best example of an experience which, in these terms, could be called 'mystic'.

Nearly everybody has a favourite piece of music which, when they hear it, affects them in some way. It could move them to joy or to tears; it could soothe or rouse their passions; it could call up a complex variety of emotions. Whatever the effect (and leaving aside music which is accompanied by a lyric), there is no rational explanation for why a series of sounds arranged in a particular order should do any of these things, and yet they do. Music in this sense is 'mystic'. Its effects cannot be explained either by studying the dots as they are written on the stave, or by somehow measuring and analyzing the sounds as they move through the air. Similarly, when Beethoven sat down and wrote, say, the Pastoral Symphony, his realization that those particular notes should be written in that particular order was also 'mystic'. If challenged to explain why he had set them in that way he would almost certainly have been at a loss, other than to say that somehow they expressed something within him that could not be expressed in any other way.

Chanting *Nam-myoho-renge-kyo* in order to 'grasp the mystic truth within you' is thus like playing a piece of music in order to experience the effect of that music. The sleeve notes on the record may help you deepen your understanding and appreciation of the piece in question, but there is no substitute for the music itself. In

---

*The letter from which this passage is taken was written to a follower in 1255, only two years after Nichiren Daishonin had declared for the first time that the ultimate truth or true Law of life is *Nam-myoho-renge-kyo*. This was a new and revolutionary teaching and Nichiren Daishonin explains here that *nam*, meaning 'devotion', is expressed by the act of chanting. Nichiren Daishonin concludes this letter by repeating *Nam-myoho-renge-kyo* twice, emphasizing that this is the correct invocation.

like manner, the 'mystic truth' of *Nam-myoho-renge-kyo* is beyond the pale of the intellect, and again, while a theoretical explanation can help you to understand, it can be fully appreciated only by chanting *Nam-myoho-renge-kyo*. This is Nichiren Daishonin's 'mystic' realization and his supreme achievement.

Bearing these points in mind, then, what exactly are the profound philosophical concepts encapsulated by the seven characters of *Nam-myoho-renge-kyo*?

MYOHO

As we have seen, *myoho* means 'Mystic Law' and expresses the relationship between the life inherent in the universe and the myriad different ways this life expresses itself. As Nichiren Daishonin explains, '*Myo* is the name given to the mystic nature of life, and *ho* to its manifestations.' In other words, while *myo* refers to the very essence of life itself, which is 'unseen' and beyond intellectual understanding, this essence always expresses itself in a tangible form, one that is capable of being apprehended by the senses. For example, although the essential nature of music is *myo*, in that it is impossible to explain *why* it moves us, the sounds of the actual notes and their effect on our emotions are nonetheless real and can be felt and are, therefore, *ho*.

The relationship between *myo* and *ho* is so all-embracing that to explain it in full would be to not only explain the whole of Buddhist philosophy, but also the whole of life. Buddhism, therefore, adopts a number of interrelated viewpoints to explain different aspects of *myoho*. For example, *myo* refers to the state of Buddhahood, while *ho* refers to the nine worlds from Hell to Bodhisattva. On one level this means that our Buddha nature is not separate from the nine other worlds we all possess and that it can only be expressed through them, as we have seen in the preceding chapter. On another level, this can also be interpreted as meaning that *myo* represents our full individual potential while *ho* represents how much of that potential we have achieved. Nichiren Daishonin explains that, as everyone possesses Buddhahood, the potential of each individual is literally limitless. He says, 'The character *myo* is rendered in Sanskrit by the word *sad*, and in Chinese is pronounced *miao*. *Myo* means "fully endowed", which in turn has the meaning of "perfection".' One way of interpreting this is to say that every person is already fully endowed with the potential to live a perfectly happy and fully creative life.

Just having great potential is no good to anybody, though, if it simply remains dormant in our lives. A potentially great pianist cannot become great unless she actually plays the piano, for instance, and nor can we improve the quality of life for ourselves and other people unless we are able to turn our potential into reality and manifest it every day in society. Nichiren Daishonin, however, also explains that 'the character *myo* means to open', which refers to the fact that we ordinary individuals *are* able to develop our full potential as human beings and thus truly open up our lives to the utmost. 'Before the preaching of the Lotus Sutra,' Nichiren Daishonin says, 'the people in the nine worlds were like plants and trees in autumn and winter. But when the single character *myo* of the Lotus Sutra shone on them like the spring and summer sun, then the flower of aspiration for enlightenment blossomed and the fruit of Buddhahood emerged.' In the light of this passage, it can also be said that *myo* refers to the fundamental state of enlightenment (and *ho* to the fundamental darkness, or delusion and ignorance), inherent in all people.

Myo also refers to death and *ho* to life. Buddhism teaches that the life-force immanent in the universe is undergoing the continuous, harmonious and eternal rhythm of *myoho*, that is, alternating between the manifest or 'seen' state, which we call life, and its latent or 'unseen' state, which we call death (see Diagram A). For, just as death is inherent in all life, so, according to Buddhism, is life inherent in all death. In other words, life-force in the state of latency, death, has the inherent ability to become manifest again as life. Hence, as Nichiren Daishonin says, '*Myo* means to revive, that is, return to life.'

This in itself is a large subject and will be discussed more fully a little later.

As you can see, *myoho* might be said to express the broad and universal principle according to which the energy of life operates in a human being, just as it does in a cherry tree, say: in the spring the sap wells up, seeping through the gnarled bare branches and along the stems to the smallest twigs so that blossoms and leaves appear, followed by fruit in abundance during the summer, only

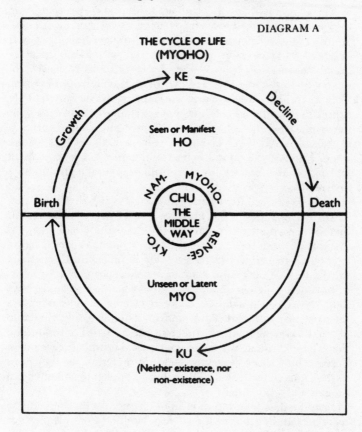

for the tree to return to its seeming lifelessness when winter comes once again. To understand better how this principle relates to life at a more individual level. Buddhism shifts its perspective and employs an explanation which is known as the Three Truths or *santai* (*san* means 'three' and *tai* means 'that which is clear or obvious').

The Three Truths

The three truths are the truth of temporary, physical or material existence (*ketai*), the truth of non-substantiality or the spiritual aspect of life (*kutai*) and the truth of the Middle Way (*chutai*), that force or energy which binds and harmonizes *ketai* and *kutai*. These are often abbreviated to *ke, ku* and *chu* respectively. To put it another way, *ke* and *ku* are two different but inseparable aspects of *chu*. According to Nichiren Daishonin, in terms of *myoho, chu* relates to *Nam-myoho-renge-kyo*, the rhythm or Law of life itself, while *ke* and *ku* relate to *ho* and *myo* respectively, the way that life expresses itself. As we shall see, however, this division is only for the convenience of explanation as all three contain the other two aspects of life. It is important to remember, therefore, that the Three Truths are not three separate things but, rather, a means of looking at the entirety of life from three different, though interrelated, perspectives.

To make this a little clearer, imagine a blank sheet of paper. This sheet of paper has two sides which we will call Side A and Side B. It is impossible to imagine Side A without Side B; one is inseparable from the other. On the other hand, a sheet of paper cannot exist *except* as Side A and Side B: indeed, if there was a third side, Side C, we would not have a sheet of paper as we know it, but something else. In other words, whether one talks about Side A, Side B or the sheet of paper as a whole, each term implies the existence of the other two and so is simply a way of talking about the same thing from a different perspective. For this reason the Three Truths are sometimes also known as the Three Perceptions. Before we get lost in technical terms, though, let us see how this concept of the Three Truths applies to an individual human life.

Imagine that John Smith is an old friend of yours. When you meet him in the street you recognize him first from his physical appearance. This corresponds to *ke*. John is more than just his physical appearance though; he has a unique character as well, which corresponds to *ku*. John's character is only known to you through his physical actions: his speech, his gestures, his eyes and facial expressions, his posture, the way he walks, the way he dresses and so on. In other words, you can only discover the *ku* of John as it becomes *ke*. On the other hand, every apect of John's appearance and behaviour – *ke* – reveals his character or nature – *ku*.

Clearly, then, the spiritual and physical aspects of John interrelate completely. Even so, they do not tell the whole story.

John's appearance and John's character are both expressions of John's life as a whole, corresponding to *chu* or *Nam-myoho-renge-kyo*. Neither John's appearance nor his character can exist without John's life, his *chu*, nor can John's life exist except as his appearance and character. If this sounds a little confusing, think back to the example of the piece of paper: John's appearance could correspond to Side A, for example, his character to Side B and his life as a whole to the whole sheet of paper. A discussion of any aspect of John implies the other two. Furthermore, John's life has a clear and unique continuity, another quality of *chu*. In other words, *chu* could also be described as our 'essential self', that aspect of our lives which keeps our physical and spiritual aspects consistent with each other through time. It is *chu*, the entity of your life, which allows you to know that you are essentially the same person now as when you were a child, for example, despite all the physical changes you have undergone and the various developments your character has been through.

To demonstrate the total interfusion of these three aspects of life – *ke, ku* and *chu* – in any individual, let us for a moment try to imagine a person who has the same appearance as John but who is not John. Let us say that, unbeknownst to you, John has a twin brother, Jim, whose character, however, is very different. Meeting Jim in the street you might at first mistake him for John because, superficially at least, he looks exactly the same (although in truth even 'identical' twins are not physically exact copies of each other). After a short while, however, you notice certain things about this person that seem to be very out of character for John: he does not usually talk that fast, for example; his laugh is normally less high-pitched; he seems to have developed an unfortunate twitch of the head, and so on. In other words, Jim cannot help but reveal *his* unique character through his 'appearance', taken in the broadest sense to mean not just his literal appearance but all aspects of his physical behaviour. So, once again, the *ku* of Jim is revealed through *ke*, both of which are expressions of Jim's *chu*, his life as a whole. Jim cannot be John, no matter how hard he tries and no matter how much he might physically resemble him because, essentially, their lives are unique to themselves. One important implication of the Three Truths, then, is that we can never become happy by wanting or trying to be someone else, nor by always acting in a way which we think is necessary to please others because, in truth, we can never be anyone other than ourselves. Nichiren Shoshu Buddhism teaches that we become truly happy and fulfilled only as we reveal more and more of our 'essential self', our *chu*, through our physical and spiritual aspects, *ke* and *ku*. This we can do by following the Middle Way or *chudo*. We will return to this subject in a moment.

The Oneness of Mind and Body

One of the most important implications of the Three Truths for the ordinary individual lies in the realization that there is no fundamental distinction between the physical and spiritual aspects of life. Instead, our mind (or spirit) and our body are merely two different aspects of our individual life and cannot be separated. This principle is called *shikishin funi*, literally meaning 'body, mind: two, not two', or the oneness of mind and body. As they are inseparable, whatever affects the mind will affect the body and vice versa. If we are unhappy or depressed, for example, our life-force will be low, we will appear less healthy and 'glowing' than when we are happy and, indeed, we may be less resistant to sickness. On the other hand, when we are sick it is very difficult not to be unhappy and depressed, depending on the severity of our sickness.

It is in illness that the inseparability of mind and body is most obvious, especially in those illnesses which conventional medicine terms 'psychosomatic' (literally, 'of mind and body'), such as eczema and stomach ulcers, which appear to have no source other than in the mind (or emotions) of the sufferer. Buddhism teaches that all illness has a spiritual, mental or emotional aspect, however, and that many contemporary diseases are primarily spiritual in origin. This is one reason why a number of diseases thought to be incurable by current medical practices are not infrequently conquered through the application of 'mind over matter'. We have seen how Angela Bolger's anger, for example, which exists in her spirit, expressed itself in her body as a sickness, epilepsy, and how she was able to overcome it through her determined and sincere chanting. Similarly, Stewart Anderson's refusal to give in to AIDS played a crucial role both in extending his life and in enriching it.

The ability to fight sickness with the mind is not restricted to those who practise Buddhism, of course, but is common to all people; this knowledge is gaining increasing recognition in the medical world. Even so, many individuals still look to outside forces, to doctors and the wonders of medical science, for cures for their illnesses, not realizing that by far the most powerful medicine lies within themselves, in their attitude to their sickness and their determination to get well again. This is not to say that the medical profession is unnecessary: indeed, Buddhism teaches that it is an extremely important and respect-worthy vocation. But if one places complete reliance on this outside force for one's well being, to be then told by as powerful an authority as a doctor that a particular condition is incurable can in itself cause a complete loss of hope and, with it, any chance of recovery. In cases like this a diagnosis can almost be tantamount to a sentence of death, or life imprisonment, by the illness in question, unless the doctor is also able somehow to rouse the fighting spirit that is inherent in every patient. The point to bear in mind here, then, is that as medicine becomes increasingly technical – increasingly concerned with the *ke* of sickness, in other words – and develops more and more drugs and machines with which to combat human suffering, so it is all the more important for increasing numbers of doctors and nurses to remember the need to treat the spirit as well as the body of all their patients. Indeed, it has been said that the doctors who get the best recovery rates from their patients are not necessarily the most skilled surgeons, or those who are most knowledgable about medicine and the workings of the body, but are those who simply care most whether or not Mr X or Mrs Y gets better again.

In the West, the mind and the body have traditionally been regarded as two separate, and often warring, entities. Arnold Toynbee sums up the dichotomy succinctly:

> Man finds himself in the awkward and embarrassing position of being an animal who is also a self-conscious spiritual being. He is aware that the spiritual aspect of his nature gives him dignity that other animals do not possess, and he feels he ought to maintain his dignity. Therefore human beings are embarrassed by those physical organs and functions and appetites that are common to them and to nonhuman animals and that therefore impugn human dignity by reminding us of our physiological kinship with brute beasts.

The inability to reconcile these two apparently contradictory aspects of human nature, coupled with the desire to maintain our fragile sense of human dignity, has been reflected in history in the tendency to elevate the spirit and deny the flesh. This can be seen most clearly perhaps in a number of the teachings of Christianity, although it is a tendency shared by Islam and some forms of Hinayana Buddhism. In the West, the desire to elevate the spirit at the expense of the flesh in the name of human dignity has at various times led to severe distortions in society and even, paradoxically, to the undeniable degradation of human dignity. The burning of heretics in Europe at periodic intervals through-out the fifteenth and sixteenth centuries, for example, could be seen as the ultimate means of punishing the flesh (albeit the flesh of others) in order to liberate the spirit. The banning of theatre, dancing and even the celebration of Christmas by Oliver Cromwell's Puritans is an example of the same tendency appearing in a milder form, as was the alleged Victorian habit of covering up piano legs in little skirts in case the sight of them should prove too provocative.

Nowadays, however, with the lessening influence of the Church, the tendency has swung the other way, so that basically hedonistic values have become dominant in western culture, as exemplified by materialism, consumerism and a greater degree of sexual freedom. With sexual 'freedom' has also come sexual confusion, both on a personal and social level: pornography and obscenity are illegal in Britain, for example, but neither society nor the law can satisfactorily define them. This confusion, it seems, is actual evidence of the continuing, though largely unseen, influence of Christian teachings in an increasingly secular society. Historically, at least, Christianity seems often to have regarded sex as a primary bestial activity (according to the Ten Commandments, rated on a par with killing), and therefore one that should be most strictly suppressed or regulated.

The Middle Way

In terms of Buddhist teachings, both individuals and societies as a whole have the tendency to veer towards either *ke* or *ku*, that is, towards either a predominantly physical or spiritual view of life. Either of these Buddhism regards as a fundamental distortion of reality and, therefore, bound to lead to suffering. To live a life of perfect balance, by contrast, in which both the physical and spiritual aspects of one's makeup function creatively, one has to follow the path of the Middle Way, *chudo*, the way which integrates and harmonizes both *ke* and *ku*. If *ke* and *ku* could be likened to two horses hitched to a wagon, *chu* would then be the driver who counteracts the tendency of the stronger horse to pull the whole wagon to one side, and thus keeps everything moving strongly forward.

Put this way the concept of the Middle Way probably sounds reasonable enough, but is it then any more profound than the age-old idea of 'moderation in all things', itself stemming from Aristotle's idea of 'golden mean', whereby (as Russell explains) 'every virtue is a mean between two extremes, each of which is a vice'? Certainly, as Nichiren Daishonin defines it, the Middle Way is, indeed, much more profound than Aristotle's 'golden mean', but to understand this one must first realize that the term 'Middle Way' has been used in a number of different senses as Buddhism has developed since the age of Shakyamuni. Generally, the term 'the Middle Way' refers to that which *transcends* the extremes of two one-sided or opposing views. This should not be confused with the idea of compromise – a means of reaching agreement by finding common ground through mutual concession – nor with simply steering a middle course, for the Middle Way in Buddhism always adds a third perspective to the two in opposition.

From this starting-point one can see that, in line with the increasing sophistication of Buddhist thought through history, the concept of the Middle Way has gradually become more and more refined. For instance, one of Shakyamuni's early teachings stated that enlightenment lay neither in a life of pleasure nor in one of spiritual austerity, but in the Middle Way between these two extremes. To tread this Middle Way one had to follow what was known as the eightfold path, that is, eight principles governing one's behaviour: right views, right thinking, right speech, right action, right way of life, right endeavour, right mindfulness and right meditation. This interpretation of the Middle Way is the one that is closest to Aristotle's 'golden mean' and the idea of 'moderation in all things', and is the one that is most often thought of in the West as representing the ultimate and orthodox doctrines of Buddhism. Shakyamuni, however, taught this idea of Middle Way only as a means of gradually raising the life-state of the people, to prepare them for his highest teaching, the Lotus Sutra, although it was later Buddhist thinkers who further refined the concept of the Middle Way on the basis of that and other sutras.

For example, Nagarjuna, an Indian scholar of Buddhism who lived sometime between AD 150–250, taught that the Middle Way is that which is neither born nor dies and which cannot be expressed by the words or concepts of existence and non-existence. It was thus Nagarjuna who developed and clarified the concept of *ku*, the nature of which we have discussed briefly in relation to the mutual possession of the Ten Worlds. According to Nagarjuna, *ku* is the true nature of all things, which he called the Middle Way. T'ien-t'ai went a stage further than Nagarjuna and said that the true nature of all things is neither *ku* nor *ke*, but that it has the characteristics of both. This Middle Way T'ien-t'ai called *chu*. Finally, Nichiren Daishonin went a stage further still and identified *chu* as the great Pure Law of *Nam-myoho-renge-kyo*, the ultimate truth of all things which is also the true nature of the life of ordinary people. He says, 'Life is indeed an elusive reality that transcends both the words and concepts of existence and non-existence. It is neither existence nor non-existence, yet exhibits the qualities of both. It is the mystic entity of the Middle Way that is the reality of all things.'

This might all seem like philosophical hair-splitting, but what it essentially boils down to is that, by finally defining the Middle Way as *Nam-myoho-renge-kyo*, Nichiren Daishonin explained how chanting this phrase can both energize and harmonize the physical and spiritual aspects of life so that, for example, through chanting, one can cure oneself of sickness or uncontrollable anger, or positively affect one's environment. Going back for a moment to the analogy of the two horses pulling the wagon, *Nam-myoho-renge-kyo* is equivalent to the driver, *chu*, and chanting therefore gives us the strength and wisdom to keep the horses of *ke* and *ku* in our own lives pulling together in the right direction. To understand how chanting *Nam-myoho-renge-kyo* can do this, one has to go a little more deeply into the concepts of *ketai*, the truth of temporary existence, and *kutai*, the truth of non-substantiality.

The Truth of Temporary Existence

Ke, as stated above, refers to life's physical aspect. In terms of the individual this means, primarily, the physical body. In a broader sense, though, *ke* includes anything which can be perceived by the sense of sight, hearing, touch, taste and smell, as well as those things which, while they may be beyond the direct reach of the senses, can nevertheless be discerned with other instruments – for example, infra-red and ultra-violet light, radio waves, microbes, planets on the outer edges of the solar system, and so on. In other words, anything that can be defined and measured quantitively falls into the realm of *ke*.

Ke is called temporary existence because, according to Buddhism, all physical existence, from the smallest sub-atomic particle to the universe as a whole, goes through the same cycle of formation (or birth), maturation (or growth), decline (or ageing) and, finally, disintegration (or death). In other words, as nothing material lasts forever, all physical existence is merely a temporary phenomenon. Indeed, Shakyamuni's last words are reputed to have included the sentence, 'Decay is inherent in all composite things', which is an indication of how central this idea of life is to Buddhist thought. The only variable in this cycle is its length. The life-span of a sub-atomic particle, for example, is infinitissimally short, in the region of one thousand-billion-billionth of a second; that of a human being varies considerably, but rarely exceeds a hundred years; while the life-span of the universe is unimaginably long.

Whether or not the universe as a whole conforms to the cycle of birth and death as postulated by Buddhism is currently a matter of intense scientific research and debate. Generally, most astronomers agree with the idea put forward by George Gamow and others in the 1940s that the universe started with the Big Bang, some ten to twenty billion years ago, when an infinitely small but infinitely dense concentration of 'something' exploded, creating matter, time and space all in an instant. What the universe consisted of before the Big Bang is shrouded in mystery: indeed, a number of physicists would argue that the question is meaningless. As recently as 1978, however, scientists were able to demonstrate that the universe is indeed expanding in line with the Big Bang theory, so much of the argument in astronomy now centres on whether it will continue to expand *ad infinitum*, or whether at some point in the distant future the universe will reach a limit of expansion and either stop or begin to contract, possibly to expand again at some date in the unimaginably distant future. Certainly, this latter forecast is what Buddhism would expect, for then the universe itself would follow the continuous rhythm of *myoho* which Buddhism perceives in all its constituent parts. In the light of modern astronomy's realization that bodies as large as stars are continually being born while others are dying (for example, the 'new' star T-Tauri and the exploded star which has become the Crab Nebula, both in the constellation of Taurus), it could be seen as a little unreasonable to suppose that the universe as a whole will prove an exception to this rule, in which case there could well be many universes. According to the most precise calculations yet made, however, as the actual death of our particular universe will not occur for anywhere between 10^{26} and 10^{76} years, the matter seems likely to remain a subject for informed speculation for quite some time to come.

Whatever may happen on a universal scale, though, the cycle of formation, maturation, decline and disintegration implies that the physical world is undergoing constant change, just as we saw that the inner world of the human being is constantly changing between the Ten Worlds. It is in this sense, then, that Buddhism regards all existence as temporary, as whatever exists at any one moment no longer exists in the same form as the next. It is said that even the cells in our own bodies are completely renewed every seven years (with the exception of brain and teeth), so that, strictly speaking, we are not physically the same person now as we were seven years ago. Ingeniously, a criminal indicted for a crime committed several years earlier once tried to use this fact in his defence, arguing that as all the cells in his body had been replaced since the crime, he was technically no longer the same man who had committed it. The judge was unimpressed.

While everybody can probably accept that the living world is constantly changing, they may have more difficulty accepting the assertion that the world of hard, inanimate, physical matter also experiences constant change. After all, even though things may eventually decay, to all intents and purposes solid objects persist as solid objects. Tables and chairs, for example, do not suddenly dematerialize, or change into other things, but remain dependably tables and chairs. At an everyday level, of course, this common-sense view is both true and adequate for an understanding of the physical world. It is not the whole truth, though, and to cling to this partial conception about the nature of physical matter limits an understanding of life as a whole. Indeed, the idea of a constantly changing physical world, and the implications that one must draw from this realization, are not the exclusive preserve of Buddhism but are supported by the discoveries made earlier this century by the pioneers of nuclear physics – Albert Einstein, Niels Bohr, Max Born, Werner Heisenberg and others. Although the conclusions drawn by these men may be well known, it is worth looking at them again to see how closely they approach the teachings of Buddhism about the nature of the physical world.

Very simply, as these nuclear pioneers probed both experimentally and theoretically deeper and deeper into the heart of the atom, searching for the smallest possible particle, the absolute primary building block of all matter and thus of the physical world, they discovered to their surprise that, at the sub-atomic level, the stable world of matter is apparently highly unstable (particles appearing and disappearing seemingly at random) and behaves in ways that by all accounts are contradictory and ought to be impossible. Indeed, so apparently unstable is the sub-atomic world that it is extremely difficult for physicists to describe it with any degree of accuracy, as accuracy needs some fixed reference point. But when even the meaning of those words is based upon a view of the world that is being fundamentally challenged, the problem of understanding becomes acute, as Jacob Bronowski describes:

> The quip among professors was (because of the way university timetables are laid out) that on Mondays, Wednesdays and Fridays the electron would behave like a particle; on Tuesdays, Thursdays and Saturdays it would behave like a wave. How could you match those two aspects, brought from the large-scale world and pushed into a single entity, into this Lilliput, *Gulliver's Travels* world of the inside of the atom? That is what the speculation and argument was about. And that requires, not calculation, but insight, imagination – if you like, metaphysics. I remember a phrase that Max Born used when he came to England many years after . . . He said, 'I am now convinced that theoretical physics is actual philosophy.' Max Born meant that the new ideas of physics amount to a different view of reality. The world is not a fixed, solid

array of objects, out there, for it cannot be fully separated from our perception of it. It shifts under our gaze, it interacts with us, and the knowledge that it yields has to be interpreted by us. There is no way of exchanging information that does not demand an act of judgement.

Interpreting this problem in the light of Buddhism, one could say that, as these and other brilliant scientists have cut matter into ever smaller fragments in their search for the ultimate 'stuff' of the physical world, *ke*, their experiments have brought them closer and closer to *ku*, the truth of non-substantiality, where something 'exists' and yet seems to defy all attempts to define the basis of its existence. It is this problem which lies at the heart of quantum mechanics, with its leptons, quarks and 'messengers', and is currently exercising some of the most highly developed intellects in the scientific community. As Paul Davies, Professor of Theoretical Physics at the University of Newcastle-upon-Tyne, remarks, finding a theory to explain the essential nature of the atom would represent 'the culmination of fundamental physics, for such a theory would be capable of explaining the behaviour and structure of all matter – in a reductionist way, of course. It would enable us to write down all of nature's secrets in a simple equation, a sort of master formula for the universe. Such an achievement would confirm the fond belief that the universe runs to a single, simple, breath-takingly elegant mathematical principle.'

The Truth of Non-substantiality

We know that *ku* refers to the 'unseen' or 'spiritual' aspects of life, to what might be called the 'nature' of things and, from a number of different examples – the flowers 'hidden' in a cherry-tree, for instance, or anger lying dormant 'somewhere' within our lives – we have seen how *ku* can be described as this state of neither existence nor non-existence. Fundamentally, the problem in trying to understand *ku* comes from applying to this concept the standards of the world of *ke*. We perceive and make judgements about the physical world around us by using the concepts of time and space, for example: three-dimensional objects share three-dimensional space and exist for a finite and measurable length of time. Einstein's theory of relativity, however, showed that these concepts have no absolute value but change in relation to each other, so that what common sense tells us about time and space is true for a certain set of circumstances – broadly speaking, for life on this planet – but is not true for all circumstances. If we could travel at or near the speed of light, for instance, both time and space would appear to change.

This was an enormous jolt to our understanding of the universe, but in *ku* not even the theory of relativity has any relevance. When we sleep, for example, we lose all sense of time, which is another way of saying that time loses all meaning; indeed, it is only by referring to the standards of *ke* when we awake – by looking at a clock, say – that we can reorientate ourselves to this world. Rip Van Winkle could not believe that his little nap was a sleep of twenty years precisely because the subjective experiences of sleeping and dreaming are experiences of *ku*, in which the standards of the 'real' world of *ke* do not apply. Yet our dreams are real experiences, ones that we know we have had, even if their link with the waking world is often, at best, tenuous. This all suggests an interesting question; if people habitually slept and dreamt for twelve hours a day – that is, if they spent half their lives with their consciousness in a state of *ku* – on what basis could anyone claim that the world experienced when awake was any more 'real' than that experienced when asleep? In short, *ku* is as 'real' as *ke*: it just happens to be real in a very different, 'non-substantial' way.

Indeed, as Yasuji Kirimura explains, the truth of non-substantiality could be said to be the basis of even the 'real' and tangible physical world:

> Buddhism explains that all forms are comprised of constituent elements which, uniting, give rise to phenomena and, separating, bring about their dissolution. Moreover, these elements themselves prove on analysis to have no fixed or absolute existence . . . It follows that ultimately no phenomena in the world can be perfectly grasped according to our concepts of 'existence'. For example, the bonding which enables molecules, atoms or nuclei to 'exist' is something which itself does not fit within the category of existence. This is what the concept of non-substantiality (*ku*) means. All things are formed from elements which are ultimately non-substantial in nature and through bonding which is also non-substantial. These then appear to us as transient phenomena in the state of temporary existence (*ke*), or constant flux.

The truth on non-substantiality does not state that 'nothing really exists', but that since all things come into existence only through their relationships with other things (what Buddhism calls 'dependent origination'), nothing exists *independently*. Thus, the essential nature of even physical phenomena lies outside the words and concepts of existence and non-existence.

Broadly speaking, this is as far as the Indian scholar Nagarjuna reached some 1800 years ago and is the point theoretical physics is approaching today. To go any further is to delve into the nature of *chu*, which Nichiren Daishonin equates with *myo*, the mystic nature of the ultimate reality of life that is beyond unaided intellectual understanding. In this sense, all the experiments and theories about the atom past and present are concerned with *ho* (what is 'seen'): in other words, with how, in this particular instance, *myo* (the unseen) becomes manifest as a proton, neutron, electron, or whatever other particles make up the *'Gulliver's Travels* world of the inside of the atom'. As Max Born conceded, beyond this point lies the realm of philosophy or, he might have added, religion. Indeed, Einstein undoubtedly came to the same conclusion, judging from his following remark: 'Science without religion is lame, religion without science is blind.' While this can be interpreted in a narrow ethical sense, a number of contemporary nuclear scientists – Fritjof Capra, for example – have taken Einstein at his word, and have begun investigating the parallels that exist between religious and scientific approaches to the ultimate reality of life.

This open-minded attitude is not without its detractors, as it challenges the distinction between 'hard facts' and supposedly woolly philosophical speculation, a distinction still taken by many scientists as an article of faith. For example, Capra's *The Tao of Physics* was ridiculed by a large portion of the scientific community when it first appeared for presuming to see similarities in the doctrines of nuclear physics and a number of 'mystical' eastern philosophies and religions. As time passes, however, an increasing number of these highly rational, highly intellectual and highly 'scientific' men and women are being won over to Capra's cause. It will be interesting to see what impact Nichiren Shoshu Buddhism will have in this area as its teachings become more widely known for, as Daisaku Ikeda has remarked, 'Science and Buddhism in no way contradict each other. I believe that as science progresses, the understanding of Buddhism will advance, and that Buddhism in turn can provide scientists with an inexhaustible source of fuel for thought. A feeling of mutual respect and sincerity is needed.' To begin to understand, however, why 'pure' science on its own is unlikely to be able to get any further in comprehending the true essence of life, we need to return to Nagarjuna and his understanding of *ku*, as this is roughly where contemporary physics finds itself.

The Unification of the Three Truths

Nagarjuna formulated his concept of *ku* on the basis of one of Shakyamuni's earlier teachings, the *Hannya* or Wisdom sutras. Put simply, this meant that Nagarjuna did not explain exactly how *ku*, life's spiritual aspect, is related to *ke*, its physical aspect, because this relationship is explained only in the Lotus Sutra. The nature of this relationship is extremely important because if, as Nagarjuna teaches, all phenomena are temporary and have no independent existence, then there is no reason other than pure chance for things to appear which share common characteristics. In other words, *ku* could become *ke* in an infinite number of different ways: there could be as many different kinds of atoms as there are atoms in the universe, for example, and no two things need ever be alike. Indeed, the chance of two phenomena resembling each other would be infinitely smaller than the chance of throwing two handfuls of confetti into the air and expecting them to fall into exactly the same arrangement. We know, however that this is not the case and that countless phenomena do share common characteristics, not least human beings.

To make this clearer, T'ien-t'ai revealed the concept of *chu*, based on the Lotus Sutra. This is known as the 'unification of the Three Truths', as it explained, firstly, that *ku* and *ke* are consistent because they are simply two expressions of the same thing, or 'entity', alternating between its 'seen' or manifest state and its 'unseen' or latent state; and, secondly, that which state this entity is in at any one time is governed by the Mystic Law. Although T'ien-t'ai never actually crystallized this Law, he did describe the relationship between *ku, ke* and *chu* and the way the Mystic Law operates in very great detail in his theory of *ichinen sanzen*, or 'three thousand worlds in a moment of life'. For example, the principle of the oneness of body and mind derives from the theory of *ichinen sanzen*. In essence, though, T'ien-t'ai explained that this principle is not only applicable to human beings but to all things in the universe. We have seen above that, in terms of the individual, the oneness of body and mind means that the body and the mind are apparently separate but are, in reality, one. In terms of the universe, though, 'body' equates to *ke*, the physical aspect of life, 'mind' to *ku*, the spiritual aspect of life, and 'oneness' to *chu*, the true essence of life. In other words, according to T'ien-t'ai there is fundamentally no distinction between mind and matter, the animate and inanimate. Nichiren Daishonin elaborates on this point in a letter to one of his followers, thanking him for a gift of rice:

> The sutras that came before the Lotus Sutra taught that all phenomena derive from one's mind. The mind is like the earth, and phenomena are like the plants growing in the earth. But the Lotus Sutra teaches that the mind is one with the earth and the earth is one with its planets . . . Therefore, it is obvious that rice is not merely rice but life itself.

The Oneness of Life and its Environment

The idea that there is no fundamental difference between mind and matter, the animate and inanimate, is probably one of the most difficult concepts that Nichiren Shoshu Buddhism teaches. For example, we tend to think of our 'life' as being somehow contained within our body, and of our environment as being outside and separate from us, but Buddhism teaches that our life encompasses our family, our friends, our immediate physical environment, our nation, our world – ultimately, even, our universe. John Donne was absolutely right, in other words, when he said, 'No man is an *Island*', for just as islands appear to be separated from each other by wide expanses of water, but at the bottom of the ocean are all part of the same earth, so people appear to be separate from one another and the physical environment around them, and yet, in the very depths of life, are all part of the great cosmic life-force. Thus, it might be more accurate to view our 'life' as consisting of the 'inner life' of the demands of our physical body, along with thoughts and emotions; and also the 'outer life' of the universe, to which we are inextricably linked and which functions to sustain our 'inner life' (see Diagram B, p. 120).

This inextricable relationship is known as the principle of *esho funi*, or the oneness of life and its environment. *E* of *esho* is a shortened form of *eho*, meaning the objective environment; *sho* is a shortened form of *shoho*, meaning subjective existence, or individual life. Nichiren Daishonin explains their relationship as follows: 'The ten directions* are "environment" (*eho*), and sentient beings are "life" (*shoho*). Environment is like the shadow, and life, the body. Without the body there can be no shadow. Similarly, without life, environment cannot exist, even though life is supported by its environment.' The assertion that environment cannot exist without life may sound strange at first, as we are all aware that there are vast tracts of wilderness – outer space, even – which seem to exist without life. These areas exist, however, only because we do: or, in the broadest sense, because life does. Daisaku Ikeda explains: 'The body moves and transforms the shadow, but at the same time, the body is in a sense created by the shadow, for the body would not be a body if it did not cast a shadow. In other words, the body is given being and identity by the environment, and vice versa.'

In this context it might be helpful to recall the words of Jacob Bronowski, that 'the world is not a fixed, solid array of objects, out there, for it cannot be fully separated from our perception of it. It shifts under our gaze, it interacts with us . . . ' Most people can go as far down the road as Bronowski takes us, for it is fairly obvious that just as our environment affects us, so we also affect it, both constructively and destructively. T'ien-t'ai's realization, however, based upon his deep understanding of the Lotus Sutra, was that the world – indeed, the universe – cannot be divorced from our perception of it at all. The world 'out there' does not simply interact with us: we and our enviroment are completely inseparable. Putting together the principles of the oneness of life and its environment and the oneness of body and mind, Nichiren Daishonin is therefore able to make the following statement: 'Life at each moment encompasses both body and spirit and both self and environment of all sentient beings in every condition of life,†

---

*The eight points of the compass, plus up and down. This indicates the entire universe.
†The Ten Worlds.

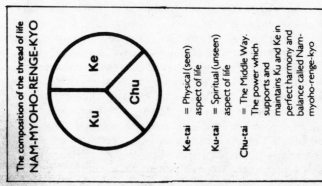

The composition of the thread of life
NAM-MYOHO-RENGE-KYO

Ku   Ke

Chu

Ke-tai = Physical (seen) aspect of life

Ku-tai = Spiritual (unseen) aspect of life

Chu-tai = The Middle Way. The power which supports and maintains Ku and Ke in perfect harmony and balance called Nam-myoho-renge-kyo.

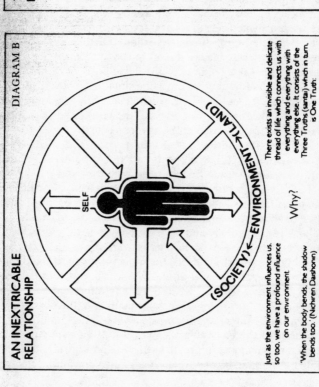

DIAGRAM B

AN INEXTRICABLE RELATIONSHIP

SELF

(SOCIETY)←ENVIRONMENT→(LAND)

Why?

There exists an invisible and delicate thread of life which connects us with everything and everything with everything else. It consists of the Three Truths (santai) which in turn, is One Truth.

Just as the environment influences us, so too, we have a profound influence on our environment.

'When the body bends, the shadow bends too.' (Nichiren Daishonin) as well as insentient beings –plants, sky and earth, on down to the most minute particles of dust. Life at each moment permeates the universe and is revealed in all phenomena.' The implication of this view is that the environment in which you find yourself at any particular moment is a completely accurate reflection of your whole life at that moment. Consider, for example, the following poem by Thomas Hardy, 'Alike and Unlike (Great Orme's Head)':

We watched the selfsame scene on that long drive,
Saw the magnificent purples, as one eye,
Of those near mountains; saw the storm arrive;
Laid up the sight in memory, you and I,
As if for joint recallings, by and by.

But our eye-records, like in hue and line,
Had superimposed on them, that very day,
Gravings on your side deep, but slight on mine! –
Tending to sever us thenceforth alway;
Mine commonplace; yours tragic, gruesome, grey.

Here are two people supposedly sharing the same objective environment – the 'near mountains'. Their life-states, however, are very different: during 'that long drive' the writer appears to have been in the state of Tranquillity or Humanity, and his companion in Hell. To the writer, therefore, the mountains were impressive but of no great significance, while to his companion they appeared Hellish. In short, the subjective reality experienced by this couple is, to all intents and purposes, of two different environments.

It is in the light of the realization that our environment is inseparable from our subjective life-state that the theory of the Ten Worlds assumes its full importance for, if you put it together with the principle of the oneness of life and its environment, it is clear that as you change yourself, through chanting, to gradually strengthen and reveal your inherent Buddhahood, so you can change the world. This happens on a number of different levels.

Firstly, your perspective changes. Nichiren Daishonin says

that the benefit of practising this Buddhism is the 'purification of the six senses', that is, the way we relate to our environment through our five senses of sight, hearing, smell, taste and touch, and the judgements we form in our sixth sense, our conscious mind, on the basis of these sensory perceptions. The Ten Worlds can thus be likened to ten different pairs of glasses. Nine of those pairs, from Hell to Bodhisattva, can give a distorted view of reality, while only Buddhahood enables us to see our life as it really is. So whereas, at one time, you might have suffered, say, from seeing things through the glasses of Hell or Hunger, now, through the glasses of Buddhahood, you do not. Jiggy Bhore's experience recounted in the preceding chapter is a good example of this.

Secondly, as you begin to view your life and environment in a different light, so you begin to desire to physically change your environment to conform with the changes that are taking place within you spiritually. For example, let us say that you have been unemployed for a long time. At first you were angry at being unable to find a job, and suffered greatly, but as time has gone on you have adjusted to your situation and, though you do not like it, you have learnt to live with it. In one sense it may even have grown quite comfortable. You have a routine, you have adapted to living on not very much money, and you have gradually limited your desires and aspirations so that, in one way or another, your horizons have become quite narrow. Although you may not consciously realize it, your dominant life-state is still the world of Hell – the dull, though bearable, ache of life lived with little hope. As Nichiren Daishonin says, 'Insects that live on smartweed forget how bitter it tastes; those who stay long in privies forget how foul the smell is.' Nevertheless, this is your reality.

When you start to chant the situation immediately begins to change. At first it might seem to get worse: however, this is only as if you have begun to notice again just how foul the 'privy' smells in which you have been living for so long. But this is necessary, as it stirs you out of an apathetic acceptance of your situation. Perhaps you get angry again and resolve that you will start to fight back against the nebulous forces that have somehow pushed you into this condition; or perhaps, as if out of nowhere, hope flares up into your life (for remember that one meaning of *myo* is 'to revive'), energizing and inspiring you to try again, to take some action to change your circumstances; or perhaps you remember the dreams and ambitions you once had, but which you have pushed to the back of your mind as the chances of ever realizing them have seemed to slip further and further from your grasp. However this inner change expresses itself, as long as you keep chanting you will not allow yourself to settle for second-best – or worse – but will keep battling until your circumstances match your heightened life-condition.

It may be, for example, that what stands between you and a better life is a lack of courage. If so, as you keep chanting *Nam-myoho-renge-kyo* you will discover that you are gradually developing courage so that, eventually, you will be able to take that step you have known for a long time you must take if you are ever going to be truly happy. Or it could be that what you lack is the life-force needed to make the great and consistent effort that your goal demands, whether it be getting a job, passing exams, fighting an illness, or whatever. Chanting will give you that life-force. Since your environment is unique to you, the effects of chanting *Nam-myoho-renge-kyo* cannot help but be tailormade to fit your own particular situation. As Nichiren Daishonin says, 'Money serves various purposes according to our needs. The same is true of the Lotus Sutra.* It will be a lantern in the dark or a boat at a crossing. At times it will be water, and at other times, fire.'

The inner change that one experiences through the practice of this Buddhism is called *inconspicuous benefit*. This is not just because it is invisible to the naked eye, but also because it accumulates gradually and you may not notice it yourself until after some time has passed. One day, you may suddenly realize that problems no longer depress or frighten you as they once did; or that you are looking forward to going to work these days; or that you worry about things much less than you used to. Inconspicuous benefit, then, relates to the unseen world of *ku* and could be said to show itself in the extent to which you can enjoy your life as a whole.

Conspicuous benefits relate to the world of *ke*, appearing in our environment as obvious and tangible improvements: better

*Here refers to *Nam-myoho-renge-kyo*.

relationships with other people, for example, sounder finances and generally improved living circumstances. As Buddhism teaches that people have both material and spiritual needs and desires, conspicuous benefits are obviously important for, without them, it is very difficult for people to be truly happy. If you never have enough money to pay your essential bills, for example, or you cannot form any consistently good relationships with other people, you cannot be said to be living a happy and fulfilled life.

At a deeper level, though, when viewed in the light of the principle of the oneness of life and its environment, conspicuous benefits can be seen as an indication of the 'health' of our inner life. This is not to say that those whose lives are rich in conspicuous benefit are somehow spiritually 'better' people than those with few such benefits, but that the lack of conspicuous benefit in our lives could be a pointer to something we need to change about ourselves. For example, people often complain of not having enough money, but as Josei Toda, the second president of the Soka Gakkai, once pointed out, money is all around us, like the air we breathe. The real problem is that, just as some people are asthmatic, so others have a problem in their inner lives which restricts their ability to attract money into their outer lives. They may have developed an acceptance of their own poverty, for instance, or an unconscious fear that having money will somehow 'corrupt' them. On the other hand, even if money is in their immediate environment, their ability to use it to enrich themselves – spiritually and materially – may be impaired in some other way. They may have a profound disrespect for it, for instance, and so squander it; or they may feel deep down that somehow they do not really deserve the cash that comes into their hands and thus get rid of it as quickly as they can. In other words, lack of money can be a symptom of a more fundamental problem as much as a problem in its own right. To look at it from a different perspective, it is only as we develop inconspicuous benefit in our lives, meaning spiritual strengths like wisdom, hope, courage, perseverance and humour, that we can truly appreciate the value of the conspicuous benefits which come our way and thus properly enjoy them. It is for this reason that inconspicuous benefit is considered to be the greater of the two, and why Nichiren Daishonin stresses the importance of purifying the six senses.

Most people can recognize that there is a close relationship between the individual and the kind of environment he or she inhabits. Whenever they move, people have a tendency to recreate around themselves the environment they are used to or feel most comfortable with, which itself is clear evidence of the truth of the oneness of life and its environment. Again, most people would agree that as one changes and develops spiritually, so one's surroundings – physical and social – quite naturally change as well. Most of what has been said so far about the oneness of life and its environment may, therefore, seem pretty commonsensical. More difficult to accept, though, is the idea that chanting *Nam-myoho-renge-kyo* in itself can have any direct effect upon the world in which we live. However, this is just what Buddhism teaches.

For example, the conspicuous benefits of chanting can at times seem almost miraculous: when the 'impossible' actually happens, or when you get exactly what you need at exactly the right time – out of the blue someone will suddenly offer you a job, say, or the money you need desperately to pay the electricity bill will suddenly arrive from an unexpected source. These things are not miracles, merely your environment reacting *directly* to your chanting. As Nichiren Daishonin explains, 'Buddhism teaches that when the Buddha nature manifests itself from within, it will obtain protection from without. This is one of its fundamental principles.' This might be a little easier to understand if we remember that the principle of the oneness of life and its environment is based on the 'unification of the Three Truths', the idea that *all* life – animate and inanimate – has a physical, spiritual and essential aspect; this means that *all* life – animate and inanimate – is capable of manifesting the Ten Worlds. Thomas Hardy and his companion in the poem discussed briefly above were not 'superimposing' their feelings onto the scene before them, in other words, but simply drawing out of that scene qualities already inherent in it. Again, this might sound like a verbal quibble but, in reality, it points up a fundamental difference of perspective. As with everything explained in Buddhist teachings, the way you look at something is of the greatest importance. In this instance, the idea that even inanimate matter possesses the Ten Worlds is the basis for explaining how chanting *Nam-myoho-renge-kyo* can put one in rhythm with the rest of the universe. Nichiren Daishonin describes this process in a vividly poetic passage:

> Once one chants *Myoho-renge-kyo*, that single sound summons forth the Buddha nature inherent in all Buddhas, all laws, all bodhisattvas, all men of Learning, all Bontens and Taishakus,* King Emma,† the sun and the moon, the myriad stars, the heavenly deities and earthly gods‡ and all beings of Hell, Hunger, Animality, Anger, Humanity and Heaven, as well as all other living beings. This benefit is incalculable and boundless. When one reveres *Myoho-renge-kyo* that is inherent in one's life as the object of worship, one's innate Buddha nature, summoned forth by one's chanting of *Nam-myoho-renge-kyo*, emerges. This is called 'Buddha'. To illustrate, when a caged bird sings, birds in the sky, summoned by his singing, gather around, and when they gather around, the bird in the cage strives to get out. When one's mouth chants the Mystic Law, his inherent Buddha nature, also summoned, will definitely emerge. The Buddha nature of Bonten and Taishaku, being summoned, will protect us, and the Buddha nature of the Buddha's and bodhisattvas, being called, will rejoice.

If we can put ourselves in harmony with the entire universe through chanting *Nam-myoho-renge-kyo*, the principle of the oneness of life and the environment implies that the opposite must also be true: namely, that if we reveal our inherent greed, anger and stupidity, rather than our Buddhahood, the environment cannot support us as Nichiren Daishonin describes here, but instead has to reflect our negativity. This may be fairly easy to see on the individual level, but less so on a national or international level. Nevertheless, the principle holds good for, on this scale, the environment reflects the sum of human negativity in the form of natural and man-made catastrophes which Buddhism calls the Three Calamities and Seven Disasters. The idea that even natural disasters are inseparably linked to human activity may be

---

*In Indian mythology, Bonten (Brahma) was the personification of the fundamental principle of the universe, Brahman; Taishaku (Indra) was the god of thunder. Both were incorporated into Buddhism as 'protective deities', i.e. positive forces of the universe (‡ below).

†The mythological Lord of Hell and judge of the dead.

‡Buddhism does not teach the existence of gods, but, in societies where they were already widely believed, adopted them to indicate the protective and creative forces inherent in life.

extremely difficult to understand, however, so we will leave it for now and return to it in a later chapter.

Theory and Practice

T'ien-t'ai's achievement in explaining the unification of the Three Truths is truly enormous. As you are probably by now very aware, however, at some levels this theoretical explanation is not at all easy to comprehend and neither, as it stands, is it of very much practical use. Nichiren Daishonin's achievement is even greater that T'ien-t'ai's because he was able to take this exceptionally profound theory and define exactly and simply how it could be used by ordinary men and women to practical effect.

To give a simple analogy, T'ien-t'ai was like a man who sees a tree standing in a field. He analyzes its form – *ke* – and realizes that within its leaves and branches there is an unseen process going on by which the tree grows – *ku*. But what is the source of this process? He deduces that it lies in the tree's roots, buried deep within the earth – *chu*.

On the basis of this a second man, Nichiren Daishonin, then teaches how, by looking after those roots through feeding and watering the earth, one can ensure that the tree as a whole will, quite naturally, grow healthily and vigorously, enjoying the benefits of sun and wind, rain and snow, until in maturity it has reached its full height and luxuriance. In other words, by identifying *chu* as *Nam-myoho-renge-kyo*, Nichiren Daishonin taught that chanting this phrase nourishes our life at its very core, enabling us to grow to our full potential whatever joys or suffering we may have to encounter. He says:

> The deeper the roots, the more luxuriant the branches. The farther the source, the longer the stream. All sutras other than the Lotus Sutra have shallow roots and short streams, while the Lotus Sutra has deep roots and a distant source. That is why the Great Teacher T'ien-t'ai stated that the Lotus Sutra would survive and spread in the evil latter age.

Put simply, T'ien-t'ai explained theoretically how the world 'interacts with us' at its most essential level and, in so doing, laid the ground-plan for Nichiren Daishonin to use when he came to explain how doing something as apparently bizarre or non-rational as chanting *Nam-myoho-renge-kyo* can change oneself and the world around one. This may be a little easier to understand by looking at the parallels between the development of Buddhism and that of science and technology, which in some ways are very close. For example, all the advances made in understanding the nature of the atom would have amounted to no more than an interesting addition to scientific knowledge and a challenging problem for contemporary philosophy, were it not for the fact that men were able to act upon those advances and, through nuclear fusion and fission, release the energy inherent in the atom. Whatever our feelings may be about nuclear energy, therefore, it is an undeniable fact that, even without understanding it, we are able to benefit from the vast body of theoretical knowledge about the workings of the atom through the simplest of acts – switching on a light, for example. Again, as scientific theory progresses, so it is able to benefit more and more people. The first computers, for instance, were large, cumbersome, crude and difficult to operate. As they have developed they have become much smaller and more sophisticated but, at the same time, much more 'user-friendly', that is, easier to work and thus available to a larger number of people. The same is true of Buddhism. Nichiren Daishonin says of *Nam-myoho-renge-kyo*: 'A law this easy to embrace and this easy to practise was taught for the sake of all mankind in this evil age of the Latter Day of the Law.'

In other words, it is precisely because the theory behind the practice of chanting *Nam-myoho-renge-kyo* is so difficult that the practice itself is so easy. So, whether or not you understand precisely what *Nam-myoho-renge-kyo* means, or how the Three Truths explain the 'mutually inclusive relationship of life and all phenomena' [*myoho*], or any of the other terms or theories explained in this book, you can still gain great benefit from chanting this single phrase, just as you can from turning on a light switch or punching a button on a desk-top computer without understanding the theory supporting them. As Nichiren Daishonin explains:

> Even though one neither reads nor studies the sutra, chanting the title alone is a source of tremendous good fortune. The sutra teaches that women, evil men, and those in the realm of Animality and Hell – in fact, all people of the Ten Worlds – can attain

Buddhahood. We can comprehend this when we remember that fire can be produced from a stone taken from the bottom of a river, and a candle can light up a place that has been dark for billions of years. If even the most ordinary things of this world are such wonders, then how much more wondrous is the power of the Mystic Law [*myoho*].

In this sense, then, one might say that chanting *Nam-myoho-renge-kyo* is the most 'user-friendly' practice you are ever likely to encounter.

Life and Death

As we have seen briefly above, one meaning of *myoho* refers to the relationship of life and death. Benjamin Franklin once said that 'in this world nothing can be said to be certain, except death and taxes'. While taxes are for most of us an unpleasant but necessary feature of everyday life, however, some people can avoid them: by employing the very best accountants, for example, or perhaps by living in parts of the world where even indirect taxation does not exist. The same cannot be said of death. There are no specialists to whom we can go who will show us ways of avoiding the inevitable when our time is up, for even the most skilled physicians can at best only postpone the moment of final reckoning. Neither is there anywhere in the world where death does not come calling. In short, death always triumphs in the end; indeed, as we shall see, for the sake of life itself, death *has* to win.

It is because everyone eventually has to die and, therefore, at some time has to confront the reality of his or her own mortality, that the mystery of death can fairly be said to represent the greatest of all the problems facing mankind. Unlike poverty or sickness, for example, no one, however fortunate, can hope to escape it. A fact less clearly understood by men and women is that death is not a problem that comes only at the end of our lives, whenever that may be. Rather, it is our attitude to death *now* – specifically to our own death – that fundamentally colours our whole attitude to life. Sometimes this is very apparent: the young Islamic extremists who willingly make themselves human bombs, for example, do so only because they have total confidence that, in dying with the name of Allah on their lips, they will be reborn at once in Paradise. Presumably, if they did not think that life after death was going to be much better than life here on earth, they would be less willing to find out so quickly.

In the West, our attitude to death, and its effect on our everyday lives, is much less obvious. In part, this is because death is often viewed as a tragedy and, therefore, a subject to be avoided in contemporary western society. Of course, everybody knows that people die – after all, death in one form or another is on the television news virtually every night – but the reality of death is these days handled almost exclusively by 'professionals': the men and women who run the emergency services, doctors, nurses, the staff of geriatric homes and, of course, those gentlemen who 'undertake' to look after all the details that death brings in its wake – such as disposing of the body, for instance. This is in great contrast to people living in less 'civilized' societies or during less 'civilized' times, who had to deal with such matters themselves. Thanks to this sanitation of death today, people can avoid having any contact with it until they experience the shock of losing a close relative or friend; most people, indeed, have never even seen a dead body.

While if may be unhealthy to be as obsessed with death as people were in the Middle Ages, it is also unhealthy to be as insulated from it as we are in the West today. Not only does such insulation mean that we can often be totally unprepared for death when it comes to someone close to us but, equally important, it can actually increase our fear of what is, after all, a perfectly natural, inescapable human phenomen. Thus, we can reach a point where we do not like to talk or even think about death. Death is horrible, embarrassing, the ultimate degradation. Why is this? What is it that caused a culture which once had such a morbid fascination with death to become almost phobic in its abhorrence of it?

In the West the answer surely lies in the gradual erosion of Christian beliefs for, ever since Copernicus challenged the Church's view of the heavens in the sixteenth century, the authority of religious dogma has been steadily undermined by scientific rationality. This process, which has continued at an even greater pace in the twentieth century, has already been described in the explanation of the Three Truths as a movement from the predominantly spiritual values of *ku* to the predominantly materialistic values of *ke*, neither of which, being extremes, can by themselves bring human beings lasting happiness. So while the benefits of science have proved enormous – for example, in enabling people to live longer and more comfortably – and should not be undervalued, in undermining Christian beliefs science has left western society without any coherent spiritual philosophy. As Bertrand Russell pointed out, the authority of science 'does not, like the body of Catholic dogma, lay down a complete systems covering human morality, human hopes, and the past and future history of the universe. It pronounces only on whatever, at the time, appears to have been scientifically ascertained.' While this approach may have many strengths, not least of which is an implied openness to new facts and theories, its inherent weakness is nowhere more apparent than in trying to understand or cope with the inescapable fact of death.

Death is a natural human event, yet it is one which is almost universally feared. This may be simply fear of the unknown, but it is a fear that will not go away just because people are now supposedly more rational and less superstitious than they once were (which is a moot point), or because the findings of science appear to be more concrete than the doctrines of the Christian Church. Moreover, while death is an event which happens to everyone, it is one about which science can offer people no answers, and certainly no consolation. Science can describe with great accuracy certain processes that the body undergoes at death but is silent as to what actually happens to the life, spirit or soul that once inhabited that body. Indeed, scientists cannot even agree about the precise moment when life ends and death begins.

Psychologically, then, the often hidden fears people have arising from ignorance of the meaning and purpose of death could be seen to threaten the very basis of contemporary western society, since death continually defies the power of science. This is a power which we have been gradually persuaded to believe inevitably brings 'progress' and happiness and which, one day, might even rule supreme, although the unbounded confidence of Russell, writing in 1957, now looks somewhat misplaced. 'Intelligence, artistic capacity, benevolence – all these things,' he asserts, 'no doubt could be increased by science. There seems scarcely any limit to what *could* be done in the way of producing a good world, if only men would use science wisely.' Yet the limits now seem to be as intrinsic to science as to men. Thus, despite the fact that the explanations offered by Christianity about death may be such that, nowadays, many people seem unable to accept them, their demise has left an unhealthy vacuum which science has been unable to fill. Filled it must be, though, for, as Daisaku Ikeda explains, 'The question of death is in itself the question of life. As long as the question of death remains unsolved, life cannot be truly substantial.' This is a realization that is hard to accept, because to do so means to look at the prevailing mores of western society through very different eyes, and to see many of our society's problems as springing, fundamentally, from the lack of a satisfactory explanation for death. Before we discuss the Buddhist view of death, therefore, it may be useful to explore this point in a little more depth.

Broadly speaking, there are currently two views about what happens to our life after death: either it continues in some spiritual form, the precise nature of which has elicited lively debate through the centuries; or there is nothingness – that is, at death our life ends for good. This latter view can be held even by those with a strong religious belief, as confidence in an after-life can sometimes evaporate dramatically as death approaches: many people may sincerely want to go gladly to meet their Maker but, when faced with the reality of dying and the alternatives of Heaven or Hell, deep in their hearts and in the knowledge of their failings and imperfections, they may also sense nothing but darkness after death. Since the decline of religious beliefs in the West, however, the increasingly dominant (though largely unspoken) attitude is that death is death and, as Hamlet says, 'the rest is silence'.

But is the rest really silence, or is there now silence simply because science, one of the dominant factors in contemporary society, is able to say very little on the question? A philosophy based on scientific materialism (*ke*) must logically say that anything you cannot see or measure – that which cannot be discerned quantitively – does not exist; therefore, nothing can exist after the decay of the material body. Equally, such a philosophy cannot pronounce on matters of the 'spirit' – *ku*.

Of course, humanity has long recognized the ephemeral nature of the physical aspect of human life; indeed, the consciousness of our own mortality is one of the qualities that sets us apart from the animal world. But for almost as long as we have been aware of the inevitabilty of our end, human beings have also speculated upon the possibility of life continuing in some form after death. This idea has occurred in different guises throughout history, at all times and in all cultures – a persistence which, if nothing else, testifies to the strength of its appeal to the human imagination; or, to put it slightly differently, how the human imagination yearns for immortality.

Modern, western man, raised on reason and a doctrine which demands scientific proof for all things, will say that because there is no hard, physical evidence of the properly dead ever coming to life again – either once and for all in Heaven or Hell, as Christianity and Islam teach, or through periodic reincarnations, as is averred by many eastern religions, including Buddhism – no such thing happens. Therefore, all doctrines which assert an after-life are either expressions of a reluctance to face the fact that life is a once only event, or are merely attempts to affect the behaviour of people living now by offering future consolation or punishment for present sufferings or wrong-doing. For example, Karl Marx criticized religion as the opium of the masses precisely because it had been used through the ages by the ruling classes, both religious and secular, to breed a passive acceptance of their lot amongst the common people, teaching them the virtue of poverty and humility and the evil of upsetting the status quo. A more blatant example of exploiting the idea of an after-life for present gain was the selling of indulgences, papal certificates which were deemed to shorten the amount of time the buyer's soul would have to spend in Purgatory before going on to Heaven.

While it is undeniably true that the idea of some form of an after-life has often been used by a number of religions to manipulate and exploit people for either political or financial ends, it is also undeniable that belief in an after-life can have a beneficial effect on the human mind. Most obviously, the idea that our actions here and now affect in some way what happens to us after death can be a source of great strength at times of severe hardship, either personal or social. A classic example of this can be found in the life of Nichiren Daishonin himself, who suffered constant harassment and persecution as a result of his efforts to spread the teachings of the Lotus Sutra and to explain the necessity of chanting *Nam-myoho-renge-kyo*. Although twice exiled and once almost beheaded, his complete conviction in the future effect of his actions, both for himself and others, enabled him, while living in the most desperate circumstances, to say, 'For what I have done, I have been condemned to exile, but it is a small suffering to undergo in this present life and not one worth crying over. In future lives I will enjoy immense happiness, a thought which gives me great satisfaction.' Thus, the confidence, or even the hope, that there is a reward awaiting us in the future is a powerful weapon in the fight against submitting to despair at any present suffering.

By contrast, the nihilistic belief that, after one short lifetime on Earth, one is consigned to the blackness of oblivion is extremely uncomfortable to sustain. Not only is the prospect of an eternity of nothingness highly unattractive to most people, used as they are to the variety of living, but, in the light of Daisaku Ikeda's remark above, the very idea of this nothingness can actually render our lives fundamentally without substance *now*. Of course, not everyone regards the prospect in this way and, as Dr Bryan Wilson has pointed out, 'some sincere and conscientious unbelievers have attained and maintained a high degree of integrity in their lives and have carried this nobility of spirit through to the end, facing death with composure and quiet resolution.' Certainly, the positive aspect of this view of death is that the real meaning of life is to be found only here and now, and that one must make the most of one's life by trying to make this world a better place, even if we are here only temporarily. This is a view with which Buddhism heartily concurs, but to which it adds the all-important dimension of the eternity of life and the universe through the endless cycle of rebirth, as we shall see shortly.

However, for those people who cannot 'attain and maintain a high degree of integrity in their lives' (and who might constitute a large majority of those living in western society today), 'Eat, drink and be merry, for tomorrow we die!' may seem to be the only feasible course of behaviour if one wants to avoid the despair that results from the idea of impending nothingness. Ironically, then, in replacing the doctrines of Christianity with those of science we may be increasing our fear and insecurity in the face of death; after all, swapping eternal bliss in Heaven (even if it may involve a preliminary period in Hell) for an increased life-span of a few more years here on Earth, most of which will be spent as a 'senior citizen', does not seem to be much of a trade-off. Perhaps it is this realization which accounts for our growing, almost manic, consumerism. Like children might feel who have been told in a sweet shop that this is their one and only chance to grab the goodies, but that they can take nothing out of the shop with them, we appear desperate in our desire to stuff ourselves with everything that is going. Moreover, by encouraging our so-called 'worldly desires', materialism afflicts not only individuals but the whole world with the three poisons of greed, anger (in the form of ruthless competitiveness) and stupidity. Indeed, as Daisaku Ikeda has pointed out, until people realize that life is eternal and indestructible, the world will never overcome these poisons.

Even more insidiously, the fear of death affects our lives in our attitude to time. In one way or another we all want more of it; it is a desire which seems so deeply rooted that we are either completely unaware of it or take it to be perfectly natural. For example, there seems to be something in the western conscious-ness which is always looking for short-cuts. Walking around the edge of a field we always think how much shorter our journey would be if we cut across the middle, and often we do. When walking, we think how much time we could save if we cycled or drove by car; when driving, how much time could be saved if we drove a faster car; when cooking, how much time we could save if we used a microwave rather than a gas or electric cooker, or if we bought pre-cooked food; when working, how much more quickly we could do our work if we had the latest computer, word-processor, tractor, and so on. When it comes to the number of ways that science and technology have devised to save time for human beings, the list seems endless.

Clearly, we place a great premium on this commodity. That we do so is almost certainly because, subconsciously, we fear our time is running out all the time we are alive. This fear can dictate many of our actions, even some of the most apparently insig-nificant. That our lifetime is limited is undeniable; no religion or philosophy teaches otherwise and the higher religions and philosophies all teach that, while we are here, we should use our time to the full. But how do we use the supposedly vast amounts of time that all the highly sophisticated artefacts of our society have managed to save for us? When Bob rushes home on the 6.16 from Charing Cross, what is it to do? Sadly, probably, just to eat something, put his feet up, then fall asleep in front of the television. Now, no one would want to deny Bob the time to rest for a bit – after all, he has probably been slaving all day at work over the latest and fastest time-saving computer – but his behaviour, and that of millions of others like him living in the West, does raise a disturbing question: has our society striven so hard and for so long to save us this apparently precious commodity – time – precisely so that we can indulge in the luxury of squandering it? Indeed, is the very idea that 'time to ourselves' is so precious a result of the notion that, as we have only one life, time devoted to other people is somehow less valuable or even wasted unless we receive a definite and quick return?

These are difficult questions, for the answers go to the very core of our view of life and our role in it. Clearly, though, the correct attitude to death must be crucial in establishing a correct attitude to life. According to Nichiren Daishonin, this must surely be to create the most value for ourselves and others, which leads to fulfilment and, therefore, happiness. But how can we formulate a 'correct' attitude to death when we have no way of knowing what happens when we die? As Daisaku Ikeda suggests, the answer lies in a more broadly-based approach:

> The inadequacies of our spiritual abilities limit our theories about the universe and about the true nature of our lives to unverifiable hypotheses. Scientific theories are subject to, and must be subjected to, theoretical and experimental tests of validity. Ways of evaluating religious hypotheses, however, are different. First, religious hypotheses must be judged on how well they explain the phenomenon of life to unaided human intelligence. Second, they must be judged on how effective they are in providing a foundation for human judgements and actions. In other words, we must ask whether scientific hypotheses are true, whereas we must ask whether religious hypotheses have any value for the improvement of the qualities of humanity.

In evaluating the hypotheses which Buddhism (or any other religion) advances about death, therefore, it would be well to bear these two points in mind. Speculation about the nature of death has formed the basis of all religions and philosophies, none of which, however, can be proved empirically. But by placing the human being at the centre of any consideration of the question, we can begin to see clearly how different ideas about death, as taught by different religions and philosophies, can and do affect the living. We have seen above, for example, how the idea of death being 'The End' has subtly, but profoundly, influenced the behaviour of people living in contemporary western civilization. Now we must turn to the Buddhist view, one which can truly liberate people from an insidious and restricting fear of death.

The Eternity of Life

When most people think about Buddhism and death the word that immediately springs to mind is 'reincarnation', with all its attendant connotations of the possibility of people being reborn as animals or even insects as some kind of punishment for actions committed in previous lifetimes. This is almost a caricature of what Buddhism teaches about death for, while it would be no exaggeration to say that the problems posed by death lie at the heart of Buddhist philosophy, the challenge of death has always been viewed by Buddhism as a means to reveal the most valuable way to live. Shakyamuni, you will remember, left the comfort of his palace to discover the answer to the four universal sufferings of mankind – birth, sickness, ageing and death – in order to then teach people how to overcome those sufferings. Similarly, although Nichiren Daishonin considered reaching an understanding of the true nature of death his greatest challenge, his desire to meet this challenge was born out of his great compassion for humanity. As he says:

> Ever since my childhood, I have studied Buddhism with one thought in mind. Life as a human being is pathetically fleeting. A man exhales his last breath with no hope to draw in another. Not even dew borne by the wind suffices to describe this transience. No one, wise or foolish, young or old, can escape death. My sole wish has therefore been to solve this eternal mystery. All else has been secondary.

Instead of dwelling on the possible vagaries of reincarnation, Nichiren Shoshu Buddhism stresses the importance of realizing deep within oneself the truth of the eternity of life. This idea is not to be confused with the Christian concept of an individual's soul living eternally after death in either Heaven or Hell; rather, the Buddhist concept of the eternity of life places the life of the individual in the context of the universe as a whole, asserting that since the entire universe exists in one form or another throughout eternity, so must all the living things contained within it exist eternally in one form or another. Thus, no living thing can be created and neither can it be destroyed. What appears to be creation and destruction is, in reality, simply the power of renewal inherent in the limitless life-force of the universe at work in an ever-changing variety of forms, like a huge kaleidoscope; neither is this process random but, rather, follows the unending cycle of birth, maturation, decline and death, according to the law of the universe, *Nam-myoho-renge-kyo*.

This profound concept of the eternity of life thus anticipates by some 3000 years the physical laws of the conservation of energy and matter. These state that neither energy nor matter are ever 'lost', but are simply converted into different forms. Coal exists as physical matter and potential energy: when burnt that potential energy becomes heat and light, which eventually become so dissipated that they cannot be seen; even so, they cannot escape from the universe as a whole. It is, therefore, no great leap to see our individual lives, composed as they are of physical and 'spiritual' energies, conforming to these laws. As Daisaku Ikeda explains:

> Our lives exist, have always existed, and will always exist simultaneously with the universe. They neither came into being before the universe, occurred accidentally, nor were created by a supernatural being. Nichiren Daishonin taught that life and death are the alternating aspects in which our real self manifests itself, and both are part of the cosmic essence.

Myoho refers to this eternal rhythm of life and death. Nichiren Daishonin says:

> *Myo* represents death, and *ho* represents life. Life and death are the two phases passed through by the entities of the Ten Worlds, the entities of all living beings which embody the law of cause and effect (*renge*) . . . No phenomena, heaven or earth, Yin or Yang,* the sun or the moon, the five planets,† or any life-condition from

*Two universal principles of ancient Chinese philosophy, the interaction of which was thought to affect the destiny of all things. Yin is the negative, dark and feminine principle; Yang the positive, bright and masculine principle.

†Only Mercury, Venus, Mars, Jupiter and Saturn were known in thirteenth-century Japan.

Hell to Buddhahood – are free from birth and death. Thus the life and death of all phenomena are simply the two phases of *Myoho-renge-kyo*. In his *Maka Shikan*, T'ien'-t'ai says, 'The emergence of all things is the manifestation of their intrinsic nature, and their extinction, the withdrawal of that nature into the state of latency.'

In other words, life and death can be likened to the black cat in the child's riddle, walking across the black and white stripes of a pedestrian-crossing and saying, 'Now you see me, now you don't.' The fact that at any one particular time we cannot see the cat (or the life of a particular person), does not mean that it does not exist. Rather, Nichiren Shoshu Buddhism teaches that, at death, life continues to exist unseen in the state of *ku* and, like the black cat on a black stripe, will definitely be seen again when it reappears in the state of *ke* at some stage in the future, when the time and conditions are right.

Now, the 'right condition' for us to see the black cat is obviously when it is on a white stripe, and to get to a white stripe from a black one, and to a black stripe from a white one, all the cat has to do is walk. Essentially the same pattern and movement applies to human life as well, though to explain how it emerges from the state of death into the state of life, and vice versa, is a little more involved. Once more we have to return to the concept of the Three Truths of temporary existence (*ke*), non-substantiality (*ku*) and the Middle Way (*chu*).

The Five Components
As applied to human life, the truth of temporary existence (*ke*) is more profound than a simple acknowledgement that human life is brief and transient. Rather, it explains that each individual life-form is the *temporary* fusion of what Buddhism terms the Five Components: form, perception, conception, volition and consciousness. A life-form appears as the Five Components come together harmoniously within the life entity or nucleus as the result of past causes and their present effects and conditions – and disappears when they disunite.

Form indicates life's physical aspect – the body – which possesses shape and colour and includes the sense organs through which one receives information about the environment. The remaining four components relate to life's spiritual aspect. *Perception* is the act of receiving information about the external world through the eyes, ears, nose, tongue and skin, and integrating them in what Buddhism terms the sixth-sense organ, the 'mind'. *Conception* is the inherent ability to form a coherent idea about what has been perceived, while *volition* is the inherent ability to take action as a result of what has been perceived and conceived. This ability to discern things in both a material and an abstract sense, to make judgements and take action, together make up the fifth component of *consciousness*.

Together, the Five Components constitute the essential elements of an individual life. We have already seen that the physical and spiritual aspects of life are inseparable, so just as it is impossible for there to be consciousness without form, perception, conception and volition, so must form have perception, conception, volition and consciousness. In other words, the concept of the Five Components teaches that, as life becomes manifest, to function effectively it must take on physical attributes – a body – and possess consciousness, perception, conception and volition. (This is one reason why Nichiren Shoshu Buddhism denies the existence of gods, ghosts and spirits except as illusions of the mind, as these beings are supposed to possess consciousness without form.)

Once again, as with the Three Truths, it is important not to view the Five Components as separate from one another, as the sentence above, 'A life-form appears as the Five Components come together . . . and disappears when they disunite', might imply, for one could just as well say that, as life appears, the Five Components appear and, as life disappears, so do the Five Components.

To understand this idea a little more clearly, let us see how it applies to a single human life. In human beings, individual life appears when a sperm fertilizes an egg. Each is a separate entity, capable for a time of separate existence, but it is only in their union that life comes into being. (Significantly, every cell in the body has the complete potential to make a whole individual, except the egg and sperm cells.) A materialist view of life would say that life is *created* at the moment of conception, but Buddhism (and the laws of the conservation of matter and energy) deny the possibility of creation as such. The difference is explained by Arnold Toynbee:

There are two possible explanations for change or novelty. It may be produced by creation – by the bringing into existence, or the coming into existence, of things that did not exist previously. Alternatively, novelty may be produced by evolution in the literal meaning of the word – that is, the unfolding of something that was contained in the package from the beginning. According to the evolutionary explanation, the appearance of change is really an illusion. Everything that exists or that is ever going to exist has been in existence from the start. All that happens is that some originally latent elements of reality are made to manifest progressively.

Needless to say, it is the 'evolutionary' view that Buddhism takes, both towards individual life and the life of the universe as a whole, as Daisaku Ikeda explains:

If the universe is interpreted in terms of no more than the concepts of non-being and being, one is forced to say that life was, and still is, being generated from non-being. Buddhism takes a different stand and posits the existence of a state of non-being that contains inherent possibilities of becoming being and thus transcends both the concept of being and the concept of non-being. Buddhist thought interprets this state as the true entity of the universe and calls it *ku* . . . The entire universe, including our earth, is a life entity: it is *ku*, which contains life. When the conditions are right for the tendency for life to manifest itself, life can be generated anywhere at any time.

The moment a sperm fertilizes an egg is, therefore, simply the 'right condition' for the tendency for human life to manifest itself. This is when life is seen, just as the black cat is seen on the white stripe. Like the black cat on the black stripe, though, life still exists even when it is not seen.

As soon as life appears it is immediately endowed with the Five Components though not, of course, in their most developed form. Nevertheless, these will also evolve as time passes. Thus, as the foetus grows physically, so gradually does its conciousness until, at birth, it is able to sustain life outside its mother's body. It is not yet independent of her but will increasingly become so as it continues to grow and its consciousness further develops. Its perception of the world around it will become clearer; it will be able to conceive increasingly sophisticated ideas (and so eventually start to talk, for example) and, of course, as anyone who has raised a small child can testify, its will, or volition, will become much stronger and more clearly defined.

Although the process may not be so clearly seen during the time in the womb, from the moment of conception to the moment of death individual life consists of the continuous interaction of the Five Components. How we perceive things influences the ideas we have about them, and vice versa, which further affects our volition or the decisions and actions we take towards them. More fundamentally, none of these actions is possible without the basic starting points of our individual body and consciousness. As Daisaku Ikeda explains, the concept of the Five Components once again finds parallels in contemporary scientific explanations of life:

> For all its impermanence, life is magnificently harmonious. Molecules and atoms are essentially inorganic, and elementary particles lack even individuality, but they combine into increasingly complex compounds until they become the genes that determine the personality of human beings. A single human being is said to have some five billion genes bearing the information necessary for his individual existence. Thanks to these genes, our bodies grow into marvellously precise complexes, we possess conciousness, and we experience happiness, anger, and the other emotions. A certain configuration and interaction of billions of particles determine how we will live and how we will react to our surroundings. Who can say the Buddhist concept of the Five Components coming together temporarily to compose a human being is not an excellent metaphor for this phenomenon?

In this light, death can therefore be defined as the moment when the Five Components no longer interact in this way. Thus, when a person dies, their consciousness disappears, along with their functions of perception, conception and volition, and after a time, their form, or body, also decays and eventually disintegrates altogether. Equally, we could say that death is the moment when, due to ageing and deficiency, the body is no longer capable of sustaining the other four components. Sometimes, that moment is utterly unambiguous. To give a somewhat gory example, a soldier who is literally blown to bits by an enemy shell dies instantly because in the single moment that his body is torn apart so must his consciousness, perception, conception and volition also disappear. At other times, it is harder to judge the moment of death because, as the body is still whole, the Five Components can be still interacting, if only intermittently – rather like a torch, whose batteries are almost run down, will occasionally flash brighter as a better connection is made within it. Tolstoy depicts the difficulty of deciding when death has come in the following passage from *Anna Karenina*, recounting the last moments, after a long illness, of Levin's brother, Nikolai:

> By the evening Nikolai could no longer lift his hands, and lay staring in front of him with a fixed, concentrated gaze. Even when his brother or Kitty bent over him, so that he could see them, he took no notice but continued looking in the same direction. Kitty sent for the priest to read the prayers for the dying.
>
> While the priest was reading the prayers, the dying man showed no signs of life. His eyes were closed. Levin, Kitty, and Maria Nikolayevna stood at the bedside. Before the priest had finished, the dying man stretched, sighed, and opened his eyes. When he had come to the end of his prayer, the priest put the cross to the cold forehead, then slowly wrapped it in his stole and, after standing in silence for a minute or two, touched the huge, bloodless hand that was turning cold.
>
> 'He's gone,' said the priest, and made to move away; but suddenly there was a faint stir in the clammy moustaches of the dying man, and from the depths of his chest came the words, sharp and distinct in the stillness:
>
> 'Not quite . . . Soon.'
>
> A moment later the face brightened, a smile appeared under the moustaches, and the women who had gathered round began carefully laying out the corpse.

In Nikolai's condition, hovering between life and death, consciousness can come and go, perception can at times appear sharp, at other times wholly obscured, the will can be stronger or weaker, and the ability to form clear ideas about what is happening can vary greatly. Only when the body has for some time shown no physical expressions of life, like breathing or warmth, and no signs whatsoever of the other four 'spiritual' components, can death be said to have arrived; even then there can be errors of judgement, as various cases of people 'returning' to life on the mortuary slab have demonstrated.

So much, then, for the moment of death. But what of the moment immediately following? Where did Nikolai's life 'go' when he died? And how does Buddhism then explain the eventual reappearance or rebirth of his life at some time in the future?

How well you understand the explanation that Nichiren Shoshu Buddhism advances for the state of death depends upon an understanding of the concept of *ku*, the state of neither existence nor non - existence. For example, we saw that the blossoms in a cherry tree in winter do not 'exist' and yet, when the time is right, they appear as if by magic out of nothing. Similarly, anger, which you know you possess, is at this moment 'somewhere' in your life, although you cannot say 'where'. You know, however, that given the right conditions it will appear as if on cue.

As we have seen, Buddhism teaches that all life in the universe is either manifest – *ke* – or unseen, in the state of *ku*. Our individual life appears as it emerges from this state of *ku*, out of the great 'sea' of life-force that pervades the universe, and at death merges back into this life-force, in the state of *ku*. If it is difficult to picture this process, it is because the state of *ku* defies the standard concepts of time and space in which our conscious minds operate. To understand 'where' our life 'goes' when we die, therefore, an analogy might prove helpful.

If you imagine the life-force of the universe as the ocean, an individual life can be likened to a single wave on the surface of the ocean. From this it follows that the single wave is in no way different from the rest of the ocean around it. The only factor that gives it a momentary identity is its physical form by which, for a short space of time, it appears defined as a wave with its own unique behaviour and characteristics. As anyone who has studied simple physics at school will know, however, the wave that is seen at the surface is merely a product of the forces and energies of a larger wave motion existing unseen within the ocean. Strictly speaking, then, we could speak of the 'seen' wave deriving from the 'unseen' wave. Finally, the concentration of kinetic energy which originally created the 'seen' wave from the 'unseen' wave will, after a time, become dissipated, and so the 'seen' wave will collapse, merging once more into the deep 'unseen' waves of the ocean from which it appeared.

In other words, at death our life does not physically 'go' anywhere because it is already concomitant with the universe, as described in the explanation above of the oneness of life and its environment (see pp. 118–127). Thus, although at death our form and consciousness no longer function, the entity of our life itself continues, in the same way that wave motion continues unseen in the depths of the ocean after the 'seen' wave at the surface has collapsed. Indeed, one could say that, just as the ocean is simply an enormous collection of harmoniously inter-related individual waves which appear and disappear according to changing conditions, and that our wave, as part of a larger, continuous wave pattern, will at some point break the surface of the ocean and reappear as a single wave again, so is the universe simply an infinite collection of harmoniously related life entities which similarly appear and disappear throughout eternity.

Entity and 'Identity'

The term 'life entity' may cause confusion for, living as we do in a society heavily influenced by Judaeo-Christian concepts, the temptation may be to say that this is just another way of describing the soul, that indestructible essence of an individual which is 'liberated' from the body at death. But the two ideas, though sharing a certain superficial similarity, are quite different. For example, according to orthodox Christian doctrines, a soul comes into being at the moment of conception and, like all aspects of life, is ultimately a result of the action of God. The soul is, therefore, completely identified with that particular, unique individual and, after his or her death, continues to exist in some spiritual realm – Heaven, Hell, Purgatory – as the essence of that person and that person alone.

By contrast, Nichiren Shoshu Buddhism teaches that the 'life entity' of an individual has existed since 'time without begin-ning', *before* the moment of conception; it appears as the result of the combined effects of all the causes carried by it from the infinite past meeting just the right conditions at that present moment; it continues unchanged throughout the individual's life; disappears but remains unaltered at death; and then reappears in a different form in the future, according to all the causes and conditions *then* prevailing.

The highest forms of Buddhism specifically deny the existence of the soul and, instead, teach what is known as the 'non-substantiality (*ku*) of persons'. This concept states that because an individual is merely the *temporary* union of the Five Components, arising only as a result of particular causes and conditions, he or she has no fixed or absolute 'self' that exists throughout time. Daisaku Ikeda explains:

> The fundamental Buddhist doctrine of causal origins interprets all things as temporary aggregations of elements instead of immutable essential entities . . . All things depend on causal relations that bring them together, and their aggregation results in a different entity that is more than a mere sum of its parts, just as water is something very different from its components oxygen and hydrogen.

This may seem a little difficult to grasp as applied to human beings, but it can be easily understood by looking at the idea of 'self', or 'identity', in the context of an individual's personal growth in one lifetime.

For example, as you get older you quite naturally undergo changes in appearance (*ke*) and character (*ku*). In other words, on the basis of *ke* and *ku* your 'identity' is not fixed but is constantly changing according to the sort of life you lead. The changes may be slight from one moment to the next but, over a number of years, they may be so marked that you could seem a completely different person. For instance, if John Smith, the healthy, kind and generous man we met earlier, for some reason becomes a heroin addict, not only can his physical appearance radically alter, but so can his character, as compassion and humanity give way to bitterness, suspicion, aggression, and so on.

Even in as extreme an example as this, when a person is totally unrecognizable as their former self, we would say that, even though his character may have changed, by *nature* he is still John Smith, essentially the 'same' man as before. This is because, despite all the changes an individual may experience, the entity or true self of his or her life (*chu*) remains constant. The nature of John Smith's *life* – his past, present and future, if you like – can belong to no one else but him. Thus, it is our true self (*chu*), the constant, unchanging entity and nature of our lives, that enables us to know that we are essentially the same people now as we were when children, despite all the changes we experience. To give an analogy, an apple tree is always an apple tree, whether the apples it produces from year to year are sometimes sweet, sometimes sour, sometimes diseased and other times perfect.

If we can accept this description of how, within a single lifetime, an individual's 'identity' *(ke* and *ku)* is constantly changing, and yet his or her life displays definite constancy *(chu),* it is no great leap of the imagination to envisage this relationship of past 'identity' (how we once were), present 'identity' (how we are now), and future 'identity' (how we may change in the future), as starting before birth and continuing after death. The only difference is that, from lifetime to lifetime, the change of 'identity' – that is, appearance and character – is even more marked than that which occurs within a single individual during a single lifetime; indeed, at each rebirth the change of 'identity' the life entity experiences is total. The innate nature of the original John Smith still exists, in other words, but in a totally different guise. Another analogy – that of the life of an actor – might help here. Consider these two speeches, taken from plays by Willliam Shakespeare:

> All the world's a stage
> And all the men and women merely players
> They have their exits and their entrances
> And one man in his time plays many parts
> His acts being seven ages . . .
>   . . . Last scene of all
> That ends this strange eventful history
> Is second childishness and mere oblivion
> Sans teeth, sans eyes, sans taste, sans everything.

>   (*As You Like It*, Act 2, Scene 7)

> Life's but a walking shadow, a poor player
> That struts and frets his hour upon the stage
> And then is heard no more.

>   (*Macbeth*, Act 5, Scene 5)

Being a man of the theatre, Shakespeare often liked to employ theatrical imagery in his dramas and the idea that life is like the performance of the play is one that crops up a number of times. Particularly noticeable in the first extract is Shakespeare's own realization that an individual's identity is not fixed but, like an actor's, changes according to the 'part' being played. More fundamentally, both passages share the idea that, when the player leaves the stage at the end of the drama, for the audience it is as if he no longer exists. Indeed, the character an actor plays does exist only when he is in front of the audience. This is a very strong poetic image for the brevity, and the huff and puff, of life. Indeed, life is like the performance of a play if you believe (as Shakespeare seems to have done) that the final curtain means for the audience just that – curtains, The End, 'mere oblivion'. Yet the 'poor player' who has strutted and fretted his hour upon the stage of life, far from being 'heard no more', simply retires from the public world, takes off his makeup (or 'identity'), then goes through the whole business again the following night. The idea of 'life being like the theatre' thus fits closely with the Buddhist notion of life and death, and one cannot help wondering if this was actually the way that Shakespeare saw it.

An actor can be likened to the entity of an individual life, for example. Being unemployed is, for our actor, like being in the state of *ku*; an actor can only be an actor – in other words, act – in front of an audience. When he does become 'manifest', by appearing on stage, he cannot do so as himself but has to appear in a particular role. This is equivalent to the fact that an individual's life entity can never be seen in itself but only in its transient identity, the form it takes in each particular lifetime. To continue the analogy, our actor can only appear on stage when all the conditions are right for him to appear: a play has to be written, the money raised, a theatre found, and so on. Most importantly, our actor has to fit one of the parts. Once the play has been cast, there is a further period of gestation – rehearsals – before the actor can at last 'be born' and play his role. How long he 'lives' is another matter, again depending upon all sorts of conditions, like how good the play is, how good the acting is, or even how expensive are the seats. But, eventually, the run of the play will end and our actor will 'die' – that is, find himself unemployed once again, in the state of *ku*, preparing for another role in another play. When he is re-employed (again, as a result of past causes, such as how good he was in his last play, and other conditions, like how 'healthy' current theatre audiences are), and then 'reborn' in a new play, he will take on a new identity whose only link with the previous one is that the same actor, or life entity, is playing it. Thus, Buddhism would agree with Shake-speare when he says:

> Life's but a walking shadow, a poor player
> That struts and frets his hour upon the stage
> And then is heard no more

But then it would add, 'till he's cast again' in some other show, for, according to the wisdom of Buddhism, life is not 'like *a* play' but is, rather, like an endless series of plays in which we are cast again and again on the basis of what we have done before. Hence, to continue the analogy, a good actor builds his own good fortune through the causes he makes in play after play. This leads to his fulfilment and happiness in his chosen career. On the other hand, a bad actor, if he is wise enough to see his limitations, may decide to change direction and earn his living in another field; whilst a lazy actor, who fails to exert himself, is most likely to suffer from short runs, long periods of unemployment and frequent descents into the bitterness and discomfort of Hell. To this, Buddhism would say, 'Such is life!'

But why do we have to die at all, if we are going to be continually reborn? Why do we not live forever and save ourselves all the trouble of worrying about death? The answer is that death fulfills in our eternal life a similar function to sleep in our present lifetime: it refreshes and revitalizes the life-force of the entity of our individual lives, giving us the power to take on a fresh, new, physical form. Without death, we would be con-demned to the sort of existence suffered by the Struldbruggs, or Immortals, as described in *Gulliver's Travels*:

> [They] commonly acted like mortals, until about thirty years old, after which by degrees they grew melancholy and dejected, increasing in both until they came to fourscore . . . When they came to fourscore years, which is reckoned the extremity of living in this country, they had not only the follies and infirmities of other old men, but many more which arose from the dreadful prospect of never dying. They were not only opinionative, peevish, covetous, morose, vain, talkative; but incapable of friendship, and dead to all natural affection, which never descended below their grandchildren. Envy and impotent desires are their prevailing passions. But those objects against which their

envy seems principally directed, are the vices of the younger sort, and the deaths of the old. By reflecting on the former, they find themselves cut off from the possibility of all pleasure; and whenever they see a funeral, they lament and repine that others have gone to an harbour of rest, to which they themselves can never hope to arrive . . .

As soon as they have completed the term of eighty years, they are looked on as dead in law; their heirs immediately succeed to their estates, only a small pittance is reserved for their support; and the poor ones are maintained at the public charge . . .

The reader will easily believe, that from what I had heard and seen, my keen appetite for perpetuity of life was much abated. I grew heartily ashamed of the pleasing visions I had formed; and thought no tyrant could invent a death, into which I would not run with pleasure from such a life.

It is precisely to avoid 'such a life' – literally, a fate worse than death – that, periodically, we cast off our ageing and increasingly inefficient bodies, rather like a snake sloughs its skin, and then, after a period of time, are reborn with a new one. To return for a moment to our analogy of the wave and the ocean, at death we no longer have the energy to sustain our physical form (*ke*) and, like the wave collapsing, we die. Our life entity (*chu*) disappears into the sea of life-force (*ku*), and eventually even all our physical remains merge with the earth. The state of death, or *ku*, is by no means static, however, but rather is a time when the life entity draws on the energy of the life-force of the universe in preparation for rebirth in another physical form. When it has generated sufficient life-force, and when all the other conditions are right, the life entity will reappear automatically in the environment exactly suited for it, pre-programmed, as it were, by all its past causes. Furthermore, the time spent in this phase of latency will depend on the amount of life-force we have at the point of death. If we are in Hell at the crucial moment, our life-force will be negligible and our time in the state of death will seem very long, as we await the power necessary for us to be reborn. If we die in the most positive and dynamic of all life conditions, Buddhahood, we can be reborn in an instant, to continue our creative purpose in life.

In short, Nichiren Shoshu Buddhism teaches that death is simply a phase in the eternal process by which an individual life entity constantly refreshes and renews itself before reappearing in a different guise. Indeed, the phrase, 'a change is as good as a rest', might have been coined to sum up the explanation that Nichiren Shoshu Buddhism gives for death, for that is just what it can be.

The notion of the life entity 'drawing on the energy of the life-force of the universe' might sound a little vague and mystical, until we realize that in sleep we are undergoing the same process, the only difference being that we retain the same (though constantly changing) physical form. What is known of the processes and function of sleep is so similar to the Buddhist explanation of death that it is worth pausing for a moment to consider it in more detail.

Sleep

Whereas dreams and dreaming have fascinated mankind for many centuries, the subject of sleep itself has attracted close attention only since the 1930s. Before then, sleep, like death, had attracted much speculation, but it was not until the discovery that the brain produces electrical waves which can be continuously recorded in patterns known as electroencephalograms (EEGs), that serious scientific research into sleep was able to commence.

Professor Alexander Borbély, Director of the Sleep Laboratory of the Institute of Pharmacology at the University of Zurich, is the author of *The Secrets of Sleep*, a layman's introduction to the world of sleep research and what science has discovered about this almost universal phenomenon in the past fifty years or so. Surprisingly, this turns out to be very little. Or perhaps it is not so surprising, in the light of what we now know about the state of *ku*, which Buddhism says the human mind enters on falling asleep. Professor Borbély's sincerely acknowledged bafflement when faced with this mysterious state is somewhat reminiscent of that experienced by the early nuclear scientists, who probed into the heart of the atom, only to find a world that refused to conform to the demands of their methods of investigation. Right at the end of the book, for example, Professor Borbély states in his conclusion:

> As we conduct our experiments, we feel in touch with a fundamental process of life. In our encounters with sleep, we are faced with a process that appears utterly ordinary yet continues to

elude our grasp. This experience conveys a sense of humility. Even if we go on using scientific methods to study the secrets of sleep, we must refrain from falling prey to arrogant expectations.

Professor Borbély does briefly discuss the superficial similarity of sleep and death, but does not explore it in any depth. Elsewhere in his book, however, the parallels between what scientists understand about sleep and the Buddhist view of death begin to emerge. For example, when explaining the relationship between sleep and the brain, Professor Borbély says, 'On the basis of our present-day knowledge, sleep and wakefulness must be considered two different but "equal" states, neither of which can be explained simply as the cessation or lack of the other . . . Overstating the case only slightly, we could say that our brain does not sleep when we do.' This is a highly significant realization for, if we substituted 'death' and 'life' for 'sleep' and 'wakeful-ness', we would have a perfect description of the concept of *myoho*. What is more, by only slightly changing the final sentence of the extract, we could say that 'our life entity does not die when we do'. In other words, the pattern which sleep follows in a living being, and which leading researchers are beginning to discern, appears to match that which Buddhism also ascribes to death.

One thing that research has clearly established is how important a good night's sleep is to the efficient mental and physical well-being of the individual, and how short is the time we can function without it. What researchers are unable to explain is exactly *how* sleep restores us. One theory suggests that we sleep in order to dream and, in dreaming, we express the unconscious or even repressed hopes and frustrations of our waking life. In this way, so the theory goes, we relieve the possibly harmful pressure these 'psychic' energies can build up deep within the mind, and so feel refreshed in the morning, in the same way that we would if we managed to work a physical illness out of our system or pluck up the courage to share with a good friend a personal problem that has caused us acute anxiety.

While there is probably a great deal in the notion that our body is refreshed through sleep because of something that happens to our mind, the idea that dreams act as a kind of routine safety-valve to relieve the pressures of everyday living does not explain why some people should then have to suffer recurring nightmares, or how in our waking moments we can be haunted by our dreams, especially those in which we have perhaps acted in ways we would never even consider in real life. For example, if a woman dreams she kills one of her children, and enjoys doing so, on waking she might feel extremely guilty at the thought that deep down a part of her self 'really' wants to commit this act. Far from relieving 'psychic' pressures, therefore, in some cases it would appear that dreams can actually increase them.

If the example of nuclear physics is anything to go by, sleep researchers may well come to the conclusion that the crucial mechanisms underlying the process of recovery during sleep lie outside the realm of science and are, therefore, beyond the reach of scientific method. Put simply, in Buddhist terms, these scientists are once again trying to use the intruments of *ke* to examine *ku*, for sleep is a 'mystic' phenomenon, in the sense discussed earlier, and *myo*, you will remember, means not only 'mystic' but also 'to revive' or 'to return to life'. To understand how sleep (and death, for that matter) refreshes the life of an individual, then, we must examine the Buddhist concept of the Nine Consciousnesses, a description of the human mind towards which some contemporary psychologists are also working. Once again, we find that the Buddhist view of life is slowly being confirmed by scientific advances made in the West.

The Nine Consciousnesses

Buddhism explains that there are nine levels of consciousness, or discernment, within the human mind; these operate together to influence our lives. The Nine Consciousnesses are the consciousness of sight, hearing, smell, taste and touch; the consciousness of the external, material world (*ke*); the consciousness of the internal, spiritual world (*ku*); the 'storehouse' consciousness; and the fundamental, 'pure' or universal consciousness, which Nichiren Daishonin identifies with *Nam-myoho-renge-kyo* (see Diagram C, p. 154). At different times, different levels of consciousness are stronger or weaker – for example, when we are awake or asleep – but all nine are inseparable and are, therefore, always a part of our lives, whether we are aware of them or not.

The first seven levels we have already encountered, for these relate to the attributes of perception and conception described

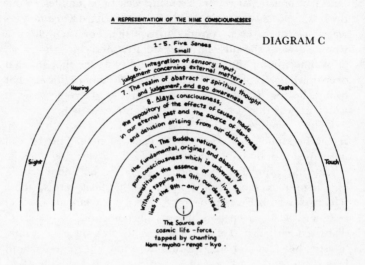

A REPRESENTATION OF THE NINE CONSCIOUSNESSES

DIAGRAM C

1 - 5. Five Senses
Smell

6. Integration of sensory input; judgement concerning external matters.

7. The realm of abstract or spiritual thought and judgement, and ego awareness

8. Alaya consciousness; the repository of the effects of causes made in our eternal past and the source of darkness and delusion arising from our desires.

9. The Buddha nature, the fundamental, original and absolutely pure consciousness which is universal and constitutes the essence of our lives. Without tapping the 9th, our destiny lies in the 8th – and is fixed.

Hearing   Taste   Sight   Touch

The Source of cosmic life – force, tapped by chanting Nam-myoho-renge-kyo.

above in the discussion of the Five Components.* We receive information about the external world through our five senses, and our sixth conciousness integrates that information, thus enabling us to distinguish between various sense-data and to 'construct' physical objects. When we pick up an orange, for example, it is our sixth consciousness which integrates the qualities of colour, shape, size, texture and smell, and enables us to judge that this is an orange we are holding and not, say, an orange-coloured ball. In addition, if an alarm clock rings while we are peeling the orange, it is our sixth consciousness that causes us to realize that the ringing is not coming from the fruit.

There is a part of our mind, however, which does not rely directly upon our senses being stimulated in order to operate. This is the 'thinking mind', our seventh consciousness, which deals with the abstract aspect of life. It is our seventh consciousness which enables us to form ideas, to imagine things, to make

*It is not unusual for Buddhist concepts to overlap, or for particular aspects of Buddhist teachings to be referred to try more than one term, as Buddhism characteristically explains the workings of life from many different, closely interrelated, viewpoints.

value judgements, to differentiate between right and wrong, to philosophize, to paint – in short, to apprehend and express the unseen, or spiritual, side of our life. So while our sixth consciousness enables us to decide, 'This is an orange,' it is our seventh consciousness that enables us to think, 'I like oranges. Oranges contain Vitamin C and therefore are good for humanity.'

It was his subjective awareness of this seventh level of consciousness that the French philosopher, René Descartes (1596–1650), considered to be the fundamental proof of his own existence, as he expressed in his well-known declaration, *cogito ergo sum* – 'I think, therefore, I am.' But whether 'pure' thought is possible without reference to the impressions and stimuli of the external world has been debated ever since Descartes coined his phrase. Certainly, Buddhism would deny the possibility, teaching as it does the inseparability of the Nine Consciousnesses. Without the external world, for example, what would the mind think about since, in the Buddhist view, the purpose of thinking is ultimately to take some sort of action? Indeed, it is even difficult to see how the concept of 'I' could exist, for this needs the idea of the existence of other people to have any meaning.

Be that as it may, when we are awake we operate primarily on the level of these seven consciousnesses. During the day we are bombarded by a myriad impressions of the external world, picked up by the first five of our consciousnesses and constantly filtered by our sixth, thus allowing us to concentrate on one thing at a time while still being aware of what is going on around us. If our consciousness were not able to operate in this way we would be overwhelmed by the sheer volume of sensory information that our physical environment throws at us from moment to moment. In addition to these impressions of the external world, many differing thoughts continually occur to us, from the extremely trivial to – possibly – the extremely profound. In other words, our waking consciousness is highly active, enabling us to interact fully with our individual environment.

When awake we are much more alert than we might think, for all the sensory impressions which our conscious mind filters out during the day, as well as even the most fleeting of our waking thoughts, are never lost but are lodged in the state of *ku*, within what Buddhism identifies as the eighth or 'storehouse' consciousness. This 'storehouse' equates to our memory, but is much deeper and more extensive than we might imagine, for it is at this level of consciousness that are recorded all our individual experiences – thoughts, words and deeds – whether we are conscious of them or not. Our dreams, for instance, often feature unknown or strange people, places, events or things which we are not aware as having made any strong impression on us but which, for some reason, have lodged themselves in our lives. Again, while some memories – of particularly significant moments in our lives, for example – can be recalled at will, other memories can come as a complete surprise. Under hypnosis, for instance, people are capable of remembering details about things that happened many years in the past – such as presents they received as young children – of which they now have no conscious recollection. Similarly, certain trivial sensory stimuli – smells and tastes in particular – can call up powerful memories of events to which we may not have given a single thought since they happened. Marcel Proust's great seven-part novel, *A la Recherche du Temps Perdu (Remembrance of Things Past)*, features one such famous incident:

> And soon, mechanically, dispirited after a dreary day with the prospect of a depressing tomorrow, I raised to my lips a spoonful of the tea in which I had soaked a morsel of the cake. No sooner had the warm liquid mixed with the crumbs touched my palate than a shudder ran through me and I stopped, intent upon the extraordinary thing that was happening to me. An exquisite pleasure had invaded my senses, something isolated, detached, with no suggestion of its origin . . . Whence could it have come to me, this all-powerful joy? I sensed that it was connected with the taste o `the tea and the cake, but that it infinitely transcended those savours, could not, indeed, be of the same nature. Whence did it come? What did it mean? How could I seize and apprehend it?
>
> I drink a second mouthful, in which I find nothing more than in the first, then a third, which gives me rather less than the second. It is time to stop; the potion is losing its magic. It is plain that the truth I am seeking lies not in the cup but in myself . . .
>
> And as soon as I had recognized the taste of the piece of madeleine soaked in her decoction of lime-blossom which my aunt used to give me (although I did not yet know and must long postpone the discovery of why this memory made me so happy) immediately the old grey house upon the street, where her room

was, rose up like a stage set . . . and with the house the town, from morning to night and in all weathers, the Square where I used to be sent before lunch, the streets along which I used to run errands, the country road we took when it was fine. And as in the game wherein the Japanese amuse themselves by filling a porcelain bowl with water and steeping in it little pieces of paper which until then are without character or form, but, the moment they become wet, stretch and twist and take on colour and distinctive shape, become flowers or houses or people, solid and recognizable, so in that moment all the flowers in our garden and in M. Swann's park, and the water-lilies on the Vivonne and the good folk of the village and their little dwellings and the parish church and the whole of Combray and its surroundings, taking shape and solidity, sprang into being, towns and gardens alike, from my cup of tea.

All this, from one fleeting sensation; but it is such small sensations which gradually lead the narrator on a grand meta-physical journey into the past, causing him to speculate on its relationship to the present and the role of the mind in linking the two. Buddhism teaches that nothing which happens in our life, however minor, escapes the eighth consciousness. Therefore, theoretically at least, we have the capacity to remember every-thing we have ever experienced, given the right external stimulus. That we normally cannot remember much of what has happened to us is simply an indication of just how deep the eighth consciousness is, and how difficult it is to plumb.

As *kutai*, the truth of non-substantiality and the condition of the eighth consciousness, does not conform to the standards of time and space, it could be described as limitless. Nichiren Daishonin, describing the essence of life, which also exists in *ku*, says: 'It is not too large to enter the seed of a flower without the seed expanding. It is not too small to fill the universe without the universe contracting.' Thus, in the light of the eternity of life, Buddhism explains that the eighth consciousness stores not only everything we have experienced in this lifetime, but everything the entity of our life has experienced since the infinite past. This has extremely important implications for, although the eighth consciousness lies below the level of our waking mind and we are not consciously aware of it during the day, the influence of this consciousness on our thoughts, words and deeds is, nevertheless, enormous, all the more so because it is usually completely unrecognized. For the moment this may be extremely difficult to understand and accept, but it will be explained more fully in the section on *renge* – cause and effect and karma.

Interestingly, the Swiss psychologist, Carl Jung (1875–1961), who with Sigmund Freud helped pioneer the exploration into the workings of the human psyche, also perceived the existence of this 'memory' inherited from the distant past; he described this in his theory of the collective unconscious. Briefly, Jung believed that, just as people share inherited physical characteristics such as arms and legs, so all people share a common and inborn pool of experience, reaching back to prehistory and even beyond. He based this idea on certain 'archetypal' images and symbols occurring independently in the dreams and fantasies of individuals and in the mythologies of whole societies, at all ages and in all cultures throughout the world. The snake, for example, seems to have a peculiar fascination for humanity, variously representing sexuality, evil, healing, instinct, duplicity, fear, impurity, corruption and the like. That a symbol like this has such a strong hold on the human imagination, and has been used to represent similar or related ideas in different cultures which have had no contact with each other, led Jung to conclude that it must be an expression of an unconscious thought that already exists in people at birth, a 'memory' which could date from the time when snakes presumably posed a real threat to our distant ancestors.

Jung's theory of the collective unconscious highlights the belief that human beings are intimately connected with the past, both their own individual past and, on a much wider scale, that of humanity as a whole. This connection is only possible because, in Buddhist terms, we all possess the 'storehouse' of the eighth consciousness which is forever recording deep within our lives the experiences registered by our first seven consciousnesses.

When we are awake, the eighth consciousness lies buried beneath the activity of the first seven levels, though it is continually taking in information and also releasing it, either as clear memories or as vague feelings, hunches, likes, dislikes, and so on. When we sleep, however, the first seven levels of our consciousness become dormant and the eighth takes over completely. The senses become dulled (though not shut down entirely, since loud noise or sudden movement can wake us), our thoughts begin to wander and, eventually, we become oblivious to the external world, losing all sense of time and space. Scientists have discovered that there are five distinct stages of sleep which recur in cycles thoughout the night and which can be judged by measuring the brain waves, eye movements and muscle tension in the sleeping person. The first four stages mark a gradual descent into deep or 'delta' sleep and are known as the 'sleep staircase'. The fifth phase is more paradoxical as it displays the almost total absence of muscle tension characteristic of 'delta sleep', the brain-wave pattern of the transitional phase between waking and sleeping and, most extraordinary of all, eye movements are even more rapid than those experienced when awake. This stage is therefore called Rapid Eye Movement or REM sleep.

Before we have been asleep for long we start to dream. At first, when it was noticed that people who were woken during REM sleep had often been in the middle of a dream, scientists thought that dreams occurred only during this phase. Later, researchers realized that we can dream at any stage of sleep, even as we are falling asleep or waking up. Buddhism explains dreaming as the various thoughts, words and deeds stored in *ku* in the eighth consciousness becoming 'liberated' as the conscious mind relaxes its grip for a few hours. When we awake again, the first seven consciousnesses reassert their control, so much so that often we completely 'forget' what we have dreamed about: that is, our conscious mind overwhelms the signals from our eighth consciousness, as it were, and we may even be deluded into thinking that we have not dreamt at all. According to sleep research, though, everybody dreams, several times every night.

We do not appear to dream continuously when we are asleep, however, and what happens to our consciousness when we are not dreaming, particularly when we are at the deepest phase of 'delta sleep', has yet to be clarified. Professor Borbély notes that a person awakened from a REM sleep 'is immediately orientated and aware of his surroundings, whereas one awakened from deep sleep experiences a period of extreme drowsiness, disorientation, and limited memory function.' Proust also recognizes this condition:

> But for me it was enough if, in my own bed, my sleep was so heavy as completely to relax my consciousness; for then I lost all sense of

the place in which I had gone to sleep, and when I awoke in the middle of the night, not knowing where I was, I could not even be sure at first who I was; I had only the most rudimentary sense of existence, such as may lurk and flicker in the depths of an animal's consciousness; I was more destitute than the cave-dweller; but then the memory – not yet of the place in which I was, but of various other places where I had lived and might now very possibly be – would come like a rope let down from heaven to draw me up out of the abyss of not-being, from which I could never have escaped by myself: in a flash I would traverse centuries of civilization, and out of a blurred glimpse of oil-lamps, then of shirts with turned-down collars, would gradually piece together the original components of my ego.

The state of complete mental 'not-being' described so graphically by Proust (and with characteristic scientific restraint by Professor Borbély) is highly significant, for it could point to a level of consciousness in 'delta sleep' which is even deeper than that experienced when dreaming. If so, this suggests evidence for what Buddhism calls the ninth, or fundamental, pure consciousness. This can be described as 'the very core of our life', or the pure, undefiled and inexhaustible life-force of the universe. In Buddhism it is equated variously with *myoho*, *chu*, the Middle Way, the true entity of life, Buddhahood, and *Nam-myoho-renge-kyo*. In other words, the ninth consciousness is the source of energy for all our mental and spiritual activity, and is the power behind the 'mechanical' energy which causes our physical selves – our bodies – to function; in short, it is what sustains us throughout eternity. When we sleep, then, there may be periods when we are able to directly 'tap into' this consciousness, the pure life-force of the universe inherent within us and of which we are a part. This would certainly account for how sleep restores our energy, since the life-force seems to come out of nowhere and miraculously revive our spiritual and physical organism.

Could it be that we are somehow 'recharged by the universe' when we are asleep? The idea may not be as fanciful as it sounds for, in quoting the following passage from the *Chuang-tzu*, a Chinese Taoist text of the third century BC, even Professor Borbély may have an inkling along these lines: 'Everything is one; during sleep the soul, undistracted, is absorbed into this unity; when awake distracted, it sees the different beings.' Again, it is tempting to speculate that it is the sudden movement from what the *Chuang-tzu* calls 'unity' to what it terms 'distraction', that accounts for the disorientation of someone roused from deep sleep, as described above.

Whatever the answer, sleep, like death, is a fundamental and mysterious aspect of all life. We go to bed tired and awake refreshed. Buddhism teaches that we die when we are worn-out and our life entity is then reborn anew. Both sleep and death thus express the continual rhythm and energy of *myoho*, the Mystic Law. The lesson here is clear, for when we are truly able to regard death as we regard sleep, as a period of rest and recuperation in our eternal lives, it will certainly hold no terror for us. Indeed, we can even look forward to it as we look forward to a good night's sleep after a hard day's work, confident that our lives will make a fresh and vigorous start next time around.

The Experience of Death

Of course, this is fine as theory, but to develop this sort of confidence in the face of our mortality, and that of those we love, is the most difficult thing imaginable, even for those who practise Nichiren Shoshu Buddhism. Inevitably, perhaps, it can arise only through an experience of death, but when one chants *Nam-myoho-renge-kyo* even death reveals its positive aspect. This idea may seem contradictory, even bizarre, but it is one which Karen Collingwood came to understand as a reality not long after she had started to chant, towards the end of 1983, when she was just eighteen. 'I was introduced to the practice by my mother,' she explains, 'who at the time was very ill with cancer. She had found that the practice gave her a great deal of help and support and had always encouraged me to chant, which I did occasionally, staring into the incense burner or out of the window, and only for about ten minutes – and I wondered why it didn't work!'

Eventually, Karen's mother became very ill and was taken into hospital. Nobody expected her to come out again, but she did, much to everyone's surprise. 'It was only then,' says Karen, 'when I suddenly realized how bad the situation was, that I began to chant with any conviction. I chanted with all my determination for my mother's recovery, and began to really attempt to learn *gongyo*, the morning and evening recitation of parts of the Lotus Sutra. This situation continued for one week.

For the first time in my life I actually wanted to stay at home with my family and give them all the help I could.'

Exactly a week after coming out of hospital, however, Karen's mother died, quite peacefully, with Karen and her father present, and a friend, an NSUK member, chanting quietly in the room. Karen's reaction to her mother's death is quite understandable: 'It seemed to me that the practice had failed. All around us people had been chanting for hours and with absolute determination for my mother to recover, but most of all, for the first time, even I myself had chanted with everything I had – and it seemed that we had failed.' A couple of days later, though, Karen's view began to change. 'Gradually,' she says, 'I began to see the benefits we had received. It was only the day after my mother's death that I was told exactly how serious her condition had been. She'd had five tumours in her spine, two of which were the size of cricket balls, and obviously she should have been in immense pain, but in fact only twelve hours before her death she had been laughing and singing with an old schoolfriend, in no pain at all! Also it was obvious that her body was weakening at an alarming rate, but her life-force at the same time was growing stronger and stronger. Maybe there was something in this Buddhism after all, I thought.'

With the encouragement of the members of her district in north London, Karen eventually began chanting again. 'I managed evening *gongyo* easily, but doing it in the morning was more difficult. It took two or three months before I could bound out of bed at 6.30 a.m., early enough to do *gongyo*, chant for half an hour as I wanted, and still be the first person ready to leave the house. My father began to wonder if this was the same person he'd had to drag out of bed at eight o'clock every morning! In fact, this was where I got my first real proof of the practice. Since I was about thirteen my father and I had only really just tolerated each other, and in the last couple of years, since my mother became ill, we'd really begun to argue. Suddenly I could see that it was my own stubborn nature, and the fact that I always thought I was in the right, which had caused these problems. I had to chant very hard to overcome this and now I enjoy a much warmer relationship with my father.'

More than this, Karen's practice has enabled her to view her mother's death, and consequently her own life, from a much wider perspective: 'I have only recently begun to understand that life is eternal and that my mother fulfilled her mission in that one lifetime. I am now looking forward, full of hope, to a lifetime working for world peace through this Buddhism. I find now that I want to do my best to give other young people some of the joy and hope for the future which I feel, and which I see as one of the greatest benefits I have received from this practice.'

'Mission' is a word which is sometimes misunderstood in relation to the practice of this Buddhism. As each person's environment – taken in the widest sense to mean friends, family, colleagues and so on – is unique to them, Buddhism equates 'mission' with the unique purpose of an individual's life, a purpose which that individual can choose through the workings of their Buddha nature and that individual alone can then fulfil. Thus, 'mission' does not necessarily mean some great and conspicuous task in society (although some people do have missions like this), nor a Messianic urge to convert the whole world to Buddhism, but rather relates to the most valuable and creative role *each person* can choose to play in the vast tapestry of cosmic life, regardless of what they believe or practise. Karen's realization that her mother had 'fulfilled her mission' was doubtless based on her subjective feeling that, as a result of her mother's practice and behaviour during her illness, Karen had come to appreciate something of the greatness of Buddhism and so began to decide upon *her* mission – to devote her life to the happiness of others.

It might be objected that the attitude to death expressed by Karen is simply one of making the best of a bad situation, and conveniently rationalizing or explaining away the failure of the practice to effect the cure for which she was chanting. This is to look at life and death too narrowly, though, for, as Buddhism regards life and death as merely two different phases experienced by the same entity of life, your death can be just as much a part of your mission as your actions in life. If death comes when you intuitively feel you have completed all you can in this lifetime, and if through your death you are able to create great value, then death itself is neither victory nor defeat but simply another phase of the eternity of life. Dr Shuhei Morita, a member of the science division of Soka Gakkai, the Nichiren Shoshu lay society in Japan, is in a better position than most to understand this point.

In the course of his work as a specialist in internal medicine he has witnessed countless experiences of Soka Gakkai members who have overcome 'incurable' illnesses such as cancer; at the same time, he has also seen cases of members who have died from such illnesses. As he explains, death itself is not the real issue, for what matters more is *how* one dies:

> All that lives must someday perish – this is a great principle of the universe. Human beings, too, have their limited life-span, and someday everyone has to die. The *Juryo* chapter of the Lotus Sutra speaks of 'bestowing longer life', and, as a benefit of faith and practice, one can indeed extend his life-span. But even so, death comes eventually.
>
> I have acutely sensed the greatness of the Daishonin's Buddhism in seeing these Gakkai members meet death from cancer. To begin with, almost none of them experience the hellish agony that characterizes cancer in its final stages, and their appearance at the moment of death is inspiring. I am always overwhelmed with awe to see them at that final moment, softly chanting *Nam-myoho-renge-kyo* and breathing gently, as though in sleep. Eyes and mouth partly open, faces bright, they radiate a sense of great peace, as though experiencing profound satisfaction at a life without regrets. Death is life's final summation, and one cannot help but feel that so splendid an attitude in facing death must testify that that person's life was also splendid. A peaceful death no doubt also indicates a fortunate life to come. Surely we can say that such a death demonstrates proof of that individual's enlightenment and change of destiny by virtue of the Mystic Law.

Only if, at the moment of death, you feel your life to have been wasted can death be regarded as a defeat, or a cause for regret. As Daisaku Ikeda explains, this is why a life spent producing value, as opposed to causing harm or even simply consuming pleasure, is ultimately one which creates the greatest happiness in the depths of an individual's life:

> Buddhism places strong emphasis on the last moment of life, for in the Buddhist view it contains the total of one's lifetime, and is also the first step towards the future. All phenomena manifest the true entity; all the acts done during one's lifetime, both good and bad, decide the way one dies. It is almost frightening, for nothing can be hidden. The way one dies, whether peacefully or horribly, is a perfect reflection of the life he has led and a spotless mirror of the future.

   This may sound very strict, even draconian in its severity of judgement. After all, everyone knows that some people die deaths which seem to bear no relationship to what they have done in life. The good may die poor, in misery or great suffering, while the rich and corrupt can sometimes die peacefully in luxury. How then can such deaths be 'a perfect reflection' of the lives these people have led? This is an extremely important question, one that goes to the very heart of the Buddhist view of life and death. To understand the reasons for this apparent inconsistency, and to further deepen our understanding of *myoho* and the eternity of life, we must now turn our attention to one of the most important aspects of Buddhist doctrine – *renge*, the law of the simultaneity of cause and effect.

RENGE

Renge means 'lotus flower'. As you may rightly conclude from the fact that the Lotus Sutra is named after this flower, the lotus is highly significant in Buddhism. There are two main reasons for this. Firstly, as we have already seen in the explanation of the concept of *soku*, the beautiful and undefiled lotus blooms in a muddy swamp and, thereby, symbolizes the emergence of our Buddha nature from the everyday problems and desires of our ordinary lives (see pp. 93–4). Secondly, because the lotus puts forth its flower and seedpod at the same time, *renge* stands for the simultaneity of cause and effect. The importance of this concept cannot be underestimated, for it is one of the central tenets of Nichiren Shoshu Buddhism.

   Cause and effect is a principle which we probably all take for granted in our lives. For example, as we grow up, we learn that different causes produce different, corresponding effects, and so try to act accordingly. Only by making the right cause will we get the effect we want. Of course, the relationship between cause and effect is often not simple or direct, especially with regard to human behaviour, but, whatever we do in life, an expectation of cause leading to effect underlies our actions. Likewise, even if we are not always consciously aware of it, we assume that every effect has been produced by a cause and, as often as not, work back from effect to cause before repeating the cause in the expectation of producing a similar effect.

This relationship of cause and effect is the basis of the scientific method that now lies at the heart of our society and is so obvious that we probably do not give it very much thought. In the past, before the rationality of science became the dominant way of looking at things, effects whose causes we did not know or understand were held to be either magic, the work of God or the inscrutable machinations of chance and impersonal destiny. Natural disasters were punishment from on high; inexplicable illness could be looked upon as the result of a spell or curse, and good or bad fortune was thought to lie in the hands of some omnipotent being.

In more recent times, of course, science has systematically demonstrated that many phenomena once thought to be either evidence of a superior, guiding intelligence, or just simply random, are now explainable as particular effects of particular causes. Thunder, for example, was once thought to be an expression of the anger of the gods; science showed it to be an effect caused by the discharge of electricity in the atmosphere. Indeed, all scientific research is based on the premise that, in the physical world at least, the fact that at any particular time a certain phenomenon has not been explained does not mean that it is, in fact, inexplicable. In other words, implicit in science is the idea that the universe is not chaotic, but ordered, and that it follows certain perceivable laws, one of the most basic of which is the law of causality. Thus, research continues into the cause of diseases such as cancer, AIDS, multiple sclerosis and the like; into the causes of mental disease, of social ills, of earthquakes, floods, droughts, typhoons and other natural phenomena; in short, scientists are exploring the operation of cause and effect in every aspect of life that can be studied, even the origins of the universe and life itself.

Though this belief in science and scientific method dominates our present society, most people are inconsistent in their attitude towards cause and effect: that is, they accept it only as far as they can (or care to) see it operating. If something happens whose cause is not obvious, or cannot be discovered even after lengthy investigation, causality is still often replaced by the idea of chance, coincidence, magic or God. For example, there seems to be no apparent cause for people to suffer from freak accidents: if someone is struck by lightning, most people would consider that person either simply unlucky or possibly, for some reason, singled out by God for that particular fate. Interestingly, the inability to discern cause and effect in all phenomena has led a number of philosophers to deduce that God must exist, if only to provide the 'First Cause' which set the whole of life into motion. As Russell notes:

> The God of the Old Testament is a God of power, the God of the New Testament is also a God of love; but the God of the theologians, from Aristotle to Calvin, is one whose appeal is intellectual: His existence solves certain puzzles which otherwise would create argumentative difficulties in the understanding of the universe.

Indeed, even some scientists still believe in God for this reason.

Many people seem to be at a transitional phase, believing in cause and effect when it can be proved beyond all doubt, and disregarding it when it cannot. Alternatively, causality is often ignored simply because it is inconvenient; in other words, when it does not fit in with any ideas we already hold strongly. For instance, if we have an unhappy relationship, we usually find it extremely hard to accept that we have made any of the causes for this suffering. On a wider scale, belief that the AIDS virus is a sign of God's wrath at homosexual wickedness will doubtless continue in some quarters until a cure is found, just as venereal disease was often thought to be divine punishment for hetereosexual immorality; that is, until it was discovered that this retribution could be sidestepped in many cases by the application of a little penicillin. On the other hand, the continuing and widespread belief in astrology is evidence of a vague feeling in many people that life is not random. Even those who read their horoscopes in the paper every day – merely, they may assure you, as a bit of harmless fun – are nonetheless expressing, if only faintly, a desire to believe that certain aspects of their personality and unexplained events in their life fit into a wider pattern of cause and effect, a pattern that can be read in the stars.

It is illogical, however, to assert that cause and effect can exist at one moment and not at the next, or in some cases but not in others. Buddhism teaches that *everything* in the universe embodies the law of cause and effect. It therefore not only denies the existence of a supreme being but also the existence of chance.

Rather, what we perceive as a chance even – the apparently random behaviour of certain sub-atomic particles, for example – is simply an effect whose cause or causes we cannot yet see or, possibly, understand. In other words, Buddhism states that there can be no effect without a cause and, similarly, that every cause must have an effect, no matter how long it may take for that effect to appear. Buddhism also asserts that there was no 'First Cause' to the universe as a whole, just as there will be no final end. The universe, permeated with life's inherent quality of renewal, has always existed; the idea that it needs a 'First Cause' simply stems from our inability to conceive of time without beginning or end.

Even so, there are certains aspects of life which do seem to operate outside the pattern of cause and effect. Why should two people exposed to exactly the same influences in life turn out so completely differently, for example? Why do 'some boys have all the luck', while others, equally able perhaps, have no luck at all? Why do some people die sudden, tragic and inexplicable deaths, just when everything in life seems to be going for them, while others, possibly less deserving, survive through the most appalling chain of accidents? Why, indeed, are some people born rich and others poor; some healthy, others crippled; some gifted, others apparently talentless? Why, in short, is there so much diversity in the fate of human beings, even from birth? What 'causes' could lead to 'effects' like these? Indeed, does not the very injustice of life argue powerfully for the existence of chance, randomness or even chaos?

The Buddhist View of Causality

Instances like these would indeed be a powerful argument for the existence of chance, except that the Buddhist concept of causality goes deeper than the cause and effect we observe in the external world of time and space. This concept involves penetrating the depths of our lives to the *inherent cause* and *latent effects* which we all experience subjectively and which are constantly interacting with the external world.

For example, generally speaking, people understand that, in the external world, cause comes first and the effect follows later. Sometimes, the two can be very close; we know that in flicking a light switch, say, we can produce almost instant illumination; but we also know that, even though the electric current may travel so fast that it appears to reach the light bulb instantly, its speed is actually finite. Consequently, there must be a minute fraction of a second between the cause – flicking the switch – and the effect – seeing the light.

At the other end of the time-scale, cause and effect can be separated by years, even aeons. Thus, in planting an acorn we are making the cause for an effect to occur at some time in the future; this complete effect, a mature, fully grown oak tree, we may not even live to witness. On a longer time-scale still, the appearance of human life on this planet came about as a result of causes that stretch back certainly as far as the beginning of our solar system, if not further, into the eternal past. Nevertheless, no matter how long or short the delay between a cause and its manifest effect, it is held that the latter always follows the former. In this sense, then, cause and effect is usually regarded as 'linear', in that one thing leads to another in an unbroken line of cause and effect relationships through time.

While this is undoubtedly true of the cause and effect we can perceive in the external world, Buddhism teaches that, at a deeper level, cause and effect are *simultaneous* for, just as this present moment is the result of all the causes made since the infinite past, so it contains everything that will create the future. As Nichiren Daishonin says, 'There can be no discontinuity between past, present and future.' In other words, Buddhism distinguishes between two different but intimately related types of cause and effect: *external cause* and *manifest effect*, and *inherent cause* and *latent effect*.

To explain this in simple terms, external cause and manifest effect can be perceived in the external world, while inherent cause and latent effect exist within our eighth consciousness as an unseen tendency. They are related in that *external cause* is whatever stimulus in our environment prompts this unseen tendency to surface in our life, while *manifest effect* is the effect that the appearance of this tendency then has on us and our environment. In other words, Buddhism explains that, in common with all phenomena, cause and effect is subject to the rhythm of life and death ('Now you see me, now you don't'), just as life and death is subject to the law of cause and effect.

In short, this means that an external cause does not lead directly to a manifest effect; this, in turn, explains why the effect of an external cause is not always immediately obvious and why the same external cause can lead to very different manifest effects, depending on the different factors or people involved. This is a very important point to grasp, as Satoru Izumi, a vice-president of the Soka Gakkai, explains:

> A problem, no matter what kind, is an effect produced by the combination of an inherent and external cause. Here is a glass of water. Let's suppose that there is some sediment at the bottom. If you stir the contents, the water will become dirty. In this case, the sediment is the inherent cause and the act of stirring is the external cause. Suppose we have a man and wife who lead a cat-and dog-existence. Each insists the other is to blame. That's like saying, 'Because you stirred the water, it became dirty.' But no matter how hard you stir, if there is no sediment the water will remain clear. People often fail to notice the sediment [in their own lives] and simply accuse others of stirring up the water. In other words, they are not aware that the cause of their unhappiness lies within themselves and that they are merely experiencing the effect of that cause after it has been activated by someone else.

Although this is one of the most crucial points to understand in the practice of Nichiren Shoshu Buddhism – indeed, in life as a whole – it is one of the most difficult for many people to accept. If it were not true, however, it would be very difficult to explain why people react so differently to exactly the same cause. The announcement that a train has been delayed, for example, can produce anger in one person, tears in another, and weary resignation in a third. Even so, it is usually very hard to accept that we suffer in direct proportion to our own inherent tendency to do so. But until we learn to accept that we become angry or upset not because of any external cause, such as our relationships with other people or our circumstances, but ultimately because of something that already exists within our own lives – the inherent cause – we can never begin to change that innate tendency and so become fundamentally happy.

We can begin to understand this when we realize that the simultaneity of cause and effect teaches that, at the very moment we take action as a result of a combination of an *external cause* and our own *inherent cause*, the *latent effect* of that action is simul-taneously lodged in our life and will appear as a *manifest effect* when it meets the right *external cause* at some point in the future. For example, let us suppose Tom says something to Dick which makes him angry. Tom's comment is the external cause, Dick's innate tendency to flare up is the inherent cause, and the manifest effect of the combination of these two causes is that Dick displays all the signs of anger: he flushes, his pulse quickens, his facial muscles tighten, and so on. If Dick then punches Tom, the latent effect of that action is immediately fixed in Dick's life in strict accordance with the effect of his punch on Tom's life. Even if he knocks Tom out and escapes immediate retribution, or if he feels that Tom deserved to be hit, the latent effect of his behaviour is actually inescapable, and *must* appear at some time in the future when it meets the appropriate external cause, be that time only moments later, after many years, or even many lifetimes.

It follows from this that the particular manifest effects we experience in our lives are all, without exception, fundamentally the result of those innate tendencies, or inherent causes, which are stored in our eighth consciousness. Daisaku Ikeda explains this point succinctly when he says:

> Human life never exists in isolation from an environment. Every activity of life occurs as the result of some external stimulus. At the same time, the true cause is the inherent cause within the human being. To give a very simple example, if someone hits you and you hit him back, the first blow is the stimulus leading to the second, but it is not the ultimate cause. You can maintain that you hit the person because he hit you, but in fact you hit him because you are you. The real cause was inside you, ready to be activated by the external cause.

Taking the logic of this statement a step further, 'every activity in life occurs as the result of some external stimulus'; if someone hits you, you are the external stimulus for that action, whether you feel it to be justified or not. This is because, deep in your life, there is a tendency – an inherent cause – which draws such behaviour towards you like a magnet. This tendency might be, for example, fear, which draws out from another person an instinctive desire to bully you. In other words, just as you hit back 'because you are you', so you are hit in the first place 'because you are you'.

This statement might seem outrageous, for it would appear to justify every act of suffering, violence or intimidation on the grounds that the victim is somehow to blame rather than the perpetrator. This reaction is understandable, of course, but it ignores the fact that the perpetrator is also subject to the law of cause and effect and so, at some time, must reap the inescapable consequences of *his* actions. In this context, it is also important to understand that Buddhism elucidates the law of cause and effect to explain *why* things happen as they do, not to justify them.

Furthermore, 'blame' is a word with strong moral overtones, while the law of cause and effect is no more moral than the law of gravity. In other words, cause and effect operates according to its own strict and inescapable pattern, regardless of what we may perceive as right or wrong. For example, Buddhism teaches that one inherent cause of suffering is our innate ignorance or stupidity. If you put your hand in the fire, for instance, you will get burnt: cause and effect. There is no point in blaming the fire for being hot or complaining that you do not deserve to suffer in this way because you are basically a good person. You suffered because inherently, in certain circumstances, you lack the good sense to see that suffering will inevitably follow the course of action you decide to take.

This example may appear trite, but we have only to consider how many times we, ourselves, have repeated mistakes which have caused us to suffer – in relationships, perhaps – to see that cause and effect follows its own logic; this may or may not coincide with our own sense of justice. For example, let us say that you have had a row with your boss, a bad-tempered and unlikeable man, over what you consider to be unfair criticism of your work. Naturally, in the drama that you re-enact that evening for your friends and family, you cast yourself as the hero and your boss as the evil villain, secure in the knowledge that 'justice' is on your side. After all, doesn't everyone agree that his criticism was wounding and unjust and that you had every right to answer him back?

You need only discover that he has a wife who is dying of an incurable illness and that he himself has developed a duodenal ulcer worrying about her, to realize that the right and wrong of the situation is less clear-cut than you thought – his mean temper could be the result of great suffering. You may then determine to be more patient and good-tempered yourself. If you never discover why he is so nasty you will forever put yourself in the right and him in the wrong – but still end up out of a job. Once again, it is only if we recognize the *existence* of an *inherent cause* for any situation, that a strong desire can develop within us to change it so that we can start to make the right *external causes* for the effects we want to see. On the other hand, if we keep getting the effects we do not want we must finally wake up to the fact that some tendency deep within us must be causing us to make the wrong external causes, no matter how we may justify our actions to ourself and others.

Although the law of cause and effect transcends any particular moral code, it is important to understand that Buddhism does teach that someone who 'slanders' or degrades life in any way by creating suffering for others, makes the external cause to experience the inevitable effect of that suffering himself at some time in the future. In other words, as in the example of Tom and Dick above, if we make the external cause for another person to suffer we simultaneously lodge the latent effect of that suffering in *our own* lives. As Nichiren Daishonin explains:

> One who climbs a high mountain must eventually descend. One who slights another will in turn be despised. One who deprecates those of handsome appearance will be born ugly. One who robs another of food and clothing is sure to fall into the world of Hunger. One who mocks noble men or anyone who observes the precepts* will be born to a poor family. One who slanders a family that embraces the True Law† will be born to a heretical family.‡ One who laughs at those who cherish the precepts will be born a commoner and meet with persecution from his sovereign. This is the general law of cause and effect.

Nichiren Daishonin is here describing the negative side of causality. Once people understand the strictness of cause and effect, however, they also realize that they can use this law to change fundamentally the basic tendency, or unhappy karma, in their lives, and so stop creating suffering for themselves and others by making the right causes to experience happiness now and in the future.

*Various rules of moral conduct taught in early Buddhist sutras. In Nichiren Daishonin's Buddhism, there is only one precept – to embrace the Gohonzon, with all that this implies.
†In Shakyamuni's Buddhism, the Lotus Sutra; in Nichiren Daishonin's Buddhism *Nam-myoho-renge-kyo*.
‡One which practises a 'provisional' or lesser teaching than is contained in the Lotus Sutra.

One step towards this understanding is to recognize clearly the difference between external and inherent cause, and manifest and latent effect, since this concept of causality can be applied to all events – from the simple and mundane to the complicated and significant, and from the intensely personal to the highly public. In attempting to analyze and understand historical events, for example, the concept of inherent cause and latent effect explains why particular effects can take so many years to become manifest: they are simply 'waiting', as it were, for the appropriate external cause. Indeed, in differentiating between the 'occasion' and the 'cause' of particular events, an historian would say, for example, that the assassination of Archduke Ferdinand did not 'cause' the First World War; rather, it was the 'occasion' (external cause) for the war to start, the real 'cause' (inherent cause) being the mutual suspicion, jealousy and antagonism of the Great Powers, built up over many years of conflict in Europe.

Applying the Buddhist view of causality to a contemporary event, very few people would have believed that the United Kingdom and Argentina would have gone to war over the Falkland Islands/Malvinas, but given the right external cause – the 'occasion' of a nationalistic government in trouble at home – the inherent cause of the conflict, the animosity generated by a centuries old dispute over sovereignty of the islands, was activated, and so war was the inevitable result (or manifest effect).

In this context, it is important to note that, although the United Kingdom ostensibly 'won' the war, in that it regained possession of the islands, the latent effect of the victory must be simply to sow the seeds of another conflict at some future date, just as this latest war was, in part, the latent effect of a conflict that occurred in 1833. In other words, according to the inescapable law of cause and effect, since the causes made in the settlement of this latest conflict once again arose from the worlds of Anger and Animality, so the latent effects of those angry and animalistic causes already exist and will become manifest again 'when the time is right' at some point in the future. In short, unless the inherent cause of the Falklands/Malvinas problem is solved – the Anger and Animality that led to the dispute over sovereignty – another war is inevitable, even though it may not occur for another 150 years or even more.

This may seem unduly pessimistic but, as we shall see later, the inescapable nature of cause and effect does not mean that we cannot change and alleviate the latent effects of past actions before they became manifest. For example, the peace that the Allies concluded with Germany in 1945 was very different from the one imposed in 1919 and has so far proved extremely durable; this shows that war need not necessarily lead to more war provided that the inherent causes of any conflict – usually anger, animality and greed – are addressed and remedied with magnanimity. In other words, if we use our innate wisdom to make the right causes for peace in the future, peace will be achieved, no matter how many bad causes have been made in the wars which preceded it.

To see how the strict law of causality can be turned to our advantage on this sort of scale, however, we must first understand the reality of cause and effect as it operates in our own lives. For Marc Bergman, a young man living in the East End of London, historically a deprived and often violent part of the capital, this understanding came only through experiencing the most dramatic and violent of situations. As he explains, 'Before I started chanting *Nam-myoho-renge-kyo* my life was very painful. In fact, it was absolute hell. I had an incredible amount of destructive anger inside me, causing rages and depressions that knew no bounds. Throughout my childhood I was teased and repeatedly beaten up. A lot of the time I was very lonely, bottling up everything inside me, only to blow up in violent fits of temper. No matter how hard I tried to break free from this unfortunate state I couldn't. I did not know then about karma, or cause and effect, so I just went on making bad causes, turning my life into what was literally a vicious circle. From the age of ten I couldn't even bring myself to call my parents Mum and Dad. I couldn't open my life to anyone at all. For the next five years or so I watched my sister, Ziggie, go through a lot of pain, especially in her relationship with my dad, who also had a lot of anger inside him, and as I grew older I mirrored this pattern almost exactly. I became rapidly more and more unhappy, insecure and fearful, with an increasing potential for violence and anger. Life never got any better, and I got steadily worse.'

Then, in 1979, Marc's family moved to the United States, to Miami in Florida. 'I thought this would be a fresh start,' he says, 'not knowing then that you carry your karma around as if it was in your suitcase. Shortly after we moved to Miami my sister went to live in New York city, and she continued to go through hell there, just as I did in Florida. And still things got worse. I got fed up with Miami and moved back to London when I was sixteen. Another fresh start? No chance. The state of Anger in me was so strong that if I went into a pub, within a few minutes someone would start to fight with me; if I got onto a train, someone opposite me would start "staring at me", and nobody would sit next to me – even in the rush hour! Every situation I found myself in had Anger at its core, and my head was like a rollercoaster always destined to jump the tracks.'

Just before Marc moved back to London, however, his sister told him about *Nam-myoho-renge-kyo*, which she had discovered in New York. Marc chanted occasionally, though usually for what he believes were 'entirely the wrong reasons'. Even so, this was to signal the beginning of a major turning-point in his life. Marc explains: 'I didn't realize that chanting even once in a while was bringing me towards the happy life I'd never known. And quite suddenly, while visiting Ziggie in New York in December 1983, I decided to practise properly and so received the Gohonzon. I did this mainly because I trusted Ziggie like I trusted no one else. Also, I could see that if I didn't change all the rubbish in my life very quickly I probably wouldn't have my life for very much longer.' For about the first five months Marc could not see any obvious benefit from practising but, as he says, 'although I was oblivious to it, an enormous inner change was taking place.'

Then, in June 1984, Marc was attacked while making a call from a public phonebox in the early hours of the morning, two blocks away from his flat in Plaistow, East London. A knife was drawn on him, acid was squirted in his eyes and he was left at 3.30 a.m. on the floor of the phonebox, unable to see a thing. 'Somehow I staggered home and and washed my eyes. I have never felt a pain so severe. After being thrown out of one hospital by an angry doctor I ended up in Moorfields Eye Hospital. At first, I was told that my eyes would be fine but, two days later, after some panic, I was admitted as an in-patient.

'The cornea in my right eye had been completely burned off. I couldn't see out of that eye, and every time I moved it I had an intense pain because my attacker had also jabbed it with the nozzle of the acid spray, damaging the muscles. After two weeks in hospital, during which time drops were put into my eye every hour, I was discharged, taking with me five different sorts of eye-drops to put in myself. I'd been told that the left eye, which had missed the brunt of the attack, would soon recover, but the right eye – well, I might go blind in that one, or even lose it altogether. This was very frightening, to say the least.' He went to stay with his parents in Miami for a couple of months to discover that, by this time, they had also received the Gohonzon, 'so I was able to chant a lot to change my life completely, and to change the problem with my eye by trying to understand why it had happened to me,' he says.

When he returned to London Marc went back to the eye hospital, where a very surprised doctor told him that the vision in his right eye had improved to between 85–90 per cent normal and that, whatever it was he was doing, he should continue. 'So I went on chanting,' says Marc, 'and now my right eye has 20/20 vision and hardly any inflammation. All I have to do now is exercise the eyelid to get the muscles working properly.' He still, however, had to deal with the root cause for everything that had happened, his overpowering state of Anger, which by now was accompanied by so much fear that he started to carry a weapon around with him. 'I continued to attract violent situations like a magnet. This showed me that the Buddhist concept of *esho funi*, the inseparability of life and its environment, is a living reality. Then I realized I had to chant to reveal my Buddha nature and so fundamentally change my karma.'

Shortly after making this determination, Marc boarded a tube train in East London. 'After a few seconds I realized that, apart from a couple of people at the far end of the carriage, I was alone with a group of about a dozen youths. They were tearing up seats, writing graffiti and generally causing havoc. One of them started giving me dirty looks and then yelling abuse at me. That sparked off his friends. I didn't return his ugly expression and obviously didn't smile. They started vying with another, saying things like, "Who's gonna stab him?" and "Who's gonna take his money, then?" I ran through various courses of action in my head. I'd actually studied karate for quite a while but I didn't want to slander their lives, or my own, by being violent. The only thing to do was chant, not aloud, but inside. Incredibly, I could really feel

Nam-myoho-renge-kyo penetrating the environment. It wasn't a case of chanting with the attitude that "If this doesn't work now, perhaps it will next week," because it had to work right there and then or I'd have been badly wounded, maybe even killed. Sure enough, within less than a minute, the youths completely changed their tone. "Oh, forget it," they said, and walked into the next carriage, probably to continue their vandalism in there.

'I found myself in situations like this nearly ten more times and I always chanted to myself. Every time a violent situation occurred, I really had to chant with my whole life to change my karma, which was obviously so deeply rooted that I needed to go through these challenges to change it. But at some point, I broke through. I can't say exactly when it was, but I know I have because, for the first time ever, I suddenly feel free to live. The only violent situations I've been in since that time have been those where I've been able to stop other people getting hurt.' Thanks to his experience, the following quotation from Hiroshi Hojo, fourth president of the Soka Gakkai, has come to mean a lot to Marc because, he says, 'it expresses exactly how I feel':

> When your very life is at stake, you struggle with every single ounce of your energy. But the battle against your own karma is even harder than that. Life and faith [in the Gohonzon] are just the same. To think that you can get through 'some way or other' just because you believe in true Buddhism is not real faith at all. When you try so hard that the sweat runs off you in streams and you squeeze out wisdom that you didn't even think you had, then you can make the impossible possible. And that's the time when the Gohonzon will protect you in every way, shape or form.

Marc knows without a shadow of a doubt what the practice of this Buddhism has meant to his life. He says, 'I feel immense gratitude at being able to chant, and have had so many benefits since changing the violent aspect of my karma, not least of which is being able to get on so much better with my parents. It seems amazing to me that I have had, and still have, so many difficulties, and yet feel so incredibly happy. But without these problems I would never be able to fulfil my desire to change the karma of East London. If it wasn't chanting *Nam-myoho-renge-kyo* I'm sure I'd probably be dead by now. I'll never give up this practice because I feel that, through it, it's possible to change absolutely anything.'

There are certain aspects of Marc Bergman's experience which some people might find a little hard to swallow, especially the acceptance that it was something in *him* which attracted all the violence he suffered from others in his environment. It is important to note, however, that his acceptance of responsibility was only the starting-point for change, and not a fatalistic resignation that this pattern of behaviour was one to which he would forever be destined. Instead, Marc resolved to root out the inherent cause in *his* life which prompted all this violence to appear.

It is in this light that his confrontation with the youths on the tube train should be seen. It was not by magic that they decided at the crucial moment to leave him alone for, by chanting when he was threatened, if only in his head, Marc was able to manifest the state of Buddhahood and so draw Buddhahood out of his environment (rather than Anger or Animality as he had in the past) just when he needed it. This may be hard to understand, because there was no obvious or external sign he was suddenly in Buddhahood rather than any of the other Ten Worlds; but then the way each one of us creates an 'atmosphere' that is sensed by other people is extremely subtle and also quite difficult to explain. The nuances of body language, for example, communicate things about ourself to others, and vice versa, of which neither we nor they may be consciously aware and yet which profoundly affect the judgements we make about each other. Beyond this, though, each time Marc revealed his Buddhahood in this way he was gradually changing the basic tendency of his life, his karma, from the state of Anger to the higher worlds of Bodhisattva and Buddhahood, because he was no longer making bad causes which would lead to yet more bad effects in the future. Each challenge was an opportunity to further strengthen this new, positive tendency and thus, in accordance with the principles of cause and effect and when his Anger had been transformed, the attacks on him stopped.

Karma

Perhaps the two most significant statements made by Marc in the telling of his experience are: 'I did not know then about karma, or cause and effect, so I just went on making bad causes'; and 'I thought this would be a fresh start, not knowing then that you carry your karma around as if it was in your suitcase.' The word *karma* has cropped up a number of times already in the course of this book and, by now, you might have a clearer idea of what if means. Buddhism teaches that everyone has karma and that until we can change those individual karmic tendencies which inevitably cause suffering to ourselves and others, we cannot become truly happy, as Marc Bergman's experience demonstrates. Although it is a belief that is probably held by at least half the world's population, karma is an idea which is still not very well understood in the West, where it is sometimes confused with fatalism, determinism and the denial of free will. So what is karma exactly?

Karma derives from the Sanskrit word meaning 'action', and refers to the fact that, due to the strict law of cause and effect, every action leads to a future action, in an unbroken chain throughout eternity. We create karma through our every thought, word and deed, and our every thought, word and deed in turn expresses our karma. Karma is not an outside force, therefore, but rather the effects of causes we ourselves have made in the past, which continue to have a profound influence on our present actions. Some of the effects of these causes are latent and have still to appear, while those which have already appeared have resulted in our present condition. Explaining this with reference to individual human life, the *Shinjikan* Sutra states, 'If you want to understand the causes you have made in the past, look at the effects as they appear in the present. And if you want to know what results will appear in the future, look at the causes you are making now.'

In a deeper sense, karma might be described as the fundamental tendency of our individual lives, or which of the Ten Worlds dominates how we think, what we say and how we act. Nichiren Daishonin explains this in terms of inherent cause and latent effect: 'Inherent cause is mind. Chih-i's* *Maki Shikan*† states "Inherent cause is what gives rise to latent effect. It is also called karma." ' In light of the oneness of life and its environment (*esho funi*) discussed earlier, Buddhism teaches that it is the fundamental or karmic tendency of an individual's life which determines the nature of the physical and social world he or she inhabits. This implies that any attempts to improve our circum-

---

*Another name for T'ien-t'ai.
†*Great Concentration and Insight* one of T'ien-t'ai's three major works.

stances are bound to end in failure if we do not at the same time reform the tendencies within us which gave rise to those circumstances in the first place. If you are so lazy or care for yourself so little that you never wash, for example, it is useless simply changing your clothes in an attempt to get rid of the smell!

To illustrate this, let us take the example of a young woman whose fundamental tendency is to be dominated by the world of Hunger – the state of life in which she constantly yearns for things she does not have and yet, when she gets them, finds herself almost immediately yearning for something else – and let us say that right now she is yearning for a steady boyfriend. This yearning rises up from her innate desire in the world of Hunger, which is the inherent cause, lying deep in her life, for all that is going to happen to her. However hard she tries, she seems unable to stop this urge and as a result, often without realizing it, she makes a multitude of external causes which express her yearning. Not only does she react to every man she sees, but she makes many other related external causes without even noticing that she is doing so: becoming flustered when she sees a man coming towards her; gazing self-consciously into the middle distance; and breathing rather heavily when she talks to him. More subtle still, she expresses her Hunger to him in every vibration and tiny action of her life, from the slight tremor in her voice to the look in her eye and the blush on her cheeks.

Naturally, such actions have an immediate effect on every man, near or far, in our young woman's entire environment, to a lesser or greater extent depending on the closeness of their life-link with her. Consciously or subconsciously, they simply cannot avoid feeling her yearning. Her face may even come into their minds when they least wish it, and her life insist on entering their thoughts. A welter of latent effects have thus been lodged in her life, to become manifest – that is to say, she will attract or draw them to her from out of her environment – when the time and circumstances are ripe.

Sadly for our young woman, they are unlikely to be the effects she wants at all. This is because, just as Marc Bergman found with his Anger, Hunger within attracts Hunger without, while often repelling those who are not hungry. Her yearning desire brings only those men who wish to devour her – the last thing she wants for a steady relationship – whilst those whom she feels she might be able to love, consciously or subconsiously make sure that they never have to cross her path. Moreover, Hunger within not only attracts Hunger without, but also thwarts her true desires, which serves further to confuse her mind and thereby causes Hunger to rise up within her involuntarily once again. Thus, she goes back to square one and starts to make the same hungry causes all over again (see Diagram D). This is why people often talk about the chain or shackles of one's karma, a very fitting and exact description. The greatness of Nichiren Daishonin's Buddhism lies in the fact that, through chanting *Nam-myoho-renge-kyo*, the shackles of one's karma are progressively weakened until they are finally severed completely. This is a point to which we will return later.

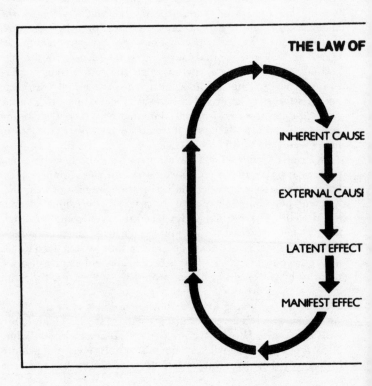

THE LAW OF

INHERENT CAUSE

EXTERNAL CAUS[

LATENT EFFECT

MANIFEST EFFEC

Clearly, the concept of karma teaches that no one is responsible for our lives except us. This applies not just to the good bits, but to everything – good, bad and indifferent – and implies that we cannot logically blame any other person for the situation in which we find ourselves at any moment. In short, karma means that everything we suffer and everything we enjoy is the result of our own actions, without exception. Of course, this would seem to ignore the fact that some people start life already at a severe disadvantage, handicapped by sickness, poverty, hunger and the like. In light of the eternity of life discussed earlier, however, Buddhism explains that the advantages or disadvantages we experience at birth are all the result of our own actions in previous lifetimes. That is to say, our life entity appears in strict accordance to the causes made by it throughout eternity.

AUSE AND EFFECT   DIAGRAM D

'What the mind has produced is internal cause and what it *will* produce is latent effect.'
(Nichikan Shonin, 26th High Priest of Nichiren Shoshu)

Arises from one of the 10 basic life-states or 'worlds', working in conjunction with our 'earthly desires' stimulated by our environment.

External action which is the vehicle for the inherent cause to produce its effect.

Lodged in the depths of our life the moment the external cause is made.

Appears on the surface of life when the time and circumstances are 'ripe'.

Because the inherent cause arises from a fundamental life tendency, the effects it produces will, in turn, trigger off similar causes. This creates the chain of destiny.

The only way to change our destiny permanently is to change our fundamental life condition to the Buddha state through chanting Nam-myoho-renge-kyo.

Naturally, this notion would be much easier to believe if we could remember all the causes we have made during our previous lifetimes, but in view of the fact that we cannot remember much more than certain key moments even in our present lifetime, memory is clearly not a very reliable criterion by which to judge the veracity of karma. Thus, a person who gets on a night-train from London to Fort William in the highlands of Scotland might go to sleep somewhere around York, say, and wake up somewhere north of Inverness. It does not matter if he cannot recognize any of the scenery out of the window when he wakes up, or remember why he is on the train, or where he is going, because he will still experience the effect of the cause he originally made – getting on the train to Fort William. As Nichiren Daishonin states, 'A person writing at night may put out the lamp, but the words he has written will still remain. It is the same with the destiny we create for ourselves in the threefold world.* Thus, just as our entity cannot escape the universe when we die, neither can it escape the consequences of all its past actions.

It is important to understand, however, that while Buddhism teaches that people suffer from the consequences of their own actions, a true Buddhist does not stand on the sidelines and simply say, 'Too bad, but it's their own fault.' Rather, remembering the story of Shakyamuni and the deer, a true Buddhist always devotes himself to taking away that suffering and giving happiness. This he does not only by taking practical action, but also by teaching others how they can change the fundamental tendencies within their lives which cause their suffering. The wider implication of this is that Nichiren Shoshu Buddhists are concerned not just with creating their own good fortune but with selflessly creating good fortune for the whole world, even if other people remain ignorant of the power of Nam-myoho-renge-kyo. As with everything else in Buddhism, this is essentially realistic because, apart from the joy and fulfilment of seeing others rid themselves of the source of their suffering through your efforts, you could never be truly content, however much good fortune you create for yourself, if your family, neighbours and fellow countrymen and women who surround you are in misery.

*The world of desire, the world of form and the world of formlessness. See also pp. 57–8

Innocence

Even so, the idea that we are all born with karma – particularly the heavy karma to experience suffering – is one which many people in the West find very difficult to accept, even upsetting or objectionable. This is understandable at first encounter. Quite apart from the difficulty of believing that we have lived before if we have no memory of it, it is even more difficult to believe that the physical circumstances of our lives, our relationships – even our parents –are determined by past causes we ourselves have made. The most fundamental of the objections to karma, however, centres upon a single word – innocence. As the notion of innocence is deeply ingrained in western civilization, firstly, with regard to justice (coupled with compassion for the innocent victims of any injustice) and, secondly, with regard to children, it is important to pause for a moment to see how it relates to karma.

In some ways western democratic society has matured from the world of Animality, in which the strong have a free rein over the weak, to the world of Humanity, in which certain human proprieties are recognized, if not always consistently applied. Through many centuries of cultural evolution, concepts of freedom, democracy, the rights of man and the protection of the weak have become not only institutionalized in the rule of law, but also entrenched in our social consciousness as to what is right and fair and proper. Of course, these notions are probably as often honoured in the breach as in the observance, but at least they reflect an awareness in western society that, by and large, people should be held responsible for their actions and that those in a position of power should not use that power without consent, or abuse it to create suffering. In other words, in the West justice is based upon the admirable ideas of human equality and personal responsibilty, from which flows the notion of guilt or innocence.

The idea of innocence as applied to children is both more obvious and more subtle. The innocence of a new-born babe is taken for granted in our culture but, in the eyes of Jacob Bronowski, this innocence stands for more than simple, uncorrupted purity:

> In scientific terms we are neotonous; that is, we come from the womb still as embryos. And perhaps that is why our civilization,

our scientific civilization, adores above all else the symbol of the child, ever since the Renaissance: the Christ child painted by Raphael and re-enacted by Blaise Pascal; the young Mozart and Gauss; the children in Jean-Jacques Rousseau and Charles Dickens . . . The real vision of the human being is the child wonder, the Virgin and Child, the Holy Family.

Bronowski saw that, while nearly all societies love and care for their children, in western society the image of the child has become invested with added significance – hope for a better tomorrow, in both the material and the spiritual sense. This dimension to childhood is apparently missing in societies where children are brought up simply to inherit existing traditions and basically defend the status quo. In the West children represent the potential for progress and development, the chance to start again, unsullied, with the pure, reforming idealism of youth. The notion, therefore, that a baby born into the terrible suffering of starvation, say, is already stained with bad karma and has itself made the causes to appear in that situation, may appear grotesque. If Bronowski is right, the implications of the concept of karma run counter in the West not only to our deeply held ideas of justice – that you are innocent until proven guilty and should suffer only for those actions that clearly and obviously trangress social mores – but also to even more fundamental ideas about the innocence of 'new life' and what it represents – purity, optimism and progress.

If we try to think seriously and unemotionally about this issue, it is clear that there can only be three possible explanations for why people experience what appears to be undeserved suffering. Either it is the will of God or some other supreme being, or it is the result of pure chance, or it is because of the karma which they thems 'ves have created. Of the first, Daisaku Ikeda states: 'It seems to me that in Christian belief, if one leads a life of agony from the day one is born to the day one dies, all one can do is reproach God for his lack of mercy. Logically speaking, it must be God who creates evil as well as good.'

On the other hand, if it is simply chance which leads individuals to experience great suffering, all one can do is either feel resentful that Fate has dealt one such a blow – and helpless to change things after the event – or lucky that it has not. Admittedly, a few individuals are able to make great efforts to alleviate their suffering in these situations, but the more usual reaction is either to sink into resignation, apathy and despair, or to become angry and look for some target against which your anger can be vented. Indeed, in situations where the suffering stems from great social injustice, embodied in social institutions such as the State, this anger has often eventually resulted in violent revolution. Unfortunately, this has also often led to even greater social injustice and suffering – as might be expected according to the law of cause and effect. Belief in randomness is a logical position to take, however, if one denies the eternity of life and the continuity of cause and effect through past, present and future.

By contrast, although the concept of karma might at first sight appear unjust or even inhumane, seen from another perspective it is extremely positive, as it offers the perpetual chance of bettering one's situation from this present moment on. As Arnold Toynbee notes: 'Actions produce consequences, and these consequences are inescapable. They are not, however, unalterable; they can be altered, for better or for worse, by further action.' In other words, karma is as much about the future as the past, if not more so. Nichiren Shoshu Buddhism teaches that we are all continually creating the future reality which we then inhabit, so no matter what our suffering, by chanting *Nam-myoho-renge-kyo* we can elevate our basic life-condition and start from this very moment to make good causes, based on Buddhahood, for our future happiness.

Although such an attitude may appear inadequate when placed against such problems as war and world hunger, Buddhism is confident that its gradual adoption by an ever-increasing number of people throughout the world will eventually change the destiny, or collective karma, mankind itself has created, resulting in the suffering that exists in the world today. As Nichiren Daishonin says:

> Little streams come together to form the great ocean, and tiny particles of dust accumulate to form Mount Sumeru.* When I, Nichiren, first took faith in the Lotus Sutra, I was like a single drop of water or a single particle of dust in all the country of Japan.

*In ancient Indian cosmology the world was divided into four continents with Mount Sumeru, the highest of all mountains, at the centre.

But later, when two people, three people, ten people, and eventually ten thousand billion people, come to recite the Lotus Sutra* and transmit it to others, then they will form a Mount Sumeru of wonderful enlightenment, a great ocean of nirvana!

Free Will

The second large question mark often placed against the idea of karma is the problem of free will. Put simply, the notion that everything we do is the result of everything that we have done up to this present moment – indeed, that even our present thoughts are the result of our past thoughts – would seem to imply that human beings have no free will and that, right now, we are little more than puppets acting out a life programmed for us since before birth, even if the programme were made by our own actions. In a culture that extols the virtues of individualism, this would be a very unattractive doctrine if, indeed, it were what Buddhism teaches. As Daisaku Ikeda explains, however, the concept of karma does not contradict that of free will:

> A man's present state is not entirely determined by the immense, indefinite plexus of karmic causes inherited from the past. The efforts he has made after this present birth also play a determining part . . . Although each human being inherits a karmic background from other existences, each is completely free to act in this world to alter it for better or worse, as he sees fit. In other words, in the Buddhist view man is innately free.

It is important to realize, therefore, that our decisions are not determined by our karmic tendencies, however much they may be influenced by them. The person who commits – or refuses to commit – a certain act, good or bad, knowing that there is an alternative course of action, has exercised a choice and, thus, his or her own free will. In the end, his karmic tendency may well have pushed him towards choosing one way rather than another, but it did not *determine* it. For example, if someone in whom Animality and Anger is a strong tendency is punched in the face, he may immediately return his attacker's blow. Nevertheless, he has made a decision, albeit a split-second one, to do so. In other words, although he is at that moment dominated by his karma,

*In Nichiren Daishonin's Buddhism, this means to chant *Nam-myoho-renge-kyo* to the Gohonzon.

his action is not determined by it because he has the possibility of not fighting back: if his attacker was also holding a gun, for instance, he would probably restrain himself. Of course, in extreme circumstances, the options one can choose are severely limited – indeed, this is one of the characteristics of the state of Hell – but, as we saw in the case of Primo Levi, even in the most hellish situations it is possible to exercise certain choices which can lead one deeper into suffering or towards eventual relief.

Furthermore, since everybody inherently possesses all the Ten Worlds from Hell to Buddhahood, the four higher worlds of Learning, Realization, Bodhisattva and Buddhahood can be drawn out, strengthened and developed in even the most apparently evil person, just as the three poisons of greed, anger and stupidity can be revealed in the most apparently noble. It is not unknown for hardened criminals to reform and become artists, social workers or priests, for example, nor for respected figures in society to become corrupted and ignoble. Thus, as we have seen through Marc Bergman's experience, if we meet the right external cause and make the right choices, even fundamental, deep-seated karma can be changed; although we must at some point inevitably experience the bad effects of bad causes we have made in the past – either in this or previous lifetimes – our actions *now* can alter and lighten how those effects appear.

Buddhism teaches that there are basically two kinds of karma –the mutable, or changeable, and the immutable. Generally speaking, immutable karma produces a fixed effect at a specific time, while the effects of mutable karma cannot be specified either in terms of how or when they will appear. Death is an example of immutable karma: it is inherent in life, and although it can be delayed, ultimately it cannot be prevented by any of our actions. Similarly, if we have the karma to suffer an incurable disease, nothing we do can stop this disease from appearing in our life if the time is right for it to appear. Habitual acts, consistently repeated, also form immutable karma in the form of equally consistent effects. For example, if you are driven by your inherent Hunger to consistently overeat, you will always be overweight; indeed, the very food which sustains your life might eventually even kill you. On the other hand, gorging yourself only occasionally will produce mutable karma, as the effect of this cause can be manifested in any number of different, short-lived ways, ranging from mere physical discomfort to severe indigestion or sickness.

Everyone's karma is a mixture of the mutable and immutable because, as Yasuji Kirimura explains:

> The degree of karma one forms depends upon the strength of one's intentions. For example, the more intense one's hatred grows, the heavier the degree of evil karma he creates. Moreover, the degree of karma formed increases as thoughts give rise to words and actions. When one feels resentment only within himself, the karma engraved in his life is relatively light. However, when he translates his rage into some physical or verbal action, he creates a heavier karma. In addition, the degree of evil karma he forms will vary according to the object of his hatred. Nichiren Daishonin states, 'To put this simply, if one strikes at the air, his fist will not hurt, but when he hits a rock, he feels pain . . . The seriousness of a sin depends on whom one harms.'

It follows from this that those of our actions which lead to little suffering produce mutable karma, while those which lead to great or continuous suffering eventually produce immutable karma.

It also follows that mutable karma can be changed through simple effort motivated by willpower. For example, if the eight-stone weakling who always gets sand kicked in his face does a bodybuilding course, he will naturally develop an appearance so formidable that his former attacker will certainly think twice about kicking sand in his face again. Through simple effort, he has changed that aspect of his karma which led him to be bullied – his physical weakness. More difficult to change, though, is that part of his nature – the inherent tendency – which has always prompted him to take revenge; in this instance by kicking sand back into the face of his erstwhile tormentor, thus creating more bad karma for himself in the future, karma which will be correspondingly more difficult to erase. Even more difficult to change would be any immutable karma he might *already* have stored in his life: to suffer from a serious illness, say, or extreme poverty, or even the inability to form satisfactory relationships with other people, and so on.

As its name implies, immutable karma is unavoidable. But why should this be so? Why can we not exercise mind over matter and, say, remain perfectly healthy throughout our lives? Again, Yasuji Kirimura explains:

Willpower operates in the conscious levels of the human psyche, while karma exists in the unconscious levels or even deeper. Clearly we need some power which can alter the flow of life itself, and that power is and always has been *Nam-myoho-renge-kyo*. With the awareness of this powerful key to our inherent inexhaustible life-force, we can be confident that we can form causes to emancipate ourselves totally from our negative karma.

In other words, chanting *Nam-myoho-renge-kyo*, and taking action based on that chanting, is the greatest good cause we can make to change even the worst karma into good fortune. As the *Fugen Sutra*, the epilogue of the Lotus Sutra states: 'If you wish to make amends for your past bad causes, sit upright and meditate on the true entity of life,* and all your offences will vanish like dewdrops in the sunlight of enlightened wisdom.' To understand exactly how chanting this phrase can have such an effect, however, we need to explore the concepts of causality and karma a little further.

Breaking the Chain of Karma
Fundamentally, all Buddhist doctrine is concerned with how one can change unhappy karma, build up one's good fortune and live a completely fulfilled life. To achieve this, early Buddhist sutras taught what might be broadly characterized as a basic morality – that by behaving well you make good causes which eventually lead to good effects. The actual reward for such virtuous behaviour in this world varies according to these early sutras, some saying that it leads to rebirth in a Pure Land where there is no suffering (which corresponds closely to certain aspects of Christian doctrine), others that it leads to rebirths in ever higher life-conditions, until one eventually achieves Buddhahood and so no longer has to be reborn into this world of suffering at all. However, all the pre-Lotus Sutra teachings agree that the effects of good causes made now do not become apparent in this lifetime.

The Lotus Sutra overturns this idea, as Nichiren Daishonin explains:

> The benefit of the other sutras is uncertain, because they teach that one must first make good causes and only then can one

---

*In Nichiren Daishonin's Buddhism, this means to chant *Nam-myoho-renge-kyo* to the Gohonzon.

become a Buddha at some later time. The Lotus Sutra is completely different. A hand which takes it up immediately attains enlightenment, and a mouth which chants it instantly enters Buddhahood, just as the moon is reflected in the water the moment it appears from behind the eastern mountains, or as a sound and its echo arise simultaneously. It is for this reason that the sutra states, 'Among those who hear of this Law, there is not one who shall not attain Buddhahood.'

In other words, chanting *Nam-myoho-renge-kyo* to the Gohonzon (cause) immediately brings to life the Buddhahood that is innate within us (effect). Thus, we can begin to experience our Buddhahood from the very moment we first chant. Moreover, because *Nam-myoho-renge-kyo* is the state of Buddhahood, not only do we reveal our Buddhahood at once when we chant this phrase, but we also simultaneously make the cause to further experience the effects of Buddhahood at some point in the future. In other words, every time we chant *Nam-myoho-renge-kyo* we are making a deposit of good fortune in our lives, which we can then draw on at a future date.

Here, then, lies the secret to changing our unhappy karma. Rather than worrying about whether we are making good or bad causes, which in itself is a cause leading to suffering, Nichiren Daishonin teaches the importance of fundamentally purifying the inner spirit that motivates various actions. To achieve this, all we have to do is chant *Nam-myoho-renge-kyo* to the Gohonzon (as part of our Buddhist practice) and so reveal our innate Buddha nature. As will be explained in a later chapter, chanting to the Gohonzon is to the development of our Buddhahood what lifting weights is to a bodybuilder; so as our Buddha nature becomes more and more apparent, and our dominant life tendency moves towards Buddhahood, we increasingly make causes that flow from this highest aspect of ourselves. As Nichiren Daishonin explains:

> The lives of human beings are fettered by evil karma, earthly desires and the inborn sufferings of life and death. But due to the three inherent potentials of Buddha nature – innate Buddhahood, the wisdom to become aware of it, and the action to manifest it – our lives can without doubt come to reveal the Buddha's three properties.*

*Enlightened wisdom (*hoshim*) relates to *kutai*; compassionate actions to relieve the sufferings of all people (*ojin*) relates to *ketai*; and the essence of the Buddha's life (*hosshin*), or *Nam-myoho-renge-kyo*, relates to *chutai*.

We still have bad karma stored in our lives – even when we become enlightened – but as our Buddhahood grows stronger we actually begin to use that bad karma to create good fortune for ourselves and others. Problems and desires make us chant rather than simply suffer, and the act of chanting both reveals and strengthens our Buddhahood there and then, and also lays down further good fortune in our eighth consciousness, which at some point in the future must in turn be revealed.

One way of understanding how chanting *Nam-myoho-renge-kyo* instantly breaks the chain of our unhappy karma is by reference to the nine consciousnesses (see Diagram C, p.154). Our karma is stored in the eighth consciousness and has a profound effect on the seven levels of consciousness that lie 'above' it. If we have a karmic tendency towards Anger, say, as Marc Bergman did, then Anger will dominate our thoughts in our seventh consciousness, as well as how we put together our view of the external world, based on our five senses, in our sixth consciousness. Incredible as it may sound, by chanting *Nam-myoho-renge-kyo* we drill down to tap our ninth consciousness, the source of cosmic life-force. This colossal life-force then surges up through the other eight consciousnesses, purifying the totality of our lives and out into our environment. Basing our lives on 'the palace of the ninth consciousness', as Nichiren Daishonin calls it, we are then able to make causes which are not dominated by our previous karmic tendencies.

Although we instantly reveal our highest selves, our own Buddha nature, every time we chant *Nam-myoho-renge-kyo*, it nevertheless takes time to achieve the state in which our highest selves, our own Buddha nature, dominates every area of our lives – ten, twenty of even thirty years of steady practice. Nichiren Daishonin guarantees that chanting *Nam-myoho-renge-kyo* will have this effect but, of course, very few people would be able to endure practising for this length of time without enjoying some reward for their efforts along the way. So, being human, we need proof of the effect of chanting in the form of conspicuous benefits. The joy of this proof deepens our faith and keeps us going long enough to appreciate the gradual accumulation of the inconspicuous benefit of the practice, which is far greater.

Nichiren Daishonin explains that there are four different ways in which chanting *Nam-myoho-renge-kyo* to the Gohonzon produces good fortune, or benefit. 'Conspicuous prayer resulting in conspicuous benefit' means that, through sincerely chanting for what you desire, you quickly achieve it. This is the benefit people often receive soon after they begin to practise; they chant for something specific, like money or a job, and get it so soon that it seems to them almost miraculous. 'Conspicuous prayer resulting in inconspicuous benefit' means that you achieve a specific desire after a lapse of time; in retrospect, however, with the wisdom of your Buddha nature, you understand why you did not achieve your desire at once.

This is rather like a ten-year-old boy being told by his parents that he cannot drive the family car, say, even though he really wants to. He may kick up a fuss at the time but, when he grows up, he sees the wisdom of his parents' refusal. In other words, this category of benefit applies to those things which come to us only when we are truly ready to create maximum value from them, not when we *think* we are ready.

'Inconspicuous prayer resulting in conspicuous benefit' refers to the support a strong and steady practice will give you by building up a 'deposit account' of good fortune. This is known as 'protection' and was the type of benefit Marc Bergman experienced when threatened by the youths on the tube train. Finally, 'inconspicuous prayer resulting in inconspicuous benefit' means that strong and steady practice carried out over a long period of time will lead to every area of your life being filled with the qualities of your true self, which is Buddhahood – wisdom, courage, compassion, purity and the joy of inexhaustible life-force. We often call this type of benefit 'human revolution'.

Nichiren Daishonin teaches that the fundamental purpose of the practice of this Buddhism is to achieve the last category of benefit. Of course, while Buddhism does not deny the value of material or short-term benefits, its real aim is to show us how we can establish a strong and solid life as a whole, in which we can overcome any difficulty that we meet and thus help establish true and lasting happiness within ourselves and in the world about us. For the more we are able to overcome our own problems through developing our Buddhahood, the greater compassion we naturally start to feel for others who are still 'fettered by evil karma, earthly desires and the inborn sufferings of birth and death', and so increasingly we begin to share the desire of all Buddhas to lead other people to enlightenment. In this day and age, that means to teach others about *Nam-myoho-renge-kyo*.

Nichiren Daishonin declared that even if we chant *Nam-myoho-renge-kyo* only once – indeed, even if we only hear the phrase – we have already created immeasurable good fortune for ourselves because that 'seed' of Buddhahood is never lost but is stored forever in our karma. It thereby becomes the cause for us to chant at some point in the future, when the time is right for us to do so, and thus eventually attain enlightenment. As the Lotus Sutra promises, 'Among those who hear of this Law, there is not one who shall not attain Buddhahood.'

However, while you automatically sow the seed of Buddhahood in your life the moment you hear or chant *Nam-myoho-renge-kyo* even once, quite how soon the seed germinates and grows into a tree of enlightened wisdom is entirely dependent upon your own freely chosen actions from that moment onwards. In other words, to attain Buddhahood demands a seeking mind, perseverance and assiduous effort. Such is the nature of *renge*, cause and effect.

KYO

Kyo literally means sutra, the voice or teaching of a Buddha. In this sense it also means sound, rhythm or vibration, and might therefore be interpreted to indicate the practice of chanting. Furthermore, since everything in the universe is essentially connected through the vibration of various different kinds of waves – light waves, sound waves, radio waves and so on – by implication *kyo* refers to the life activity of universal phenomena and indicates that everything that exists, has existed or will exist is a manifestation of the Mystic Law. In terms of human life, Nichiren Daishonin explains *kyo* thus: 'Once you realize that your own life is the Mystic Law, you will realize that so are the lives of all others. That realization is the mystic *kyo* or sutra.'

In addition, the Chinese character for *kyo* originally meant the warp in a piece of woven cloth, and so *kyo* later came to take on the meaning of the thread of logic, reason, the Way or the Law. It was, therefore, also used in the sense of a teaching to be preserved. Putting these various meanings together, Nichiren Daishonin further states, '*Kyo* denotes the voices and sounds of all living beings. One interpretation says, "Voice makes an essential part of Buddhist practice." This is called *kyo* and the three existences of life are also called *kyo*.' Fundamentally, then, *kyo* refers to the continuity of life throughout past, present and future, and in the title of the Lotus Sutra, *Myoho-renge-kyo*, indicates that the ultimate truth of life as expounded in the Lotus Sutra is itself eternal and unchanging.

As we have seen, Nichiren Daishonin defined that truth as *Nam-myoho-renge-kyo*. To explain it, however, he often employed the teaching of *ichinen sanzen*, developed over 600 years earlier by T'ien-t'ai on the basis of his own enlightenment through the Lotus Sutra. This profound and complex theory has been mentioned a number of times in the course of this book and various aspects of it have already been examined in some depth, such as the mutual possession of the Ten Worlds, the Three Truths, the Five Components and the simultaneity of cause and effect. A discussion of *kyo*, the Buddha's teaching, therefore seems an appropriate point to complete the picture.

Ichinen Sanzen

The term *ichinen sanzen* literally means 'three thousand realms in a moment of life', and explains the variety of ways that life expresses itself from moment to moment. *Ichinen* (literally, 'one

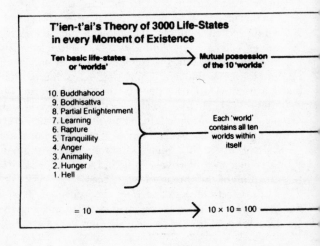

T'ien-t'ai's Theory of 3000 Life-States in every Moment of Existence

Ten basic life-states or 'worlds' ⟶ Mutual possession of the 10 'worlds'

10. Buddhahood
9. Bodhisattva
8. Partial Enlightenment
7. Learning
6. Rapture
5. Tranquillity
4. Anger
3. Animality
2. Hunger
1. Hell

Each 'world' contains all ten worlds within itself

= 10 ⟶ 10 × 10 = 100

mind' or 'life-moment') refers to the unchanging entity of life, and *sanzen* (literally, 'three thousand') to the various forms that this entity can take. As Nichikan Shonin (1665–1726), the twenty-sixth high priest of Nichiren Shoshu, explains:

> 'Three thousand realms in a moment of life' has two meanings according to the Lotus Sutra: 'to contain' and 'to permeate'. The entire universe is contained in each life at every moment of its existence. Conversely, each life-moment permeates the entire universe. The life-moment is a particle of dust holding the elements of all worlds in the universe. It is a drop of water whose essence differs in no way from the vast ocean itself.

While the general meaning of this passage may not be too difficult to grasp, the idea that at any single moment our lives both 'contain' and 'permeate' the entire universe is one that certainly does stretch our capacity to truly understand. Realizing this difficulty, T'ien-t'ai broke down the relationship between an individual life-moment and the universe into 3000 separate parts which, together, make up a completely integrated and harmonious whole (see Diagram E, p. 196). In other words, the number 'three thousand' is not arbitrarily chosen to mean simply 'very many', but is the result of a precisely analyzed formula. This formula gives us a way to comprehend the magnitude of

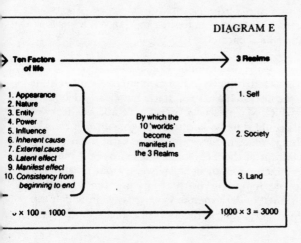

DIAGRAM E

Ten Factors of life ──────────────→ 3 Realms

1. Appearance
2. Nature
3. Entity
4. Power
5. Influence
6. Inherent cause
7. External cause
8. Latent effect
9. Manifest effect
10. Consistency from beginning to end

By which the 10 'worlds' become manifest in the 3 Realms

1. Self
2. Society
3. Land

∪ × 100 = 1000 ──────────────→ 1000 × 3 = 3000

ichinen sanzen, as Nichiren Daishonin explains at the beginning of one of his most important treatises, *The True Object of Worship*:

> Volume Five of the *Maka Shikan* states: 'Life at each moment is endowed with the Ten Worlds. At the same time, each of the Ten Worlds is endowed with all the others, so that an entity of life actually possesses one hundred worlds. Each of these worlds in turn possesses thirty realms, which means that in one hundred worlds there are three thousand realms. The three thousand realms are all possessed by a single entity of life. If there is no life, that is the end of the matter. But if there is the slightest bit of life, it contains all the three thousand realms . . . This is what we mean when we speak of the "region of the unfathomable".'

Quite probably you can follow this somewhat technical passage until mention of the 'thirty realms', which we have not yet encountered or at least not in these terms. For an explanation of the mutual possession of the Ten Worlds see pp. 78–82 to refresh your memory before continuing, as *ichinen sanzen* can only be fully grasped on a theoretical level if the meaning of each of its constituent parts has been properly digested. Even then, a theoretical understanding of *ichinen sanzen* is still only a partial one, as T'ien-t'ai suggests by his reference to the 'region of the unfathomable'. We will return to this point later.

What, then, are the 'thirty realms'? This is a term arrived at by bringing together two different but related concepts: the Ten Factors of life and the Three Realms of existence. To avoid becoming hopelessly entangled in figures and jargon, let us look at these two concepts separately.

The Ten Factors of Life. In our examination of the Ten Worlds we saw that our lives as individuals change moment by moment from one life state to the next. Each of these states has clearly definable characteristics which were described in some detail; the theory of the Ten Worlds could thus be said to highlight the *differences* in our subjective experience of life with each passing moment. By contrast, the concept of the Ten Factors stresses what remains *constant* in our moment to moment existence, no matter which of the Ten Worlds we happen to be in at any one time. In other words, the Ten Factors describe the various ways in which the Ten Worlds invariably express themselves and the mechanism by which we change from one life state to the next with each passing moment.

The Ten Factors are taken from a passage in the *Hoben* (second) chapter of the Lotus Sutra, which reads: 'The true entity of all phenomena can only be understood and shared between Buddhas. This reality consists of appearance, nature, entity, power, influence, inherent cause, relation [external cause], latent effect, manifest effect, and their consistency from beginning to end.' Of this passage Yasuji Kirimura comments:

> The *Hoben* chapter analyzes the true entity, that is, the essential characteristic common to all the Ten Worlds, and defines it as the Ten Factors of life . . . This is the one ultimate truth to which Shakyamuni became enlightened, the truth which he reveals for the first time in the *Hoben* chapter in order to enable all people to attain Buddhahood just as he did.

Clearly, an understanding of these Ten Factors is very important. But what exactly do they mean? The first three of the Ten Factors, appearance, nature and entity, are simply different names for *ke, ku* and *chu*; the four factors referring to causality have been discussed in the preceding section on *renge*. Here, then, let us look at the remaining three factors – power, influence and 'consistency from beginning to end'.

Power equates with energy and refers to the potential or strength inherent in individual life to achieve something or affect the environment. Power might, therefore, be called individual life-force and is expressed both in one's physical and spiritual functions. *Influence* is what is produced when power, the potential to create something, is manifested either physically or mentally. Nichikan Shonin states: 'Influence is the use of thought, word or deed to create good or evil.' As Daisaku Ikeda notes, however, power and influence 'are not necessarily always proportional to each other. In some cases, inherent power is great, but the resulting action is small; in others, the inherent power may be small, but the action large. This is no doubt due to the qualitative changes power undergoes from one state of existence to another.' For example, a person of great talent who is always depressed, say, and lives almost constantly in the state of Hell, in which life-force is negligible, will be able to exert very little influence on his environment, even though he has great potential which might be more fully revealed if his life state were higher. As it is, he may find it very hard even to relate to others, simply because he is unable to manifest his inherent power. On the other hand, someone of little talent but who is dominated by the world of Humanity, say, who is always bright and cheerful and finds it very easy to get on with people, will reveal a greater proportion of his inherent power and will therefore have a greater effect on his environment.

Referring to the nine factors so far discussed, a commentary by Miao-lo* on one of T'ien-t'ai's major works states:

> Appearance exists only in what is material, nature only in what is spiritual. Entity, power, influence and relation [external cause] in principle combine both the material and the spiritual. Inherent cause and latent effect are purely spiritual; manifest effect exists only in what is material.

The last of the Ten Factors, *'consistency from beginning to end'*, is best explained by describing how the other nine factors work together, for it underlines the point that all the factors from 'appearance' to 'manifest effect' make up one harmonious whole. For example, let us say that Jane's boyfriend has just walked out on her (external cause), drawing out in her the world of Hell (inherent cause). Jane will look as if she is suffering (appearance) because, in the depths of her life (entity), she is very unhappy. Just how she expresses that suffering depends on her character (nature), but undoubtedly her life-force (power) will be low and so any action she takes (influence), the exact form of which is determined by her past relationship with her boyfriend (latent effect), will, by her own standards, inevitably be weak (manifest effect).

In other words, the tenth factor, 'consistency from beginning to end', means that when Jane is in the state of Hell every aspect of her life – the other nine factors, in other words – is consistent with that state. She cannot at the same moment feel desperately unhappy and yet have great life-force; neither at that moment can she appear joyful. Of course, if the pain lessens momentarily due

---

*(711–82): sixth head of the T'ien–t'ai sect in China, who restored the sect and wrote profound commentaries on T'ien-t'ai's three major works. The one referred to here is the *Hokke Gengi Shakusen (Annotations on the Profound Meaning of the Lotus Sutra)*.

to some other external cause – a call from a sympathetic friend, for example – she may be able to 'put a brave face on it' and perhaps even fool other people that she is not suffering at all. Bearing in mind the mutual possession of the Ten Worlds (which gives us the hundred worlds), this may be the very way in which Jane's personal Hell reveals within it the world of Bodhisattva, as she does not want anyone else to suffer simply because she is suffering; or it may be that her Hell also reveals the world of Anger, as she is too proud to let others see that she is upset over a man.

The important point to remember about the Ten Factors, though, is that however much Jane might subtly change from moment to moment, her life state will always express itself absolutely consistently, from how she appears to the causes she makes and the effects she experiences. As Nichikan Shonin explains, 'Appearance is the beginning and manifest effect is the end. Consistency from beginning to end is the unchangeable entity of the Middle Way, permeating all the other nine factors.' That is to say, just as the Middle Way (*chu* of *ku, ke, chu*) integrates and harmonizes the physical and spiritual aspects of individual life, so it ensures the consistency of its operation with regard to power, influence and cause and effect.

Clearly, the theory of *ichinen sanzen* is already becoming quite complex for, as each of the hundred worlds also possesses the Ten Factors, we have now 1000 possible different ways in which life can express itself from moment to moment. This is sometimes known as the 1000 factors. Even so, we know that life is more complex still, for no two people are ever alike: Jane's boyfriend walks out and she falls apart, but when Sally's boyfriend leaves, she sheds a brief tear, puts on her party gear and quickly goes out to find another one. In other words, Jane's sojourn in Hell is much longer than Sally's, just as her Rapture and Hunger may be less dominating, and so on. In short, we have seen that the highest teachings of Buddhism discern patterns which are common to all life – the Ten Worlds and the Ten Factors – but how do they explain individuality, the 'how and why' of the obvious differences that exist between people? The answer to this question lies in the theory of the Three Realms, the final piece of the jigsaw puzzle of *ichinen sanzen*.

The Three Realms of Existence. The Three Realms are the realm of the Five Components, the realm of sentient (animate) beings and the realm of the (inanimate) environment. In human terms these Three Realms correspond to the individual, society and the physical environment.

The *realm of the Five Components* explains individual uniqueness. We have already discussed these Five Components – form, perception, conception, volition and consciousness – in terms of life and death (see pp. 139–145), and have seen how, at the moment a sperm fertilizes the egg in the womb (external cause), an individual life entity (*chu*) that was formerly in its unseen state (*ku*) becomes manifest (*ke*) – that is, endowed with the Five Components – in strict accordance with the karma it has formed in its previous existences. Form relates to the physical aspect of life, the other four components to its spiritual aspect, and because these are but two different aspects of the same entity, they are completely harmonious and inseparable. In other words, at the very moment an individual life appears it possesses unique characteristics, both physically and spiritually, as a result of its past karma. Moreover, at the moment of birth, the development of that individual's uniqueness accelerates, through the workings of the Five Components, in reaction to his or her environment. As Daisaku Ikeda explains, 'Each person's personality is differentiated from other personalities by the action of these components, for they determine how he will respond to reality and, hence, what reality is to him. Through the function of the Five Components, an infinite variety of mental and physical activities becomes possible.'

With these remarks in mind, one easy way of understanding the Five Components is to view them as the essential attributes we need in order to deal with life: the ability to be 'alive' or 'awake' (consciousness); the ability to sense objects and events in our environment (perception), form coherent ideas about those objects or events (conception) and then make decisions about them (volition). All these mental and spiritual activities are 'housed', as it were, in the body (form), and at the same time work to sustain that housing. Armed with these attributes, the exact nature of which differs from person to person, each of us is then able to interact uniquely with the rest of the world – the realms of sentient beings and the environment.

The *realm of sentient beings* is quite simply the world of different individual humans, animals, birds and insects; in other words, all living things other than trees and plants which, lacking a brain and a central nervous system, come within the *realm of the environment*, along with rocks, water, air and all the other elements that make up the non-sentient, physical world.

The exact constitution of these two realms – the social and physical environment – is also uniquely different for each individual. On one level, this is a reflection of the laws of physics, one of the most basic of which states that no two bodies can occupy the same space at the same time. This means that even if, say, three people were standing in a small and completely bare room, at any one moment each person would have a slightly different perception of reality from the other two: how they see the room would depend upon precisely where they were standing, for example, while, no matter where they were standing, no one could see themselves as the other two can see them.

On another level, the uniqueness of each individual's social and physical environment is a perfect reflection of his or her unique personality. 'Birds of a feather flock together' is a fitting description for how we tend to seek, consciously or otherwise, the company of those whose life states correspond to our own and, quite naturally, also inhabit the physical environment best suited to that society. For example, people who like huntin', shootin', and fishin' feel most at home when huntin', shootin' or fishin' together in the depths of the countryside; those who absolutely adore 'style' will most likely be found in the more Bohemian parts of large cities. Put a person from either group in the social or physical environment of the other and he or she will most probably feel decidedly uncomfortable. Of course, as we tend to have a number of different aspects to our personality, at different times different social and physical environments will appeal to us, depending on our life state at that moment. Nevertheless, our predominant 'persona' will determine the social and physical realms within which we spend the greatest portion of our time.

Furthermore, the scope or extent of the realms which we inhabit depends upon our dominant life state. For example, conscious only of his pain, a person in extreme suffering will be almost totally oblivious to his physical surroundings and the people within it. In that sense, his world will seem incredibly small and restricted. A person in Buddhahood, on the other hand, is concerned with the well-being and happiness of all living things, firstly within his or her immediate surroundings but, ultimately, throughout the whole world and the entire universe. By implication, this means that someone in whom Buddhahood is dominant is also deeply concerned about the well-being of the physical environment itself. In short, as we manifest each of the Ten Worlds in the way that is unique to our personality, through the actions of the Five Components, so the realms of sentient beings and the environment alter accordingly. Thus, the Three Realms can be seen as the theoretical basis for the concept of *esho funi*, the inseparability of the self and its environment. Every individual has a unique self, matched by a unique living and physical environment which changes in direct response to the changes which occur within that individual, and vice versa.

The Implications of Ichinen Sanzen

Seen from the viewpoint of the individual, *ichinen sanzen* explains theoretically how, by changing yourself, you change the world about you. This is perhaps not so difficult an idea to understand or accept, although some people might question the extent to which the weak are able to effect any meaningful change in situations of great suffering. As was explained in the Introduction, however, fundamentally the weak suffer precisely because they are weak; this implies that by becoming stronger – changing themselves – they too can change their environment.

Ichinen sanzen can also be seen from the viewpoint of the realms of sentient beings and the environment, for not only do individuals possess the hundred worlds and the Ten Factors, but so does society and so does the land. In other words, *ichinen sanzen* explains how not only single individuals, but groups of individuals and even the inanimate physical environment, can all manifest the hundred worlds, experience the effects of karma, and so on.

Let us look first at how *ichinen sanzen* applies to society. Starting on a fairly small scale, we can see how a group of football supporters, for example, can all experience Rapture when their team wins and Hell when it loses. Similarly, if their team does well in a knockout competition, they will all share in the karma or destiny of that team, following it around the country from match to match and, if it reaches the final, will all participate in some way in its ultimate success or failure. Of course, different individuals within the group will fulfil different roles but, insofar as they identify with their team, all share a common destiny. In this sense, then, a group of football supporters is like one large life entity and, as such, will together be able to reveal any of the hundred worlds in accordance with the Ten Factors – cause and effect, power and influence, and so forth. Moreover, as one entity, they will also possess an effect their own unique physical environment: football stadia, special trains and coaches, particular pubs and the like.

Increasing the scale, members of the same nation, while being many different individuals, also share common attributes. Most of the French, for example, live in France and speak French. They have their own history, their own unique institutions, their own culture and so on. In short, as a society they have characteristics which differentiate them from other societies just as surely as their own personal characteristics differentiate individual French men and women from each other. Increasing the scale again, the French have much in common with many other Europeans which they do not share with, say, most Asians or Africans: physical features and cultural heritage, to name but two. Indeed, we have only to increase the scale once more to see that all human beings are members of one enormous society and that, in the broadest sense, we *homo sapiens* have as much in common as we have differences.

This has important ramifications, for although the society to which we feel we belong is simply the group with which we choose to identify at any particular moment, at different levels we share a common destiny with other members of our various social groupings, whether we like it or not. For example, let us consider an imaginary Frenchman – Henri Dupont. Knowing nothing more about him, Henri is immediately identified with two groups – 'the French' and 'men' – both of which, by themselves, have an enormous bearing on his personal karma, regardless of any other aspect of his individuality. For example, if the French government breaks off diplomatic relations with another country, Henri will not be able to visit that country, even if he personally has no quarrel with anyone in it; and if his government then decides that France will go to war with that country, he cannot avoid becoming involved in one way or another simply because he disagrees or because he voted for the Opposition during the last election. As an able-bodied male he might even be called on to risk his life fighting for his country; indeed, even if he declares himself a pacifist he will still be subject in one way or another to the collective karma of his society to suffer war. To take another example, the passengers on the *Titanic* came from all walks of life, and many would have felt that they had absolutely nothing in common with each other, yet they did share one thing: the karma to be on the *Titanic* when it struck an iceberg. It is impossible to know how each individual had created that karma and, in a sense, it is irrelevant. The important point is that, quite unknowingly, all the individuals on that ship together comprised a society which experienced a common fate.

In short, viewed from the aspect of the realm of sentient beings, *ichinen sanzen* teaches that we are all part of many different and overlapping societies – family, friends, colleagues, neighbours, men, women, adults, children and so on – and that our own personal karma and identity is inextricably linked with that of other people, both individually and in groups. This is one reason why Nichiren Shoshu Buddhism teaches the necessity of individuals identifying with the largest possible group – humanity as a whole – because whatever happens to one sub-group within humanity will inevitably affect all the others, even if that effect is not immediately apparent. For many years this inextricable relationship may not indeed have been very obvious, but now that the world is so tightly knit together, both by a global economy and a highly efficient communications system, it is becoming increasingly clear that any problems affecting people in one part of the world soon lead to repercussions in another.

Of course, as long as the problems of others do not directly affect our lives many of us believe that they can be ignored. Over 700 years ago, however, Nichiren Daishonin pointed out the dangers inherent in such a short-sighted perspective. Writing of thirteenth-century Japan, then undergoing a series of seemingly endless natural and man-made disasters, he observed in the *Rissho Ankoku Ron (On Securing the Peace of the Land through the Establishment of True Buddhism)*, 'If the nation is destroyed and families are wiped out, then where can one flee for safety? If you care anything about your personal security, you should first of all pray for order and tranquillity throughout the four quarters of the land, should you not?' One has only to substitute 'world' for 'nation' and 'land' for these words to apply directly to the global turmoil which is the current shared karma of mankind. Either way, the implication is clear: in the final analysis, we sink or swim together.

It is when we come to consider *ichinen sanzen* from the viewpoint of the physical environment, the last of the Three Realms, that the greatest problems of understanding usually arise. It is not hard to see why, as the following passage from Nichiren Daishonin's *The True Object of Worship* demonstrates:

> Question: What is the difference between the principle of the one hundred worlds or the one thousand factors, and that of *ichinen sanzen*, the three thousand realms of life?

> Answer: The former concerns only sentient beings, the latter applies to both insentient and sentient beings.

> Question: If insentient beings possess the Ten Factors, is it correct to assume that plants and trees have minds and can attain Buddhahood like sentient beings?

> Answer: This is a matter that is difficult to believe and difficult to understand . . .

Difficult though it may be, the highest levels of Buddhist philosophy do teach, not that non-sentient things have minds but that they, too, are capable of 'attaining Buddhahood'. But how can inanimate objects reveal the Ten Worlds or the Ten Factors? The answer is that by themselves they cannot, of course, as they are incapable of making the necessary effort. They can, however, reveal the Ten Worlds as they are acted upon by living beings. Take a knife, for example. A person can use it to commit suicide: this is the Hellish aspect of a knife. A knife can be used to cut up food, thus revealing the world of Hunger within it. Someone might carry a knife to make him feel strong and so manifest its inherent Animality; and if he then uses the knife to threaten or injure another person, he would reveal its Anger. In Tranquillity a knife lies in the dark of a kitchen drawer and could reveal Rapture if it is needed to cut open a longed-for parcel or letter. In

Learning it could be used to dissect an animal in a biology class, and in Realization to carve a statue. A surgeon performing an operation reveals the world of Bodhisattva in a knife, while someone in Buddhahood might use a knife in any number of ways to create value – to illustrate a particular teaching, for example, or, in Nichiren Daishonin's case, to create an object of worship, the Gohonzon, to enable other people to reveal their own Buddha natures.

Explaining this point, Nichiren Daishonin says:

> Both the Buddhist and non-Buddhist scriptures permit wooden or painted images to be used as objects of worship but T'ien-t'ai and his followers were the first to explain the principle [*ichinen sanzen*] behind this act. If a piece of wood or paper did not have both a material and spiritual aspect, or lacked the inherent cause to manifest a spiritual nature, then it would be futile to rely upon it as an object of worship.

This difficult concept might be easier to understand if we leave aside objects of worship, for a moment, and concentrate instead on the subject of painting and painters, taking as an example a well-known painter like Van Gogh.

As most people know, Vincent Van Gogh (1853–90) lived and worked for most of his short life in extreme poverty, supported financially by his brother, Theo. Although his pictures now fetch millions, in his time his work was ridiculed as wild and undisciplined and, consequently, sold very poorly. Van Gogh was a highly emotional man, at times experiencing heights of the greatest rapture and, at others, the depths of deepest depression. But even though it eventually led to his suicide, Van Gogh's emotional instability was also the key to his greatness as a painter. Towards the end of his life particularly, he reacted strongly, even violently, to his physical surroundings and increasingly painted the world he felt, as much as the world he saw. That is to say, in Buddhist terms, each time he painted a picture, Van Gogh depicted not only the subject of his painting – sunflowers, a starry night, a cornfield – but also his own acutely experienced life state. Of course, all painters do this to a greater or lesser degree, but a major part of the enormous appeal of Van Gogh's works lies in the passion of the man: indeed, his intensely emotional approach to painting pioneered a whole new school of art, the expressionist movement.

Here, though, we face a paradox: it is an inescapable fact that all Van Gogh's paintings are mere combinations of oil pigments on canvas – in other words, material objects – and yet they are capable of producing in those who see them the same life state Van Gogh experienced when he painted them, be it Rapture, Tranquillity, Hell or whatever (although obviously experienced in a way unique to each particular individual). According to the principle of *ichinen sanzen*, this is only possible because these material objects – oil paints and canvas – also possess a spiritual nature which can be revealed when the circumstances are right: that is, when an artist uses them to express his own spirit.

This is what Nichiren Daishonin means when he says in the passage quoted above: 'If a piece of wood or paper did not have both a material and spiritual aspect, or lacked the inherent cause to manifest a spiritual nature, then it would be futile to rely upon it as an object of worship.' A painting is not 'an object of worship' (though great works of art can almost fulfil this role for some people), but the principle is exactly the same. Analyzed in terms of the Ten Factors, Van Gogh's painting, 'Sunflowers', obviously possesses 'appearance', but it also has 'nature' or spirit, because both are expressions of the 'entity' of the picture, an entity which perfectly matches the entity of the life state of Van Gogh when he painted it. The 'power' of the picture becomes 'influence' when it is activated, as it were, by the 'external cause' of someone looking at it. The 'inherent cause' is the totality of all the acts Van Gogh made to produce the painting, including those which he made before he first put brush to canvas, the 'manifest effect' is the reaction it produces in the person who sees it, and the 'latent effect' can be judged by the fact that the painting continues to grow in fame and value; finally, these nine factors are all quite clearly 'consistent from beginning to end'.

It is no great leap to apply this principle to inanimate objects on a larger scale, for example, to architecture. Buildings can make people feel happy or miserable because they too possess the Ten Worlds and, through the workings of the Ten Factors, naturally must reflect the life state of the architects and planners who are responsible for them. Thus, if these men and women regard people merely as 'units' to be housed, they will design and build accordingly, and the people who then live in those houses will inevitably sense that they have somehow been dehumanized. Consequently, they will feel oppressed and depressed by their surroundings and may even feel the urge to vandalize them or cover them with graffiti. Indeed, it is possible to interpret even these acts as attempts to humanize the environment, as they can at least be considered signs of a human presence, albeit a negative one. Good architecture has the opposite effect, of course, and reflects a sensitivity to the need of people to feel 'spiritually' comfortable within their environment, just as much as they need to be physically comfortable.

Finally, that this principle also applies to the natural environment is clear from the everyday experience of many ordinary people, encapsulated in the words of such great poets as William Wordsworth:

> My heart leaps up when I behold
> A rainbow in the sky

We are moved by nature not simply because we are emotional creatures but because the natural world also possesses the Ten Worlds, revealed to us when we are in the right life state. Yasuji Kirimura explains:

> When a sentient being attains Buddhahood, the same state of life is simultaneously manifested by its surroundings, bringing out Buddhahood from within insentient beings in accordance with the principle of the oneness of life and its environment. For example, when a sentient being who has attained Buddhahood sees a mountain, the mountain appears as the entity of Buddhahood. However, when another sentient being in the world of Hunger sees the same mountain, it appears to him as the entity of Hunger.

One is reminded here of Thomas Hardy's poem, 'Alike and Unlike', discussed earlier, and, indeed, one of Wordsworth's most famous works, 'Intimations of Immortality from Recollections of Early Childhood', also deals with the relationship between the natural world and his changing vision of it. Here is just the first verse:

> There was a time when meadow, grove, and stream,
> The earth, and every common sight,
> To me did seem
> Apparelled in celestial light,
> The glory and the freshness of a dream.
> It is not now as it hath been of yore;-
> Turn wheresoe'er I may,
> By night or day
> The things which I have seen I now can see no more.

Analyzed in terms of the mutual possession of the Ten Worlds, Wordsworth's predominant state, Realization, has moved from Rapture, when everything seemed bathed 'in celestial light'; to Hell, as he mourns the passing of this Rapture, interpreted as the loss of 'vision'; until, by the end of the poem, he seems to be approaching a sense of his own Buddhahood:

> Thanks to the human heart by which we live,
> Thanks to its tenderness, its joys, and fears,
> To me the meanest flower that blows can give
> Thoughts that do often lie too deep for tears.

If 'the meanest flower that blows' can act as the external cause to prompt these profound thoughts in Wordsworth, it must inherently possess the quality to do so; or, to put it another way, for Wordsworth to be able to perceive whatever quality he sees in that flower, the flower must be capable of displaying it. In short, for Wordsworth's natural environment – the meadows, groves and streams of the Lake District – to be capable of matching every changing nuance of Wordsworth's life state, it too must possess the hundred worlds and Ten Factors.

So, when Nichiren Daishonin says that 'if the minds of the people are impure, their land is also impure, but if their minds are pure, so is their land. There are not two lands, pure or impure in themselves. The difference lies solely in the good or evil of our minds,' he is not simply making a statement that applies to pollution of the natural environment, or how we physically alter our surroundings to suit our changing life states. Rather, he is referring to the indissoluble bond between the living and the non-living aspects of the world in the very depths of life, first clarified by T'ien-t'ai's theory of *ichinen sanzen*. This is a very important point to remember when we come to discuss the object of worship, the Gohonzon, and examine Nichiren Daishonin's attitude to other religions and philosophies, particularly with regard to the principle of the Three Calamities and Seven Disasters as explained in his *Rissho Ankoku Ron* (see Chapter 6).

Given the extreme difficulties posed by some aspects of *ichinen sanzen*, 'clarified' may not be exactly the right word to use here. Even if the general sense of what has been said is clear, the breadth and depth of *ichinen sanzen* is impossible to grasp with the intellect alone. If we are confined to the world of Hell, for example, our conscious experience of life will be a fraction of the three thousand worlds, and even in the higher life states we may not consciously experience many more. To all intents and purpose, then, for all people of the nine worlds from Hell to Bodhisattva, *ichinen sanzen* is pure theory. To be truly enlightened – that is, to understand the totality of *ichinen sanzen* with our lives rather than our heads – we must be able to experience the 'three thousand worlds in a moment of life'. In other words, T'ien-t'ai's philosophical theory has to be translated into action, in a way open to ordinary men and women who have families, work and a myriad other aspects of daily life to which to attend. It was Nichiren Daishonin's great realization that it is precisely in this context that *nam*, the word mentioned at the beginning of this chapter, at last reveals its full significance.

NAM

The concept of *nam* is so important because the deepest meaning of this word encapsulates both the action we need to take, and the attitude we need to develop, if we are to attain Buddahood in this lifetime. In other words, *nam* might be said to indicate how to practise the Law revealed in the Lotus Sutra and analyzed by T'ien-t'ai in terms of *ichinen sanzen*, three thousand realms in a moment of existence.

In this light, it is worth re-examining a passage from Nichiren Daishonin's writings which we encountered at the beginning of this chapter: 'People place the word *nam* before the name of all deities and Buddhas in worshipping them. But what is the meaning of *nam*? This word comes from Sanskrit and means to devote one's life. Ultimately, it means to offer our lives to the Buddha.' At first glance, this would seem to suggest that we have to be prepared to sacrifice ourselves, either literally or figuratively, to receive any benefit from the practice of Buddhism. Once again, however, the problem of truly understanding this concept lies in language for, as we shall see a little later, the English word 'devotion' cannot adequately convey the profundity inherent in *nam*. Indeed, in the passage quoted above, the phrase 'and means to devote one's life' is a rendering of the more difficult 'and is translated as *kuei-ming* in Chinese and *kimyo* in Japanese'. To understand *nam* more fully, therefore, it might be helpful to look at how this Sanskrit word is expressed in Japanese.

Kimyo is a word made up of two separate characters, as Nichiren Daishonin explains: 'In the phrase "to dedicate (*ki*) one's life (*myo*)", *ki* indicates the physical aspect of life, and *myo* the spiritual aspect.' From this passage we can see that, in practical terms, *ki* might be said to refer to 'action', and *myo* (a different *myo* from that of *myoho*) to the 'spirit' or 'attitude' underlying it. From this single word, *kimyo*, we can therefore draw a number of important conclusions with regard to the practice of Buddhism.

Firstly, in terms of 'action', there is the necessity of practising Buddhism exactly as the Buddha teaches. In a famous letter to a follower, a samurai called Niike Saemon-no-jo, Nichiren Daishonin says, 'Faith in this sutra means that you will surely attain Buddhahood if you are true to the entirety of the Lotus Sutra, adhering exactly to its teachings without adding any of your own ideas or following the arbitrary interpretations of others.' This may sound rather strict, restrictive or even intolerant, used as we are in the West to arguing freely and openly and then coming to our own conclusions about the more abstract and debatable aspects of life, but it is entirely reasonable. If you want to learn how to drive a car, for example, you could get together with others who cannot drive, argue about what one has to do, and then, on the basis of what you have decided, get behind the wheel. Of course, you will probably have an accident as a result. You are much more likely, however, to ask someone who can already drive to teach you. What is more, when you are learning you will naturally follow your instructor's directions to the best of your ability. If you are told that to drive a car you need to use the steering-wheel, clutch, brake, accelerator and gears, it would be absurd to decide that, just to be original, you will never use the steering-wheel, say, or the brake only when you feel like it. In other words, the Buddha is in the position of the driving-instructor and, being already enlightened, teaches those who want to attain the same life-condition exactly how they can do so, always keeping their ultimate happiness in the front of his mind.

This is not to say that the Buddha cannot be questioned or challenged. Indeed, virtually all the sutras taught by Shakyamuni arose out of questions that were put to him and, in the very same letter to Niike, Nichiren Daishonin says, 'Have the priest who is my messenger read this letter to you. Trust him as a priest with enlightened wisdom and ask him any questions you may have about Buddhism. If you do not question and resolve your doubts, you cannot dispel the dark clouds of illusion, any more than you could travel a thousand miles without legs. Have him read this letter again and again and ask whatever questions you wish.' Once again, though, the attitude of the questioner is of paramount importance. Someone whose questions arise from a sincere desire to understand is much more likely to comprehend the answer than a person who questions with the aim of denigrating Buddhism or showing off his or her supposed superiority.

Not only must we practise – that is, take action – exactly as the Buddha teaches, but *kimyo* implies that we must also gradually cultivate the same attitude as the Buddha. This does not mean that, as Buddhists, we should all share the same opinions, but that our basic attitude to our lives – and the lives of others – should be one of the deepest respect and compassion. This is probably one of the hardest aspects of practising this Buddhism. As Nichiren Daishonin points out time and time again in his writings, however, we can gain little in terms of elevating our life state, accumulating benefit and establishing unshakeable happiness, if our actions are not matched, or are even contradicted, by the spirit with which we perform them. For example, in a reply to a letter from another of his followers, Nichiren Daishonin says, 'There is a difference if one chants the *daimoku* [*Nam-myoho-renge-kyo*] while acting against the intent of this sutra [the Lotus]. There are many forms of slander that go against the correct practice of this sutra.' He then lists the Fourteen Slanders – arrogance; negligence; arbitrary, egotistical judgement; shallow, self-satisfied understanding; attachment to earthly desires; lack of seeking spirit; not believing [the Buddha's teachings]; aversion; deluded doubt; vilification; contempt; hatred; jealousy and grudges – and comments, 'Since these Fourteen Slanders apply equally to priesthood and laity, you must be on your guard against them.'

While the Fourteen Slanders point out the ways in which we can undermine any action we might take to create value, a sentence from the Lotus Sutra sums up the attitude we should adopt if we want automatically to avoid committing any of these slanders: 'Single-mindedly yearning to see the Buddha, they do not begrudge their lives.' This sentence, which might be said to express perfectly the spirit of *nam*, or *kimyo*, can be interpreted on a number of different levels.

In one sense it means that you can only attain Buddhahood by practising for the whole of your life: indeed, no one who is truly enlightened would ever consider giving up the practice, any more than a hungry man would consider giving up food just because when he eats he loses his hunger for a time. As Nichiren Daishonin says, 'To accept is easy; to continue is difficult. But Buddhahood lies in continuing faith.' In other words, enlightenment is not a goal you reach and then stop, but a condition of life which demands continuous effort to sustain. In a way, the relationship of enlightenment to the continuing practice of Buddhism is rather like riding a bicycle. The balance is possible by virtue of the forward motion, which means you can stay on only for as long as you keep turning the pedals. If you stop, you may keep going for a while, thanks to the momentum you have already built up, but eventually you will fall off. Similarly, if you stop practising Buddhism you will not be able to manifest your Buddha nature. It follows from this that, in another sense, this sentence from the Lotus Sutra means that, in order to see the Buddha – that is, your own Buddha nature – you must not begrudge making the necessary, life-long effort. This might sound like an unbelievably demanding austerity until you remember that one of the many benefits of the practice is an enormous increase in life-force which, in itself, enables you to keep going, just as physical exercise makes you fitter and thus able to do more.

On a deeper level, this sentence implies that you can only see your own Buddha nature as you begin to perceive the truth of cause and effect. In personal terms this means seeing your own karma, accepting that you have made all the causes for your life as it is at this moment, and that it is therefore useless blaming other people or external factors for those aspects that cause you unhappiness. If you decide not to begrudge the reality of your life but take full responsibility for it in this way, you can choose to use those very sufferings to reveal your Buddha nature by chanting *Nam-myoho-renge-kyo* to overcome them, no matter what your situation.

This fundamental change of attitude can be seen in the experience of Satoru Izumi, outlined in the preface to his book, *Guidelines of Faith*: 'I took faith in Nichiren Shoshu when I was twenty-nine. At that time I was in the depths of misery. I used to think there was nobody in the world more unhappy than me.' Satoru's mother had died when he was three and, to avoid complicated family ructions, he was raised by his grandparents. 'My grandfather was a very good-natured man. He had acted as a guarantor for some of his friends, and when he died he left behind a huge debt. All the family property changed hands. I was only twenty years old then.'

Being his grandparents' heir, naturally enough Satoru had difficulty coping with this sudden loss. 'I resented everyone and everything in the world,' he says. 'Why did I have to suffer such misfortune? People said that good deeds are rewarded and evil deeds are punished, but I couldn't believe it. My grandfather had lived honestly and worked hard since his youth. For generations my family had served as chief parishioners, both for the Buddhist temple and the Shinto shrine in the village. My grandfather, too, had done everything he could for the temple, for the shrine, for the village, the school and so on.' But all this had seemed only to have led to the ruin of the family. Bitterly, Satoru concluded that there were no gods – and no Buddhas either – and developed a deep cynicism about religion in general. He explains: 'Every Buddhist or Shinto priest I met said that his was the best religion in the world. To me they all seemed to be seeking only their own interests. How could there be so many "best" religions? I gradually came to believe that the only thing I could rely on in this life was my own effort. I was later to learn that this itself was an erroneous conclusion, a reaction to the false religions of my family, but I had no way of knowing this at the time. "From today on," I told myself, "I'll save money every day, no matter how little, and depend on no one but myself." Thus I entered a new period in life.'

In due course he married and his wife bore him a son. 'I was overjoyed,' he says, 'but my joy was shortlived, for our son died four days later. Earlier I had lost my mother and now I had lost my child. Why so much misery? I kept asking myself this question. Then the following year my wife fell ill and had to be hospitalized. There went all my hard-earned money. My misfortunes would not cease.' Worse was to follow, as the Izumis' first daughter, born in the year that followed, turned out to have cerebral palsy. Satoru plumbed new depths of unhappiness, even briefly considering killing his child to put her – and him – out of their misery.

A friend had told him about Nichiren Shoshu some time before but, despite his various misfortunes, Satoru had shrugged him off, having by now developed a strongly fatalistic attitude to life. As he explains, however, his crippled daughter radically altered his way of thinking: 'I could no longer say, "What will be will be," or "Don't bother. Let things go their own way." I had a child with a disease which the doctor had pronounced incurable. I would try everything – anything – which people suggested might help, I decided. Then, even if my daughter were to die, I could say to her, "I've done everything a parent could, I've made sure you've had all the medical care available, I've tried whatever people said might help for your illness. There is nothing more I can do for you. Please resign yourself to your fate." '

His friend kept talking to him about Nichiren Daishonin's Buddhism and Satoru started to consider it in this new light: 'What if I rejected that religion and my daughter died? Wouldn't I regret it for the rest of my life, thinking, "I wish I had taken faith in it. She might have been cured"? I must be free of regret when I die. All right, I decided, I would take faith in Nichiren Shoshu for the sake of my poor child.

'Nichiren Shoshu is the true Buddhism of Nichiren Daishonin. At first I had no idea why it was "true", but I didn't care as long as it was powerful enough to cure my child's illness. Now, as I look back, I realize that had it not been for my paralyzed daughter, I would not be what I am today. To me she was what Buddhism terms a "good influence".' A 'good influence' or a 'good friend' in Buddhism is anyone or anything which enables you to meet *Nam-myoho-renge-kyo*, or deepen your faith in it and thus attain enlightenment. As Satoru explains, a 'good influence' can at first sight often appear the worst possible disaster: 'The direct cause for my conversion was my ailing daughter. Viewed from a broader perspective, however, there were other factors, too. My mother died when I was three. When I was twenty, my grandfather died, leaving a huge debt. All our property changed hands. My son died four days after birth. Then my daughter was born, handicapped by an incurable disease. All these misfortunes, I think, combined to make me take faith in true Buddhism. I'm convinced that all of them – my mother, my grandfather, my son, my daughter – appeared in this world in order to lead me to the Gohonzon.'

Looking back from the viewpoint of over forty-five years of practice, Satoru Izumi is able to say with some authority, 'As long as you maintain an indestructable faith, you will never fail to transform adversity into happiness, just like poison changed into medicine.' This is the attitude of 'Single-mindedly yearning to see the Buddha, they do not begrudge their lives.' Indeed, it would not be too much to say that only with such an attitude can one ever hope to overcome all the hardships life can throw at you and thus attain Buddhahood. As Nichiren Daishonin says, 'I, Nichiren, have called forth Buddhahood from within my life by living this sentence.'

In this sense, not to begrudge your life essentially means that, by giving everything to the practice of Buddhism, through the law of cause and effect you quite naturally gain everything. But what exactly is the 'everything' you give and gain? Quite simply, what you give is that which is most precious to you – your life itself – and what you gain in return is the immeasurable treasure of enlightenement, both in this lifetime and throughout eternity. Of course, it is extremely difficult to understand that it is possible to 'give your life' and yet make no sacrifice. Nichiren Daishonin explains:

Some may have wives, children, retainers, estates, gold, silver or other treasures according to their status. Others have nothing at all. Yet, whether one has wealth or not, life is still the most precious of treasures. This is why the saints and sages of ancient times offered their lives to the Buddha, and were themselves able to attain Buddhahood . . .

Yet even common mortals can attain Buddhahood if they cherish one thing: earnest faith. In the deepest sense, earnest faith is the will to understand and live up to the spirit, not the words, of the sutras . . .

Therefore, saints consecrated themselves by offering their own bodies, whereas common mortals may consecrate themselves by the sincerity with which they give. The precept of donation expounded in the seventh volume of the *Maka Shikan* in effect teaches the spirit of offering.

It is very clear from this passage that it is the attitude underlying our actions – in short, living moment by moment with a wholehearted 'spirit of offering' – which fundamentally creates benefit in our lives; a point perhaps worth bearing in mind whether one practises Buddhism or not.

This brings us to another important implication of *kimyo*, namely, that although there are specifically religious practices involved in Nichiren Daishonin's Buddhism – particularly chanting *Nam-myoho-renge-kyo* and performing *gongyo* twice daily before the Gohonzon – it is impossible to draw any rigid distinction between the practice of Buddhism and daily life. This is borne out by the practice in our own homes, within our daily routine and in the midst of our daily reality. In other words, *kimyo* means that, in the final analysis, Buddhist practice only has any meaning as it improves every aspect of our everyday lives and that, in turn, our everyday lives become a perfect reflection of our attitude to the practice. For example, the benefits we receive from our practice, like greater wisdom and increased life-force, naturally affect all areas of our life and work while, if we begrudge making the effort to chant, it is highly likely that we begrudge making any effort for which we cannot see an immediate, short-term reward.

This complete identification of a religion with every aspect of daily life is a concept that is now uncommon in the West, except insofar as religious morality or commandments have attempted to regulate the behaviour of individuals, usually as a means to achieve social harmony. While it is true that there are still certain groups of Christians for whom prayer and worship are highly prominent – in monasteries, for example – or who consciously try to 'live' the Gospels in their daily lives, most ordinary people generally draw a distinction between the religious and secular aspects of life. Although often somewhat blurred, this distinction perhaps finds its clearest expression in Jesus Christ's admonition for Christians to 'Render unto Caesar that which is Caesar's, and unto God that which is God's.' Thus, although the moral code by which the vast majority of people live in the West is founded on Christian ethics, many fewer apply Christianity assiduously to all facets of daily life, and fewer still in the pure, anti-materialistic spirit of its founder.

This distinction between the religious and secular aspects of life can also be seen in the word 'devotion', which is why it cannot convey the true meaning of *nam* or *kimyo*. In one sense, 'devotion' refers to the act of consciously worshipping something, and so is primarily spiritual or religious; in another, it refers to the attitude of wholehearted dedication to something, which can have either religious or non-religious connotations. As a Christian, one can therefore be devoted to God in both the former and the latter senses, but one can be devoted to one's wife, husband, family, work – even one's garden or car – only in the sense of being dedicated. Indeed, in Christianity the worship of any 'graven image' is specifically forbidden. In other words, although religion and daily life overlap in many areas, because Christianity draws a fundamental distinction between humanity and divinity, they can also come into sharp conflict: witness the Catholic Church's attitude to birth control, for example, or the argument in the Protestant Church about the changing role of women, especially with regard to their ordination. In short, Christian purists would like daily life to be subordinate to religion, while others feel that religion should serve daily life, even if that means interpreting religion more liberally than the purists would like.

By contrast, we have seen that the highest Buddhist teachings state that, fundamentally, there is no distinction between the spiritual and physical apsects of life. In other words, because the Lotus Sutra teaches that the essential reality of life is in no way

different from all the infinite ways in which life expresses itself, to
'devote oneself to the Lotus Sutra', the literal meaning of *Nam-
myoho-renge-kyo*, does not mean to devote oneself just to the
practice of Buddhism, but rather to life as a whole. Nichiren
Daishonin puts this succinctly in a letter to one of his closest
followers, in which he compares the superiority of the Lotus Sutra
over previous teachings: 'In contrast, the sixth volume of the
Lotus Sutra reads, "No affairs of life or work are in any way
different from the ultimate reality" . . . whereas [other sutras]
relate secular matters in terms of Buddhism, the Lotus Sutra
explains that secular matters ultimately are Buddhism.'

In Nichiren Daishonin's Buddhism, then, the profound meaning of *nam* is once again an expression of the Middle Way,
encompassing and transcending both the religious and secular
aspects of 'devotion'. It means that to chant *Nam-myoho-renge-kyo*,
the religious aspect of the practice of Buddhism, is to worship and
express gratitude for the entirety of universal life; it also means
that, in its highest condition, Buddhahood, all the actions that
makes up one's entire life have as their underlying motive the
creation of happiness for oneself and for others, and are thus also
dedicated to life as a whole. Indeed, Nichiren Daishonin teaches
that, in its deepest sense, *nam* or *kimyo* means to fuse our lives with
the eternal, immutable truth of *Myoho-renge-kyo* and, through this
fusion with the ultimate, universal truth, simultaneously draw
from within ourselves inexhaustible wisdom in response to the
ever-changing circumstances of our daily lives.

But how do we do this? The simple answer is by sincerely
praying – that is, chanting *Nam-myoho-renge-kyo* – to the
Gohonzon. Daisaku Ikeda explains:

> Nichiren Daishonin, the Buddha of the Latter Day of the Law,
> embodied the fundamental Law of the universe in the form of a
> scroll or mandala. In one's prayer to that mandala, the act
> through which devotion takes place, the external cosmos and the
> inner realm of the mind are perfectly fused, enabling one to
> establish a correct rhythm in the course of life and daily existence.

By now, you will probably have some understanding of the
incomparable depth of meaning contained in the phrase *Nam-*

myoho-renge-kyo. In the light of this passage, though, it is clear that the Gohonzon, the true object of worship to reveal our Buddha-hood, plays a central role in the practice of Nichiren Daishonin's Buddhism. This will be discussed in the following chapter.

Part Two
Buddhism in Daily Life

'The true path of life lies in the affairs of this world.'
Nichiren Daishonin

3

The Gohonzon

The Gohonzon is the prime point of faith, practice and study in Nichiren Shoshu Buddhism. Before we discuss the Gohonzon in any detail, it might be well to remind ourselves of the basic aim of all Buddhist teachings, that is, to lead all people to the understanding that they inherently possess Buddhahood, the highest condition of life, and that by developing their Buddhahood they can establish a life of indestructible happiness, charged with wisdom, courage, compassion and life-force. All Buddhas appear in order to teach people this truth. Even though the truth remains the same, however, exactly how it is taught varies from Buddha to Buddha and from age to age. For example, Shakyamuni led many different kinds of people towards enlightenment during his life, in many different ways, through pre-Lotus Sutra teachings which were suitable for that age. Just before he died he taught the Lotus Sutra which expounded, for the first time, his own complete experience of enlightenment. The Lotus Sutra also dealt with the transmission of the essence of the true teachings, not only to this age in which we all now live (which he named the Latter Day of the Law), but 'for ten thousand years and more into eternity'. T'ien-t'ai, on the other hand, aware that when he lived the Latter Day of the Law had not yet begun, taught his enlightenment through the doctrine of *ichinen sanzen*.

At the heart of Nichiren Daishonin's Buddhism lie what are known as the Three Great Secret Laws. They are called 'secret' for three reasons: firstly, because they are 'hidden' within and 'between the lines of' the *Juryo* (sixteenth) chapter of the Lotus Sutra; secondly, because they cannot be understood by the intellect alone and are therefore beyond the grasp of ordinary people; and thirdly, because they were not revealed by any Buddha who lived before Nichiren Daishonin. This is not to say that Buddhas such as Shakyamuni and T'ien-t'ai were not aware of the Three Great Secret Laws: they were, and referred to them – albeit obliquely – in many places in their various teachings. They were also well aware that it was not yet time for them to be revealed – that is, during the Latter Day of the Law which would start some 2000 years after the death of Shakyamuni. Thus, until Nichiren Daishonin appeared in thirteenth-century Japan, no Buddha had considered the time to be right for the Three Great Secret Laws to be revealed. Although the significance of these Three Great Secret Laws is not easy to appreciate at first, together they comprise the supreme apex of Buddhist teachings. This is something which gradually becomes clearer as one continues to practise and so experiences their workings within one's own life and circumstances.

The Three Great Secret Laws are the *invocation*, the chanting of *Nam-myoho-renge-kyo*; the *object of worship*, the Gohonzon; and the *sanctuary*, the place where the object of worship is enshrined. Nichiren Daishonin established the invocation on 28 April 1253 when he chanted *Nam-myoho-renge-kyo* for the first time, and the object of worship on 12 October 1279 when he inscribed the Dai-Gohonzon (*Dai* in this context meaning 'great' or 'original'). He entrusted the establishment of the high sanctuary to his followers, 'when the time is right'. This was fully achieved only as recently as 12 October 1972, when the Dai-Gohonzon was enshrined in a great building known as the Sho-Hondo, found at Taiseki-ji, the head temple of Nichiren Shoshu Buddhism, located, in accordance with Nichiren Daishonin's wishes, at the foot of Mount Fuji in Japan.

As it is obviously impractical for all Nichiren Shoshu Buddhists to practise regularly to the Dai-Gohonzon, successive high priests of Nichiren Shoshu are charged with the responsibility of inscribing smaller replicas of it, which are then available to all those who are prepared to make the commitment to protect and practise to their own, individual Gohonzon for the rest of their lives. In this, the successive high priests are following the instructions and example of Nichiren Daishonin who inscribed Gohonzons for those of his followers with strong faith, both before and after inscribing the Dai-Gohonzon. Nowadays, these individual Gohonzons take the form of a scroll of rice paper which is inscribed by the high priest and then printed under the supervision of Nichiren Shoshu priests by means of a woodblock process, again onto rice-paper scrolls. The Gohonzon we each receive is then enshrined in our own home in a special cabinet called a *butsudan* (literally, 'place of the Buddha'). Thus, as far as our own, individual Gohonzon is concerned, our home becomes the sanctuary, the place where we practise true Buddhism.

So far in this book we have concentrated our attention on *Nam-myoho-renge-kyo*, the invocation or *daimoku* of Nichiren Shoshu Buddhism. Since *Nam-myoho-renge-kyo* is directed to the object of worship and the sanctuary is built to enshrine it, however, the object of worship actually encompasses all Three Great Secret Laws; thus the Gohonzon is also called the One Great Secret Law. In the final analysis, then, all Buddhist teachings are expounded to explain the eventual revelation of the Gohonzon; all study of those teachings untimately leads to an understanding of the Gohonzon; and to have faith in the Gohonzon – that is, to practise to it – for the whole of one's life, is to attain enlightment. The Gohonzon is therefore the single most important object in Nichiren Shoshu Buddhism.

Objects of Worship

So what is the Gohonzon and how does it merit the great importance that Nichiren Shoshu Buddhism places on it? The Gohonzon can be explained in a variety of ways – what it looks like, what it represents, what it does and so on – and in his different writings Nichiren Daishonin employs all these approaches to convey to his followers the Gohonzon's deep significance. Let us start with the word itself: Gohonzon. *Honzon* literally means 'object of fundamental respect', and *go* means 'worthy of honour'. Together they signify that the Gohonzon is the true object of worship.

There are a number of implications in this title which some people living in the West might find difficult to accept. For a start, brought up as we are in a predominantly Christian tradition (even if we do not practise Christianity ourselves), the idea of worshipping any object might seem alien or even suspect. After all, not only do the Ten Commandments specifically forbid the setting up and worship of graven – that is, carved – images, but in this scientific age there may appear to be something rather primitive in the act of investing inanimate objects with a power science cannot confirm they possess.

Nichiren Daishonin realized, however, that it is an ingrained trait in all people to desire an 'object of worship', or something to which they can devote themselves, and that if they do not already have such an object they will feel compelled to make one up for themselves. This can clearly be seen in various religions. For example, a Catholic Church usually contains statues and paintings of Christ, the Virgin Mary and a whole host of saints, which express a deep-seated desire in ordinary people to have a physical object upon which they can focus their reverence. The Protestant wing of Christianity, while more visually austere than its Catholic counterpart, still allows the Cross to be worshipped as a central symbol of Christ's suffering and sacrifice; and even many earlier forms of Buddhism, based on the pre-Lotus Sutra teachings, have as their object of worship statues of Shakyamuni Buddha – sitting, lying or standing – despite his express injunction to worship the Law and not his person.

This desire for an object of worship does not hold good just for religion for, whether one is consciously aware of it or not, everyone in everyday life also has an 'object of worship' or devotion. Its form may be more diverse or more abstract, but it fulfils exactly the same function as an object of worship in religion: that of providing a central focus upon which people can concentrate their desires, hopes, ambitions – in short, their lives. Thus, for many people their husband, wife or family can be their fundamental object of devotion, the thing they value above all else; for others it can be money or career, possessions, intellect, a boy or girlfriend, pop or film stars, even pets. In other words, an 'object of devotion' in everyday life is that thing for which each person truly lives, upon which, therefore, they base their happiness and which has a profound effect on every aspect of their daily lives. Often, we do not realize what our own personal 'object of devotion' is until we lose it: when our partner suddenly leaves us, for example, or our car is stolen, a sparkling career falters and so on. At that moment, and though we may not think of it in these terms, we are also painfully aware of the extent to which we have made our happiness reliant on something external to ourselves.

Of course, no one can exist in isolation and Nichiren Shoshu Buddhism does not teach the severing of attachments as a path to happiness but, by recognizing the natural, human need for an object of devotion, in inscribing the Dai-Gohonzon Nichiren Daishonin provided the 'true' object of worship which puts all our other desires into their correct perspective. To call any object of worship 'true' may sound somewhat dogmatic, but this is based simply on the effect that chanting to the Gohonzon has on our lives, enabling us to begin to experience real, solid and dynamic happiness, perhaps for the first time. In other words, the Gohonzon is called the *true* object of worship because it is able to reorientate the lives and give happiness to *all* people.

This is because, unlike secular objects of devotion, the Gohonzon remains constant and absolute both in appearance and meaning, is utterly pure and utterly reliable and, because it embodies such profound principles, is capable of providing life-long support and sustenance. Explaining this point to a female disciple of his, Nichiren Daishonin says:

> A woman who devotes herself to this Gohonzon invites happiness in this life; and in the next, the Gohonzon will be with her and protect her always. Like a lantern in the dark, like a strong supporting arm on a treacherous path, the Gohonzon will protect you, Lady Nichinyo, wherever you go.

Great as the Gohonzon is, it is also vital to understand that it is not a god, nor any form of external force which grants wishes like a genie, but is simply an object which draws out from deep within us qualities – namely, the Buddha nature – that we already inherently possess. Nichiren Daishonin is absolutely clear on this point, as when he says, 'Never seek this Gohonzon outside yourself. The Gohonzon exists only within the mortal flesh of us ordinary people who embrace the Lotus Sutra and chant *Nam-myoho-renge-kyo*.' Thus, like a mirror, the Gohonzon which Nichiren Daishonin first inscribed reflects the Buddahood within us.

In this context, it is also important to realize that the way in which one reacts to any object of devotion – if it is made by a human being – depends not just on what it is supposed to represent but also on the state of life of the person who created it. A golden statue of Shakyamuni Buddha, for example, could reflect the state of Hunger, the desire for material wealth in the person making it, while a statue of Christ on the Cross might well reflect the anguish and guilt, the state of Hell, subconsciously experienced by the sculptor. In worshipping these objects, then, one could be unknowingly strengthening in oneself a tendency towards one of the lower conditions of life, despite the sincere effort one may be making to appreciate, say, the Buddha's wisdom or Christ's compassion. In contrast, the Gohonzon was inscribed by Nichiren Daishonin himself, desiring nothing other than the happiness of all human beings, and therefore reflects *his* life state. Consequently, it gradually strengthens in all those who continue to chant to it the tendency towards the highest state of life, Buddahood. This is a subject to which we shall return shortly.

As Daisaku Ikeda points out, however, suspicion towards religious objects of worship is not unjustified:

> All religions have objects of worship which are usually expressions of some supernatural or external power governing life and human destiny. People have a subservient attitude in prayer when asking for salvation, forgiveness and compassion or, in some cases, try by subservience to satisfy those powers and avoid their wrath. Such attitudes have contributed to creating the special position of the clergy as intermediaries between man and his object of worship. The pursuit of external objects, symbolizing the supernatural, inevitably leads to the formation of a strict hierarchy in the religious world.

It is important to note here that each person who receives the Gohonzon is able to practise to it directly, without the need for any intermediaries. Thus, the main function of the priests in Nichiren Shoshu is to ensure that the original purity of Nichiren Daishonin's teachings is not distorted by arbitrary or shallow interpretation, thus guarding the Three Treasures of the Law: *Nam-myoho-renge-kyo* of the Three Great Secret Laws, the Buddha (Nichiren Daishonin) and the Priest (specifically, the second High Priest, Nikko Shonin, who ensured the transmission of the Law into the future after Nichiren Daishonin's death).

Similarly, while the various lay organizations of Nichiren Shoshu Buddhism, which together comprise the Soka Gakkai International, exist to help each member gain the greatest benefit from their practice of this Buddhism, in the end it is each person's individual struggle in front of their own Gohonzon which leads to their enlightenment. As Daisaku Ikeda notes:

> Essentially, man acquires power through his own training. Machines, facilities and advice from others are all only external aids which help him develop his potential. A world record in sports is made with the help of excellent facilities, scientific research and well-trained experienced coaches. But the athlete himself has to achieve the record. This is much more true in faith.

Kanjin

A phrase Nichiren Daishonin uses to describe the Gohonzon is *kanjin no honzon*, meaning the 'object of worship for observing one's mind (or life)'. T'ien-t'ai had taught a kind of meditation as a means of 'observing one's mind and finding the Ten Worlds within it', but it was extremely difficult and time-consuming and thus limited to a very few practitioners. The Gohonzon, on the other hand, being itself the physical embodiment of the state of Buddhahood, enables us to 'find the Ten Worlds' within our own lives simply by chanting to it. In other words, just as a mirror can show us that we look like physically, so the Gohonzon is a mirror which enables us to 'see' our lives in terms of the Ten Worlds. In this way we can open up those areas of our lives that have formerly been hidden to us: the way we think, for example, what our true values are (as opposed to those we think we live by), what we most want from life and, perhaps, what we most fear.

When we first start chanting to the Gohonzon what has, until then, been obscure to us may very well be those karmic tendencies which cause us to suffer, and so we will probably determine that these are what we must change if we are to become happy. Fundamentally, though, *kanjin* means to see in the clear mirror of the Gohonzon that our true nature is nothing other than Buddhahood. Thus, from one viewpoint, the Gohonzon is the object which Nichiren Daishonin gave to show us ordinary men and women that we are Buddhas and that, in the deepest sense, happiness consists of becoming totally convinced of this. From another viewpoint, however, it is also the means by which we can become convinced of our Buddha nature and begin to act on that conviction. In other words, just as a pianist needs a piano first to realize he possesses a talent to play it and then to develop that talent further, so we need the 'instrument' of the Gohonzon to first see and then develop our own innate Buddhahood. So, whereas the Lotus Sutra states that one can attain enlightenment not through the intellect, but only through faith, Nichiren Daishonin reveals that, ultimately, 'faith' means 'embracing the Gohonzon' – that is, determining to practise to it exactly as he taught for the whole of one's life. Thus 'faith', 'embracing the Gohonzon' and becoming enlightened to the Mystic Law, are all one and the same thing.

Indeed, were it not for the 'mirror' of the Gohonzon it would be impossible for us living in this age to change our karma and attain Buddhahood. This is because, although chanting *Nam-myoho-renge-kyo* by itself creates good fortune in the form of conspicuous benefit, unless we can first see that there are fundamental karmic tendencies within ourselves which cause us to suffer, we will never summon up the desire to challenge and change them. For example, chanting *Nam-myoho-renge-kyo* by itself may bring you a wonderful partner, but if you still have a very jealous nature, say, it is likely that your new relationship will quickly sour and you will lose him or her. In this ever-changing world, it is only by being able to refer constantly to the unchanging state of Buddhahood embodied in the Gohonzon that we can draw forth our own Buddhahood, again and again, to reflect on the deep, underlying causes of our actions. In this way, through our repeated chanting to the Gohonzon, we gradually make Buddhahood the dominant karmic tendency in our lives, just as a nail repeatedly brought into contact with a magnet will itself become magnetized. Hence, as Nichiren Daishonin states in the *Rissho Ankoku Ron*: 'You have transformed yourself through your association with me and, like the bramble growing in the hemp field, you have learned to stand up straight!'

The Oneness of the Person and the Law

How is it possible for the Gohonzon to work in this way? The lines just quoted from the *Rissho Ankoku Ron* give us a clue for, as already mentioned, the Gohonzon not only embodies the Law of *Nam-myoho-renge-kyo*, but also the life of Nichiren Daishonin. He says elsewhere, 'I, Nichiren, have inscribed my life in *sumi*,* so believe in this Gohonzon with your whole heart.' This might sound a little strange until we remember the example of Van Gogh discussed in the previous chapter. Just as Van Gogh expressed his life state in the form of the pictures he painted, which act as the external cause, when we look at them, to call up the same life state from ourselves, so Nichiren Daishonin expressed his life state of Buddhahood in the form of the Gohonzon, the external cause to call up our own Buddhahood when we chant to it, whether our conscious mind is aware of it or not. Indeed, when we begin to practise we cannot possibly understand this Gohonzon intellectually, any more than we can read at birth. Just as we first learn to speak and only begin to match written symbols with spoken words as our consciousness develops so, as we chant, our Buddha nature (which intuitively recognizes the Gohonzon when we first meet it) gradually leads our conscious mind to the point where it, too, can recognize the Gohonzon. As Nichiren Daishonin explains, 'There is a clear distinction between a Buddha and a common mortal, in that a common mortal is deluded, while a Buddha is enlightened.'

If we chant to the Gohonzon consistently, then our continual association with the 'life' of Nichiren Daishonin will eventually raise our own life state until it is on a par with his, so that we are able to reveal from within ourselves those qualities which characterized his life: profound wisdom, deep compassion for the suffering of ordinary people, and an indomitable fighting spirit, the product of great courage and life-force. In this way, the Gohonzon acts rather like a favourite teacher, one to whom we keep returning until we have absorbed everything he or she can teach us, the only difference being that what the Gohonzon has to teach is literally inexhaustible. Of course, our 'continual association with the life of Nichiren Daishonin' does not mean that we will start to take on Nichiren Daishonin's personality or imitate the life he led, any more than looking at Van Gogh's paintings will make us behave like him. Rather, we each experience

---

*A very black ink used in Japanese calligraphy.

Buddhahood and translate it into action in a way which is unique to our own individual lives, as explained by the theory of *ichinen sanzen* (see pp. 196–212).

That Nichiren Daishonin was able to inscribe the Gohonzon demonstrates the principle of the *Oneness of the Person and the Law*. The Person is Nichiren Daishonin, the Law is *Nam-myoho-renge-kyo*, and their oneness is the Gohonzon. In the strict sense, the oneness of the Person and the Law means that Nichiren Daishonin's predominant life state was Buddhahood from the very beginning: he did not have to become enlightened through studying Buddhism, but rather confirmed through his study of the sutras what he had already intuitively understood. In other words, Nichiren Daishonin was enlightened at birth and, as soon as he became fully aware of this, as early as before his sixteenth birthday, he also realized that he had to devote the rest of his life to teaching others how they could reach the same enlightenment. As he says, 'From the moment I was born until today, I, Nichiren, have never known a moment's ease; I have thought only of propagating the *daimoku* of the Lotus Sutra.'

The principle of the oneness of the Person and Law is also another way of saying that all ordinary people are potentially Buddhas and that, although the Law exists eternally, Buddhism does not exist apart from human life; thus, the Person is essential to teach it. This principle is evident in every character written on the Gohonzon. For example, down the centre of the Gohonzon, in characters bigger and bolder than the rest, is written *NAM-MYOHO-RENGE-KYO NICHIREN,* highlighting the fact that Nichiren Daishonin himself was a human being and subject to all the joys and sufferings that other human beings experience. The Gohonzon is also a graphic representation of the reality of life when it is in the state of Buddhahood and in total harmony with the Law of universal life, for these bold characters are surrounded by many smaller ones which represent all the other aspects of life, both positive and negative; all the forces of the universe which affect us, such as the sun, the moon and the stars; the various profound principles we set in motion when we start to chant to the Gohonzon; and the benefits we will receive as a result of our practice.

We have already met many of the aspects of life depicted on the Gohonzon. For example, the Ten Worlds appear, including the

Three Evil Paths of Hell, Hunger and Animality. This is very important, as it shows with absolute clarity that even the Buddha still possesses these lower life states. In a life dominated by Buddhahood, however, all the nine worlds work to create value. The Gohonzon clearly illustrates the proper relationship of the nine worlds to Buddhahood, as they cluster around *Nam-myoho-renge-kyo* like minor planets around the sun. As Nichiren Daishonin says, 'Illuminated by the five characters of the Mystic Law, they display the enlightened nature they inherently possess.' By contrast, if any of us were capable of absolutely truthfully depicting our life states as Nichiren Daishonin did, it is probable that we would place one of the six lower worlds from Hell to Rapture in large, bold characters down the centre – or possibly the worlds of Learning, Realization or Bodhisattva – whilst *Nam-myoho-renge-kyo* would appear to be insignificant by comparison (if, indeed, it could be seen at all). If we were to do this we would be wrong, though, for Nichiren Daishonin taught that *Nam-myoho-renge-kyo* is always shining brilliantly in the heart of our lives, even though all we may see are the dark clouds of our unhappy karma which obscure it.

Every facet, shade and colour of universal life – positive and negative – is represented on the Gohonzon which, nevertheless, is still a depiction of Nichiren Daishonin's life as a human being –an enlightened human being, it is true, but a human being nevertheless. He was well aware that his life – all life – naturally contains good and bad, darkness and light. Hence, in inscribing the Gohonzon, he gave all human beings an object to which *anyone* can relate, exactly as they are, without guilt or shame or feeling that they have to beg forgiveness for qualities which are inherent in all life, not just their own. Thus, whatever state is dominant in our lives when we first chant *Nam-myoho-renge-kyo,* our continual practice gradually supplants it with Buddhahood, until our lives perfectly match, or fuse with, the Gohonzon. In this way, Nichiren Daishonin opened up the way for all people to attain the supreme happiness of enlightenment in their own lifetime.

The Ceremony in the Air

Of course, anyone can claim that an object they have made is, endowed with special properties but that does not mean that it is, or that the maker is special in any sense. How, then, are we to know that Nichiren Daishonin was qualified to inscribe this 'true object of worship'? Furthermore, if the Gohonzon is a representation of Nichiren Daishonin's life, what is its relationship to Shakyamuni's supreme teaching, the Lotus Sutra? These are crucial questions which go to the very heart of Nichiren Shoshu Buddhism – indeed, all forms of Buddhism.

Firstly, we should remember that Buddhism teaches the strict operation of a universal law of cause and effect. One does not first have to believe in any claim that Nichiren Daishonin makes about the Gohonzon for it to work, therefore. Rather, 'having faith in the Gohonzon' means simply chanting to it sincerely and consistently over a freely chosen period of time to see for oneself what effect it has on one's life; as in any experiment, one follows the procedure exactly as laid down by the experiment's creator and then compares the results against the claims. This is the actual proof referred to earlier (see p. 30).

The relationship of the Gohonzon to the Lotus Sutra, and how Nichiren Daishonin was qualified to inscribe it, is a little more difficult to understand but, essentially, everything hinges on an event called the 'ceremony in the air', described in the Lotus Sutra from the second half of the *Hoto* (eleventh) chapter, through to the *Zokurui* (twenty-second) chapter. In these chapters, by means of a breathtaking allegory, Shakyamuni describes – amongst other things – how he foresees the Lotus Sutra being propagated far into the future.

The 'ceremony in the air' starts when a great assembly of bodhisattvas, gods and other beings, gathered together at Eagle Peak* to hear Shakyamuni preach the Law, are startled by the appearance from beneath the ground of an immense Treasure Tower, as great in height as the radius of the earth and encrusted with rare and dazzling jewels; this tower hangs suspended in mid-air above them. Shakyamuni subsequently summons an enormous number of Buddhas from throughout the universe to Eagle Peak – an indication that what he is about to say is of unparalleled importance – and then ascends into the air himself, whereupon the doors of the Treasure Tower open to reveal

---

*A mountain to the northeast of Rajagriha, the capital of Magadha in ancient Indian, where Shakyamuni expounded the Lotus Sutra. It symbolizes the Buddha's land, or the condition of Buddhahood. Also known in English as Vulture Peak.

another Buddha, called Taho, seated inside. Shakyamuni sits in the Treasure Tower next to Taho, raises the entire assembly into the air, and then begins to preach.

He describes how difficult it will be to teach the Law after his death and how those who try to propagate it will be harassed and persecuted by three types of enemies – ignorant lay people, arrogant and cunning priests, and religious leaders who, fearing they will lose status or profit, mislead the secular authorities and cause them to attack the votaries of the Lotus Sutra. Then, in the *Yujutsu* (fifteenth) chapter, countless Bodhisattvas of the Earth spring up out of the ground and, led by a supreme leader, Jogyo, and three other great bodhisattvas called Mughengyo, Anryugyo and Jyogyo, are entrusted by Shakyamuni in the *Jinriki* (twenty-first) chapter with the mission of teaching the Law contained in the Lotus Sutra during the Latter Day of the Law some 2000 years after his death. The 'ceremony in the air' ends when Shakymuni returns the entire assembly to Eagle Peak, all the Buddhas he had summoned go back to their own parts of the universe and the Treasure Tower returns to beneath the earth.

What are we to make of this extraordinary event, even though we realize that it never happened but is an elaborate allegory of deep significance? (Indeed, that Shakyamuni raises the assembly into the air, so that they are not on Eagle Peak when he preaches, indicates that the Law he expounds is not to be associated with any particular time in history or geographical location, but is both eternal and universal.) Everything that occurs during the 'ceremony in the air' has a profound meaning. For example, as explained earlier, Shakyamuni used the appearance of the Treasure Tower to demonstrate the vastness of the life condition of the Buddha. As Nichiren Daishonin says, 'In the Latter Day of the Law, there is no Treasure Tower other than the figures of the men and women who embrace the Lotus Sutra. It follows, therefore, that those who chant *Nam-myoho-renge-kyo*, irrespective of social status, are themselves the Treasure Tower and likewise themselves are Taho Buddha.' In the Treasure Tower, Shakyamuni himself represents the subjective wisdom (*chi*) inherent in each one of us, arising from our Buddhahood. Taho represents objective reality (*kyo*), the good fortune people can draw into their lives from their environment through manifesting the wisdom and compassion of their Buddhahood. Shakyamuni joining Taho in the Treasure Tower represents the fusion of wisdom and reality; in other words, our realization of the true nature of life or enlightenment.

As explained earlier, the four leaders of the Bodhisattvas of the Earth represent great qualities possessed innately by each human being. *Jogyo* represents the inexhaustible life-force of the true self; *Muhengyo* the confidence and freedom that comes from a deep understanding of the eternity of life; *Anryugyo* the indestructible happiness that is established through the practice of true Buddhism; and *Jyogyo* the purity of a life in which the three poisons of greed, anger and stupidity have been conquered. Finally, the people who rose up out of the Earth to follow the supreme leader, Jogyo, correspond to the men and women who now, and in the future, chant *Nam-myoho-renge-kyo*. In the due course of time it is the task of all the assembled Bodhisattvas of the Earth, whom the sutra describes as being equal in number to the sands of 60,000 Ganges Rivers, to spread the Law entrusted to Jogyo to the whole of mankind during the Latter Day of the Law, and so secure a peaceful and happy world.

What has all this to do with the Gohonzon and Nichiren Daishonin? The Gohonzon is a figurative representation of the 'ceremony in the air' and, in inscribing it, Nichiren Daishonin was therefore basing the true object of worship on the precise moment when Shakyamuni reveals his enlightenment and preaches the Law; in other words, on the most important moment of the most important of Shakyamuni's teachings. Nichiren Daishonin explicity states, 'The Lotus Sutra ... explains the Gohonzon in the eight chapters from the *Yujutsu* through to the *Zokurui* chapter'; and in another writing says of the Gohonzon, 'This mandala is in no way Nichiren's invention. It is the object of worship which perfectly depicts Lord Shakyamuni in the Treasure Tower and all the other Buddhas who were present, as accurately as the print matches the woodblock.' In short, by basing the Gohonzon so closely on the 'ceremony in the air', Nichiren Daishonin was not only drawing a direct line between Shakyamuni's Buddhism and his own, but was clarifying the object of worship and the Law which Shakyamuni indirectly hinted at during that eternal and universal ceremony.

Thus – although this is virtually impossible to understand until one experiences it – when we chant to the Gohonzon we, too, become participants in this timeless event. In the deepest sense, this is how we are able to change our karma: by touching eternity. Josei Toda, second president of the Soka Gakkai, stated: 'Devoting oneself to the Gohonzon and chanting *Nam-myoho-renge-kyo* is the way to change one's destiny for the better. All the causes and effects in between disappear, and a common mortal since time without beginning emerges.' Commenting on this passage, Daisaku Ikeda adds:

> When we sit upright facing the Gohonzon, a common mortal since time without beginning and the Buddha since time without beginning sit facing one another. That moment of relation provides a sublime seat where you join your palms together to become one with the true entity of all phenomena. It contains the overflowing power to embrace, integrate and motivate all exist-ences. This is what is meant by 'all the causes and effects in between disappear, and a common mortal since time without beginning emerges.'

To explain this from another perspective, Shakyamuni can be said to have taught the Buddhism of the 'harvest', or True Effect, while Nichiren Daishonin teaches the Buddhism of the sowing or True Cause. In other words, in the Lotus Sutra Shakyamuni describes from his own experience what it is like to be enlightened – the effect or 'harvest' of seeds sown in the past – but he never spells out how he reached this state, other than by referring to the practice of 'bodhisattva austerities', implying practice under a great master. Nor does Shakyamuni explain exactly the Law that he had realized. Nichiren Daishonin, on the other hand, states that this Law was, and always will be, *Nam-myoho-renge-kyo*. By teaching that anyone who chants this phrase to the Gohonzon can become enlightened in one lifetime he reveals it as the cause for all people to attain Buddhahood, the seed that must first be sown if one wants to harvest enlightenment.

Nichiren Daishonin was qualified to inscribe the Gohonzon for two main reasons. Firstly, Shakyamuni declared in the Lotus Sutra that the teaching for the Latter Day of the Law should not appear until at least 2000 years after his death and that the 'votary of the Lotus Sutra' would not appear until then either. It was because Nichiren Daishonin began teaching *Nam-myoho-renge-kyo* at the right time that he was later able to say:

> Had it not been for the advent of Nichiren in the Latter Day of the Law, the Buddha would have been a great liar and the testimony

given by Taho and all the other Buddhas [during the 'ceremony in the air'] would have been false. In the twenty-two hundred and thirty years since the Buddha's death, Nichiren is the only person in the whole world to fulfil the Buddha's prophecy.

Secondly, only Nichiren Daishonin experienced all the persecutions that Shakyamuni predicted the votary of the Lotus Sutra would have to suffer to fulfil his mission, a point he makes in a number of his writings. The facts of Nichiren Daishonin's life are a matter of undisputed historical record so, although some may argue as to their interpretation, in the light of what is written in the Lotus Sutra it would be difficult to answer Nichiren Daishonin when he asks:

> Who is it who is cursed and spoken ill of by the populace? Who is the monk who is attacked with swords and staves? Who is the monk who, because of the Lotus Sutra, is accused in petitions submitted to the courtiers and warriors? Who is the monk who is 'again and again banished', as the Lotus Sutra predicted? Who else in Japan besides Nichiren could fit this description? . . . Who, then, is the votary of the Lotus Sutra?

In other words, if the Lotus Sutra is documentary proof of what Shakyamuni foresaw for the votary of the Lotus Sutra, Nichiren Daishonin is actual proof that Shakyamuni was right. Indeed, it was only when he escaped execution by the sword through an extraordinary occurrence, that Nichiren Daishonin decided he had truly 'lived' the Lotus Sutra by confirming all its predictions and was, therefore, unquestionably qualified to start inscribing the Gohonzon for his closest followers.

Eight years after his attempted execution, in 1279, Nichiren Daishonin finally inscribed the Dai-Gohonzon, the establishment of which he himself considered to constitute the fundamental reason for his life. He says: 'The Buddha [Shakyamuni] fulfilled the purpose of his advent in a little over forty years; T'ien-t'ai took about thirty years, and Dengyo,* some twenty years . . . For me it took twenty-seven years.' While on one level this is a statement of simple fact – Nichiren Daishonin inscribed

---

*(767–822): founder of the Tendai sect in Japan, based on T'ien-t'ai's doctrines. Dengyo was thus the first in Japan to establish the Lotus Sutra as the highest Buddhist teaching, though later heads of the sect became confused on this point and the sect itself fell into decline.

the Dai-Gohonzon some twenty-seven years after first declaring *Nam-myoho-renge-kyo* in 1253 – on a deeper level, it testifies to the enormous importance of the Dai-Gohonzon. His reference to such major figures as Shakyamuni, T'ien-t'ai and Dengyo not only places his achievement in inscribing the Dai-Gohonzon directly in the historical flow of Buddhism, but also alludes to the basic method by which all Buddhas expounded their teachings – preparation, revelation and transmission.

First they prepare their listeners for what is to come, then, when they judge that the time is right, they reveal the teaching and, finally, they urge their listeners to transmit the teaching to others in the future. The length of these three periods can vary considerably. Thus, Shakyamuni taught the Lotus Sutra only after preparing his disciples for more than forty years (and predicted that its significance would not be fully realized until more than 2000 years after his death), T'ien-t'ai revealed the doctrine of *ichinen sanzen* only after teaching for more than thirty years, and Dengyo was able to establish T'ien-t'ai's Buddhism in Japan only after struggling for almost twenty years to convince the Japanese, particularly Buddhist priests, of its superiority.

In Nichiren Daishonin's case, living as he did at a time when Buddhist teachings were in a state of utter disarray and confusion, it took twenty-seven years for him to prepare his followers to receive his ultimate teaching. During these years he had to make sure that they had grasped certain cardinal points about Buddhism for, if they had not, they would have failed to appreciate the deep significance of the Dai-Gohonzon. For example, they first had to understand that the Lotus Sutra is foremost among Shakyamuni's teachings, and that Shakyamuni himself said that the Lotus Sutra is the only teaching which would be able to lead people to enlightenment in the chaotic first 500 years of the Latter Day of the Law. Then they had to learn that to chant *Nam-myoho-renge-kyo is* to practise the Lotus Sutra in the Latter Day of the Law. Finally, they had to recognize that, by fulfilling the predictions made in the Lotus Sutra, Nichiren Daishonin had demonstrated that he was indeed its votary. Only when enough of his followers had become fully convinced of these points, had deeply understood the mission of all Buddhas to save others from suffering, and had themselves developed a profound enough sense of mission to withstand the persecutions they too were now undergoing, did Nichiren Daishonin on 12 October 1279 then inscribe the Dai-Gohonzon, the true object of worship for attaining Buddhahood. This marked the revelation phase of his teaching.

Nichiren Daishonin inscribed the Dai-Gohonzon primarily out of his desire to lead to enlightenment all those people who would live after his death (which occurred exactly three years later on 13 October 1282), and so the Dai-Gohonzon functions not only to reveal the ultimate truth but also to transmit it far into the future. As he says, 'If Nichiren's compassion is truly great and encompassing, *Nam-myoho-renge-kyo* will spread for 10,000 years and more, for all eternity, for it has the beneficial power to open the eyes of every living person in Japan*, and it blocks off the road that leads to the hell of incessant suffering.' In other words, as the physical embodiment of *Nam-myoho-renge-kyo*, the Dai-Gohonzon exists as the eternal cause to awaken the Buddhahood dormant in all people throughout the world. In describing the Dai-Gohonzon's greatness, Nichikan Shonin, the twenty-sixth high priest of Nichiren Shoshu, states:

> This is the origin of all Buddhas and sutras and the place to which they return. The blessings of the myriads of Buddhas and sutras throughout space and time, without a single exception, all return to this Gohonzon, which provides the seed of Buddhahood and is hidden in the [Lotus] sutra, just as the tree's hundreds and thousands of branches and leaves all return to the same root. This Gohonzon provides great and boundless benefits. Its mystic functions are vast and profound. So if you take faith in this Gohonzon even for a while, no prayer will go unanswered, no sin will remain unforgiven, all good fortune will be bestowed, and all righteousness proven.

In this light it is clear that, in time, people everywhere will come to recognize the establishment of the Dai-Gohonzon as an achievement unparalleled in the history of mankind, surpassing any other before or since.

---

*Nichiren Daishonin makes it clear in a number of his writings that he revealed the Three Great Secret Laws for the sake of all humanity but, to explain his Buddhism to a specifically Japanese audience, he would sometimes stress the benefits of practice as if from the viewpoint of the Japanese nation alone. Here, however, 'Japan' indicates the whole world.

4

The Essentials of Practice

There are three essential aspects to Nichiren Daishonin's Buddhism: *faith*, which means to determine to attain enlightenment through practising to the Gohonzon for the whole of one's life; *practice* for oneself and others, which means to perform *gongyo* twice a day and to chant *Nam-myoho-renge-kyo* 'to your heart's content', while making efforts to teach others about this Buddhism and to work for their fundamental happiness whether they practise Buddhism or not; and *study*, which means to read and try to understand the profundity of the teachings of Nichiren Daishonin. Underlining the importance of these three aspects, Nichiren Daishonin states:

> Believe in the Gohonzon, the supreme object of worship in the world. Forge strong faith and receive the protection of Shakyamuni, Taho and all the other Buddhas.* Exert yourself in the two ways of practice and study. Without practice and study, there can be no Buddhism. You must not only persevere yourself, you must also teach others. Both practice and study arise from faith. Teach others to the best of your ability, even if only a single sentence or phrase.

Since faith, practice and study form the basis of Nichiren Shoshu Buddhism, let us look more closely at what they mean.

*The protection both of one's own inherent wisdom and the physical environment.

FAITH

Faith is the most important aspect of Nichiren Shoshu Buddhism. As Nichiren Daishonin indicates in the passage above, faith gives rise to practice and study, and practice and study in turn serve to deepen one's faith. It must be understood, however, that in Nichiren Shoshu Buddhism faith does not mean blind belief in something, but the basic desire and determination to become enlightened, no matter what, and, through this enlightenment, to contribute to establishing a peaceful and happy world. As Daisaku Ikeda explains:

> Faith means to believe in the Dai-Gohonzon and devote yourself to it confidently and courageously, no matter what waves and storms may buffet you, no matter what criticism and vilification or persecution may assail you, and no matter what karma may confront you. This is the path toward Buddhahood. If you are convinced of this, it can be called faith.

In this sense, faith in Nichiren Daishonin's Buddhism is comparable to faith in many other areas of life. For example, anyone who wants to achieve something that demands they make the effort to develop themselves can only do so because, fundamentally, they have faith in themselves and their abilities. This is so whether one wants to become a doctor, musician, scientist, politician, athlete, or whatever. Indeed, if one does not have this faith in oneself, or if it is shaken by some event or the lack of immediate success, one will never achieve that on which one has set one's heart.

In another sense, faith could be said to form the basis of all our actions, in that we have to have faith in a myriad different ways simply in order to live our daily lives. For example, when we get on a bus we have faith – albeit unconsciously – that the bus driver will take us where we are meant to go; that he will drive carefully and that the bus itself is in a safe and roadworthy condition. It would be ridiculous if, every time we caught a bus, we questioned the driver as to his intentions and examined the wheels to make sure that they were tightly secured to the axles. In this sense, faith can be equated with trust, which is essentially what it means in Nichiren Daishonin's Buddhism. We trust that by practising exactly as Nichiren Daishonin taught, we will be rewarded with the life-condition of Buddhahood, as he promises.

In Buddhism, however, as in ordinary life, trust has to be earned. If we have faith in bus drivers, ultimately it is because, generally speaking, the wheels do not fall off buses and they do get us to where we want to go in one piece. It is the same with Nichiren Daishonin's Buddhism, only with the added advantage that, as we begin to see that our lives are improving – slowly but steadily – and that Nichiren Daishonin is therefore keeping his promise, our faith and trust in his teachings gradually deepen. In other words, we can become convinced of the truth of Nichiren Shoshu Buddhism only through the accumulation of our own experiences, which arise quite naturally as a result of our practice. Thus, faith cannot exist without practice and study, and one can no more 'believe' in Buddhism, if one does not practise it, than one can 'believe' in one's skill as a cook, say, if one never does any cooking. In short, faith, like cooking, exists only in action. By definition, then, it is also impossible to practise without faith – even if, initially, the faith you have is only in the person who first tells you about *Nam-myoho-renge-kyo*.

Nichiren Shoshu Buddhism is founded on one very simple premise: that faith finds expression in everyday reality or, to put it slightly differently, that Buddhism equals daily life. In other words, we practise the Buddhism of Nichiren Daishonin in order to live the most valuable possible lives as individual human beings; this means working to create the greatest possible value for ourselves and those who share our environment. The most important thing to establish, therefore, is the quality of our lives from moment to moment, whether at any given moment we are cleaning the house, working in an office, spending time with friends, chanting or any other activity. Indeed, as we spend much more time in activities other than chanting, it only makes sense that the benefits we gain from the physical practice of this Buddhism must be applicable to all other areas of our lives. If this were not the case, the implication would be that we could be happy only in front of the Gohonzon, which is not what Nichiren Daishonin teaches at all. However, he does teach that in order to learn what he calls 'the art of living' – how to improve fundamentally the quality of life for ourselves and others, so that we can become truly happy and fulfilled in this lifetime – we must follow the practice he prescribes.

PRACTICE

As we have seen, the practice of Nichiren Shoshu Buddhism falls
into two parts: practice for oneself and practice for others. Strictly
speaking, we cannot compartmentalize our practice in this way
as we are each inseparable from our own unique environment.
Thus, as we gain benefits from our practice, so we quite naturally
begin to benefit others. For example, if someone who has always
lacked money changes this aspect of his karma, he will no longer
rely on his friends or family for support and so will cause those
people less worry. Conversely, through teaching others about
Nam-myoho-renge-kyo we can help them to change those areas of
their karma which cause them to suffer, and so gain the benefit of
seeing them become happy too. In the same way, we need to
study not only to understand how Buddhist concepts apply to our
own lives, but also to explain Buddhism effectively to others who
wish to learn about it. Indeed, study for the sake of intellectual,
theoretical satisfaction has no place whatsoever in Nichiren
Daishonin's Buddhism.

Practice for Oneself

Bearing these points in mind how, first, does one 'practise for
oneself'? The most basic practice of Nichiren Shoshu Buddhism
is to chant *Nam-myoho-renge-kyo*. If you want to chant, all you have
to do is sit or kneel upright, with your hands together and eyes
open, and simply repeat this phrase out loud over and over again,
in a rhythmical manner, with a clear and relaxed voice. In
pronouncing *Nam-myoho-renge-kyo*, all the vowels are short and
each syllable is pronounced separately, thus: Nam-myo-ho-ren-
ge-kyo, *Myo* and *kyo* are both spoken as one syllable – m'yo, k'yo
(this latter as in To*kyo*) – and the *n* and *g* in *renge* are both hard, as
in Be*n* and *g*et. If you do not have a Gohonzon you will find it
easier when you start chanting to face a blank wall, as this will
help your mind to cease wandering and concentrate on the sound
of chanting. The speed and volume at which you chant are not
important (except you should not upset your neighbours): what
does matter is the rhythm and pronunciation of your *daimoku*
(each *Nam-myoho-renge-kyo*), the firmness of the vibrations of your
voice and the sincerity with which you chant.

Sincerity may be the last thing you think you are experiencing when you begin to chant, as it is not unusual for people to feel a little foolish or embarrassed at first. After all, this action is probably one that is completely outside the range of your previous experience and you may even wonder, at first, quite why you are behaving in this apparently bizarre manner, or what your friends would say if they saw you. Sincerity in this context, however, ultimately means the strength of your desire to put Buddhism to the test, so if you chant with the attitude of 'Single-mindedly yearning to see the Buddha', any feelings of embarrassment will quickly evaporate as you begin to experience your own Buddhahood for the first time.

When and where you chant are entirely up to you, although obviously it is better to choose a time and place that allows you to concentrate. How long you should chant is again your decision, although, as already mentioned, Nichiren Daishonin encourages us to chant to our 'heart's content'; this can vary according to our specific needs and the demands of our daily schedules. It is best, however, to establish a regular and consistent practice in which at first we chant for, say, ten minutes each morning and evening, as this matches the basic daily rhythm of our lives. As you begin to experience the effect of chanting you might quite naturally want to increase the amount of chanting you do; or at times – during a crisis, for example – you may be encouraged to do more chanting by other people. This is because they know from experience that, at such times, one needs to be able to draw hard on the qualities of Buddhahood that extra *daimoku* gives one. Once again, though, just how much effort you put into your practice is ultimately determined by no one but you.

People often worry about what they should be thinking when they chant, but there are no hard and fast rules on this score. Generally, it is a good idea when you begin each chanting session to try to concentrate on establishing a precise and clear rhythm and to listen to the sound of your *daimoku*. Then, quite naturally, any problems you may be facing, or your current preoccupations or desires, will probably come into your mind as prayers, to be bathed, as it were, in your own intuitive Buddha wisdom. Gradually, as you repeat this process, you will find that the decisions you start to make (not while you are chanting, but in your daily life) will be based more and more on this wisdom – an expression of your true self – and you will begin to orientate your life towards the kind of happy future you begin to realize could be yours. Chanting, however, does not always work in exactly this way. For example, through chanting at times you will be able to re-inspire yourself with the courage and confidence to keep battling when things look black; at other times you will be able suddenly to see a solution in what seemed like a hopeless situation; or at times you may simply be able to keep fatigue at bay to finish an urgent task. In short, chanting *Nam-myoho-renge-kyo* to the Gohonzon is designed for any problem or circumstance, no matter how insignificant it might seem, like getting up on time; or however overwhelming or awesome, such as the problem of world peace. Finally, in the same way as when we began, we should listen to our voice chanting during the last few moments of our *daimoku* when, quite naturally, we can feel joy rising up within us; indeed, ideally we should continue to chant until we feel this joy welling up from deep within our lives.

In order to see for ourselves that there is no limit to what we can chant for, we are encouraged to set specific goals when we practise, in any area of our lives that is causing us to suffer. Naturally, these goals are as varied as the people who set them – a job; somewhere better to live; more money; overcoming an illness; a better relationship and so on – and although they can often be quite self-centred when we start to chant, they mark an important initial step in proving to ourselves that the practice works. Once we have gained this proof, so our practice tends increasingly to turn outwards, towards practising for the happiness of other people or overcoming our own weaknesses or failings. But whatever form our desires may take, the most important thing to remember is to chant regularly and whole-heartedly so that we can steadily build up the inner strength – the life force – we need to overcome any obstacle to happiness that life might throw at us, at any time, on any day.

It is partly to support the regularity of our practice of chanting *daimoku* that we perform *gongyo* twice a day. As already explained, *gongyo* literally means 'assiduous practice', and is the profound ceremony all Nichiren Shoshu Buddhists perform every morning and evening to the Gohonzon. Although the precise form of *gongyo* was established only after his death, Nichiren Daishonin himself indicated that it should be based on the recitation of part of the

Hoben (second) and whole of the *Juryo* (sixteenth) chapters of the Lotus Sutra, followed by the chanting of *daimoku*. Daisaku Ikeda briefly explains why Nichiren Daishonin chose these two chapters:

> Regarding the meaning of the recitation of the *Hoben* and *Juryo* chapters of the Lotus Sutra during *gongyo*, these two chapters are the apex of all the teachings expounded by the Buddha Shakyamuni. In other words, these two chapters are the gem of all the sutras – the soul of the so-called eighty thousand teachings.* The true aspect of the universe and all the principles of life are expounded in them, including the three truths of non-substantiality (*kutai*), temporary existence (*ketai*) and the Middle Way (*chutai*); the Buddha's three properties of the Law, wisdom and action; eternal life permeating the three existences of past, present and future; the Ten Worlds; and the principle that earthly desires are enlightenment.
>
> Whether or not you understand their meaning, when you recite these two chapters of the Lotus Sutra daily you are conducting a ceremony, consciously or unconsciously, to confirm and actualize all the principles that permeate both your life and the universe. In other words, because of the mystic power of the Dai-Gohonzon, you can experience the fusion of the Law which exists within your life and throughout the universe. When you do *gongyo*, you are officiating at a ceremony that sheds light into your life as a common mortal because it shares the state of Buddhahood with the Gohonzon. Moreover, chanting *daimoku* after reciting the sutra is instrumental in enabling the universal principles to function to the fullest in your favour. In other words, you can enjoy the benefits of the ultimate principles expounded in true Buddhism as you bring them gloriously into play through your *daimoku*.

To learn *gongyo* you will definitely need help from someone who already knows it (and who will almost certainly be a member of one of the various Nichiren Shoshu lay organizations around the world), especially as *gongyo* is recited in the language of Kumarajiva's translation of the Lotus Sutra, namely, classical Chinese pronounced according to Japanese phonetics. Initially,

---

*All the teachings which Shakyamuni expounded during his lifetime. The figure is not intended to be literal, but simply indicates a large number.

this may appear somewhat daunting, but everyone who starts to learn *gongyo* eventually masters it, mostly within a few weeks. Again, at first glance it might seem strange or illogical to perform this ceremony in a language no one understands, but there are actually very good reasons for this.

Firstly, it should be remembered that *gongyo* constitutes an intrinsic part of the *practice* of Nichiren Shoshu Buddhism and that, even though at first we may not intellectually understand what we are doing, if we keep making the cause of doing *gongyo* regularly, we will gain the effect of seeing growth in all areas of our lives. Nichiren Daishonin explains this using the analogy of a baby who, with no conscious understanding of what it is doing, instinctively takes its mother's breast and gains nourishment as a result. To give another analogy, if we want to develop ourselves physically, we quite naturally take exercise, even though very few of us will bother to learn exactly how making such effort leads to the physiological changes our bodies experience in becoming fitter and stronger. *Gongyo*, too, is an exercise, one we perform twice daily, only not just for our bodies but to purify our lives as a whole. Similarly, just as one does a 'warm-up' to prepare oneself before any strenuous exercise, so the effort of concentration we have to make in the supporting practice of reciting the sutra enables us to gain the maximum benefit from the primary practice of chanting *Nam-myoho-renge-kyo* which follows. Our lives are by then purified and in perfect balance.

The practice of morning *gongyo* charges us with the qualities of Buddhahood for the coming day, while evening *gongyo* allows us to use those same qualities to reflect on the day that has just passed, recharge ourselves for the rest of the time we will remain awake, and look ahead to that which we wish to achieve the following day after we have refreshed ourselves with sleep. Of course, we can *study* the meaning of the passages from the Lotus Sutra which we recite during *gongyo* – indeed, we are positively encouraged to do so – but this is done solely to support the daily practice of it. In short, although we can quite quickly experience the beneficial effect of performing *gongyo*, we can fully understand it only through both practice and study, though once again, this understanding arises gradually, over a period of time.

The second reason why *gongyo* is not performed in the practitioner's mother-tongue is that not only would it be more difficult to recite rhythmically in another language, but any translation would invariably – and considerably – lengthen it. Here, for example, are the first few lines of *gongyo* from the *Hoben* chapter, followed by their literal English translation:

> *Niji seson. Ju sanmai. Anjo ni ki. Go sharihotsu. Sho-but chi-e. Jinjin muryo. Go chi-e mon. Nange nannyu. Issai shomon. Hyaku-shi-butsu. Sho fu no chi.*

> At this time the World-Honoured One serenely arose from meditation and addressed Shariputra: 'The wisdom of all Buddhas is infinitely profound and immeasurable. The portal of this wisdom is difficult to understand and difficult to enter. Neither men of Learning nor men of Realization are able to comprehend it.'

The literal translation of any part of the Lotus Sutra only hints at the profundity of meaning lying below the surface, as we have already seen in our examination of the title, *Myoho-renge-kyo*; so even these few lines quoted above can be interpreted from a variety of different viewpoints and at greatly varying depths. It is much better, then, to leave Kumarajiva's translation as it is so far as the *practice* is concerned for, deep within our lives, our Buddha nature understands and responds to it. Even so, the *study* of it can be – and is – pursued in many different languages in order to satisfy our intellects, our conscious, thinking minds.

This last point brings us to the third reason why *gongyo* is performed in a language nobody speaks (for even to the Chinese the characters are ancient and not commonly in use today): paradoxically, it enables Nichiren Shoshu Buddhists of all nationalities to participate in this most profound ceremony together, wherever they are in the world and whenever such opportunities arise. Nichiren Daishonin's Buddhism has for one of its goals the overcoming of petty differences between peoples based on nationality and race and, for a religion to be universal, this ability for all people to worship together in the same way is crucially important. Currently, some twenty million people in 115 different countries across the globe perform *gongyo* twice a day, every day of the year, and, as time passes, are being joined by an ever-growing number of others. Part of the reason for this steady growth lies in the fact that everybody learns – and benefits from

– the same practice. Just as the Gohonzon remains constant and absolute, for all people in all times, so does *gongyo*.

The Power of the Negative Force of Life

An important thing to remember when you chant is that, every time you do so, you are engaged in a battle to overcome the negative and destructive influences that exist within your life. These influences, which are quite natural and inherent in every aspect of life, are called in Buddhism by a variety of names – fundamental darkness, illusions, devils and demons, obstacles – and can appear either as internal forces, such as laziness, fears and doubts, or as external opposition, such as the ridicule or criticism of your Buddhist practice by other people. However this negativity manifests itself, it will always touch on your own, unique areas of weakness – your personal Achilles heel – and so always work to weaken your faith and stop you revealing your Buddhahood. In other words, because you are making the supreme good cause for your happiness by starting to practise, it is perfectly natural that the negativity within and around you will try to stop you from doing so. As Nichiren Daishonin explains:

> The doctrine of *ichinen sanzen** revealed in the fifth volume of the *Maka Shikan* is especially profound. If you propagate it, devils will arise without fail. Were it not for these, there would be no way of knowing that this is the true teaching. One passage from the same volume reads, 'As practice progresses and understanding grows, the three devils and four obstacles† emerge, vying with one another to interfere ... You should neither be influenced nor frightened by them. If you fall under their influence, you will be led into the paths of evil. If you are frightened by them, you will be prevented from practising true Buddhism.' This quotation not only applies to Nichiren but also is the guide for his disciples.

Therefore, it is only by continually challenging and over-coming this negative force, both within yourself and in your environment, through chanting *Nam-myoho-renge-kyo*, that you

---

*Here indicates *Nam-myoho-renge-kyo*. Nichiren Daishonin uses this term to emphasize the direct relationship between his Buddhism and T'ien-t'ai's.
†A categorization of the various obstacles and hindrances which trouble one's practice of Buddhism, such as doubt, fear, sickness, opposition from one's family and so forth. Also called *sansho shima*.

can become truly happy because, at root, it is this very negativity which restricts your life and makes you suffer. On the other hand, as Nichiren Daishonin points out, if we never had anything to fight there would be no way of seeing for ourselves just how effective this practice is: as he says in another writing, 'Only by defeating a powerful enemy can one prove his own strength.' Fundamentally, the 'powerful enemy' is nothing other than our own illusions and our 'strength' simply our Buddhahood. To practise Nichiren Daishonin's Buddhism is therefore to engage in a battle for your own lasting happiness – a battle between the Buddha, the creative force of life, and the 'devil', its destructive opponent. Buddhism teaches that it is the eternal struggle between these two opposing forces which creates the very energy of life itself. Thus, even the 'devils' have an important function in life and must therefore exist innately within us all.

This point is clearly illustrated in the experience of Marina Cantacuzino, the development of whose practice is by no means unusual. She started to chant very soon after learning about *Nam-myoho-renge-kyo*, but it was only after practising for some eighteen months that she began to feel as if she was doing it from her own desire, rather than out of a sense of obligation of some kind. As she says, 'I realized that just because my feelings towards the practice had often been negative, full of criticism, doubt and fear, this did not mean that the cause was to be found in the practice itself. My attitude was just a symptom of my own negativity which had always held me back and came from the very depths of my being.'

Marina had started chanting when she was in America with her husband, Dan, visiting his brother who had been practising strongly for about three years, 'At that point I felt very relaxed about it,' she says. 'Everyone seemed friendly and the philosophy made sense. I was just a visitor and I enjoyed being an onlooker. I wanted it to stay that way.' When they returned to England, though, they both joined their local NSUK group and began attending meetings regularly; at this time the first wave of negativity hit Marina: 'It was all right as long as we were visitors but, as soon as we became official group members, as it were, the panic set in. I didn't want to commit myself. I wanted to remain on the fringe of things.'

Matters got so bad that she used to dread answering the phone in case it was someone asking her to go to a meeting. When she did go, it was not because she wanted to but because she feared some kind of retribution if she failed to turn up. But even when she did attend, Marina still suffered: 'At district meetings I hated most of all the introductions because I felt all I could say with honesty was my name and where I lived; unlike everyone else I could not claim that chanting *Nam-myoho-renge-kyo* had changed my life. I can see now that everything about my practice was faint-hearted, so how could I possibly have expected to feel the change inside which I so desired?' She would often leave meetings feeling not only depressed, but filled with a kind of fear – as she puts it, 'a fear of the unknown, of feeling out of place and out of touch. I felt I was unlike everyone else there.'

Despite everything, however, Marina continued to practise with the result that she was slowly able to get to the root of why she felt as she did. She explains: 'I think a lot of my negativity towards the practice was due to a kind of cultural allegiance. I felt by embracing Buddhism I was rejecting my past; having been raised as a Catholic and having always been very close to my mother, it also felt like a rejection of her.' In addition, she worried that by joining an organization she would, as she puts it, lose her 'edge'. She says, 'I thought NSUK would make me speak and act like everyone else and rob me of my identity. I did not realize then that *Nam-myoho-renge-kyo* is not a path but is life itself, which includes all things and all different kinds of people. It includes my individuality, my political beliefs and even my Christian up-bringing.'

Another way in which Marina's negativity towards Buddhism expressed itself was in her attitude to it when with friends and family. As she explains, 'Because I lacked self-confidence I often worried about what others thought. In the past, my moods, my happiness, my self-respect (or lack of it) were all determined by what others had said or done to me. So I became what you could call a "closet chanter". I never chanted when I was staying in other people's houses and I avoided talking about it to people I thought would be sceptical or think me peculiar. Occasionally, out of a sense or duty, I forced myself to talk to others about Buddhism, but it was always disastrous because it did not come from the heart. I said what I felt I was supposed to say because, in an awful kind of way, I felt I had to apologize for what might appear to be the eccentricities of the practice and justify my involvement with it.'

Needless to say, just before receiving her Gohonzon, Marina went through terrible doubts. 'I felt completely trapped,' she says, 'and the goodwill of everyone in my district only made me feel more pressurized. Of course, I had a perfect right to say "No", but somehow I knew that to say "No" to the Gohonzon would be a backward step, leaving me in a position of deadlock and unable to change the things in my life which I did not like. In the end I adopted a "Well, why not?" attitude, and told myself that I'd return it within a year if nothing good had happened.' But even after receiving the Gohonzon, at first Marina could not bring herself to accept the fact that she was actually practising Buddhism, even going so far as to disguise the area where her Gohonzon was enshrined when friends came round, afraid that it looked too 'religious'.

After a year with the Gohonzon, however, her basic attitude had changed. Now she says, 'Because I am more sure I am doing the right thing, I leave everything as it is and I don't mind what people say. A few people still think it's weird or freakish, but whereas in the past this would have immediately weakened my belief and made me think they had a point, now it does not in any way undermine my faith, but just makes me all the more determined to prove the power of the practice through my own life. I can see that my old attitude was once again a reflection of my tendency to sway with the wind, believe whoever happened to be talking at the time and never stick to my own convictions.' Summing up, Marina realizes that learning to 'stand alone' – that is, establishing a solid practice through overcoming some problem or area of weakness within oneself – is only the first step towards a completely fulfilled existence. As she says, 'I don't necessarily have all the answers now, but I do feel completely confident in my practice. I can say with truth that I do it because I want to do it, because it has enabled me to understand why I am like I am, and how I can get rid of the negativity and fear in my life which had plagued me for so long.'

Everyone who chants continues to battle with the negative side of life, though as their faith grows they become swifter and more skilled in taking control of it. Likewise, those who decide at some point to challenge the influence of this negativity are able, like

Marina, to come to a much higher condition of life as a result. This is exactly what the process of 'human revolution' is all about – turning the 'poison' of one's negativity into the 'elixir' of enlightenment. Nevertheless, since it is an essential component of life as a whole, the dark side of life never completely disappears, but is always present in some form – to keep us on our toes, as it were. Even so, after some years of chanting, the negativity which those who practise have to contend with may often not be so much their own but someone else's, or that expressed collectively in society as a whole. Indeed, it is because we cannot be truly happy in an unhappy and negative world that, from the very outset of our practice, we are taught Nichiren Daishonin's emphasis on practice for others as being of equal importance as practice for oneself.

Practice for Others

If the ultimate aim of 'practice for oneself' is our individual 'human revolution' – conquering the negative aspects of our character and developing wisdom, courage, compassion and joy – the ultimate aim of 'practice for others' is *kosen-rufu*. *Kosen-rufu* literally means to 'widely declare and spread'; in other words, to propagate this Buddhism throughout the world.

Nowadays, in the West at least, there is a certain amount of suspicion towards any sort of religious proselytism, especially when it concerns so-called 'new religions'. Undoubtedly, this suspicion is well founded, for there are numerous instances of gullible people being tricked out of their money by religious charlatans; or even out of their lives, as demonstrated by the case of Jim Jones and the mass suicide at the People's Temple in Guyana. Nichiren Shoshu Buddhism, however, opens one's eyes to the vulnerability of people in this respect because, tradition- ally, religious teachings have so often placed emphasis on self- sacrifice as a virtue. Jim Jones and his flock were an extreme example of the effect of such teachings.

In the practice of Nichiren Daishonin's Buddhism there is no such thing as self-sacrifice, since practice involves enlightenment to the universal law of cause and effect. Thus, one discovers that 'practice for others', based on the profound compassion of *jihi* – the desire to help others overcome their sufferings and gain lasting happiness through practising this Buddhism – is in fact the most pure and noble of all causes. This reaps the most pure and noble of all rewards: the purification of one's own unhappy karma, entirely through one's own efforts. A follower of Nichiren Shoshu Buddhism might well decide to live amongst the poor, for example, not in order to share their poverty but to help them to become 'rich', both in spirit and in satisfying their daily material needs.

Viewed from this perspective, *kosen-rufu* might be described as the cumulative effect of many individuals freely deciding to undertake their own human revolution. Moreover, the international movement for *kosen-rufu* is in strict accordance with the Buddha's will. For example, in the *Yakuo* (twenty-third) chapter of the Lotus Sutra, Shakyamuni states: 'In the fifth five hundred years after my death, accomplish worldwide *kosen-rufu* and never allow its flow to cease.'

In the broadest sense, then, practice for others consists of any action one takes that leads another person, either directly or indirectly, towards their own eventual enlightenment. This is called *shakubuku*. The most direct *shakubuku*, of course, is to tell others about chanting *Nam-myoho-renge-kyo* and explain the Buddhist view of life. While some people are willing to try chanting simply because they are told about it in this way, others are more sceptical. Generally speaking, these people will begin to practise only because, over a period of time, they come to respect someone they know who is chanting and trust him or her as a person of good sense, warmth and understanding. Indeed, there are numerous cases of people starting to practise only many years after first learning about *Nam-myoho-renge-kyo* but who, during the whole of that period, have nevertheless been keeping a watchful eye on their friend, relation, colleague or neighbour who does chant. From this it follows that showing proof of the benefits of practising this Buddhism, particularly in the form of our own human revolution, in itself constitutes *shakubuku* when it gradually convinces others of the power of *Nam-myoho-renge-kyo*.

From this it can be clearly understood that Nichiren Shoshu Buddhism sees *kosen-rufu* as coming about by entirely natural, peaceful methods. Essentially, this means that others are persuaded to practise Nichiren Shoshu Buddhism only when they become convinced by one or more of the three proofs mentioned in the Introduction. That is to say, through *documentary* proof – the written evidence that all Buddhist teachings lead to the Lotus Sutra and from there to *Nam-myoho-renge-kyo* and the Gohonzon – people will realize that Nichiren Daishonin's Buddhism represents the correct and orthodox Buddhist practice for this age and for all types of people, whatever their background. Through *theoretical* proof – learning about the profound principles of Buddhism – people will gradually come to understand that *Nam-myoho-renge-kyo* perfectly elucidates the mysteries of life and death. Most importantly, through *actual* proof – witnessing the change in those who practise – more and more people will come to see how chanting this phrase can radically alter a person's life for the better. In other words, just as scientific discoveries may initially shake the way ordinary people look at the world, but are gradually accepted as true because they can be proved empirically, so, in time, will Nichiren Shoshu Buddhism be accepted as a matter of common sense simply because so many people will have proved it for themselves. Nichiren Shoshu Buddhists consequently feel no need to coerce others into practising this Buddhism or to be intolerant of those who practise other religions and philosophies.

Of course, this is not to say that in teaching others about this Buddhism one should not explain the differences between Buddhist concepts and the doctrines of other religions, nor correct misconceptions that even other Buddhists may, in all good faith, hold about Buddhism. Indeed, Nichiren Daishonin was unpopular among the established Buddhist sects of his day precisely because he was able to point to the sutras and show exactly where the doctrines on which these sects were based fell short of the highest Buddhist teachings. As Daisaku Ikeda explains:

> In propagating true Buddhism we must take into consideration the two types of country mentioned in the writings of Nichiren Daishonin: the country which is ignorant of true Buddhism and the country which actively slanders the Law.* Moreover, we must take into consideration the two different viewpoints in the interpretation of the *myo* of *myoho* or the Mystic Law: the *myo* of comparison and the all-encompassing *myo*. The former means to

---

*A country which slanders the Law is that in which Buddhism is established, but which fails to recognize the supremacy of the Lotus Sutra. See also Chapter 6.

show that the Mystic Law is superior when compared to all other teachings, while the latter means to show that the Mystic Law encompasses and integrates all laws and teachings and that, based upon it, all other teachings reveal their true meaning as partial aspects of this ultimate truth.

Despite the incredible opposition he faced, Nichiren Daishonin had such confidence in the all-encompassing nature of the Mystic Law that he knew everything he was teaching would eventually be proved correct and accepted by a large proportion of mankind. As he says:

> Only I, Nichiren, at first chanted *Nam-myoho-renge-kyo*, but then two, three and a hundred followed, chanting and teaching others. Likewise, propagation will unfold in this way in the future . . . At the time of *kosen-rufu* the entire Japanese nation* will chant *Nam-myoho-renge-kyo*, as surely as an arrow aimed at the earth cannot miss its target.

This passage also highlights the strongly democratic nature of the movement for *kosen-rufu*: ordinary people tell their friends and family about what they have experienced through chanting *Nam-myoho-renge-kyo*; some of those friends try it and tell their friends; and so the Law is spread quite naturally on the basis of person-to-person communication.

That Nichiren Daishonin's confidence in *Nam-myoho-renge-kyo* was not misplaced is evidenced today by the steady growth of his Buddhism worldwide and its appeal to many ordinary people from all races, cultures and social classes. In the West, we naturally tend to associate Buddhism with the Orient and, currently, the majority of those practising Nichiren Daishonin's Buddhism are indeed to be found in the Far East. It is envisaged, however, that before long the balance of Nichiren Shoshu Buddhists will even out across the globe.

Fundamentally, Nichiren Shoshu Buddhists believe that a lasting world peace will be established only when enough people – ordinary, down-to-earth people like those whose experiences you have read in the course of this book – learn to live their daily lives according to the profound philosophy of Nichiren Daishonin's Buddhism; a philosophy which, while respecting the

*Here refers to the whole world.

fundamental dignity of all life, is powerful enough to release in ordinary people the strength with which to overcome their sufferings, and flexible enough to allow everyone to express and develop their own individuality.

It would be a mistake to suppose that the achievement of *kosen-rufu* implies that everyone must practise this Buddhism for world peace to come about – indeed, Nichiren Shoshu Buddhists recognize that such a thing will probably never happen. What they do foresee, though, is the existence of a large minority of people who chant *Nam-myoho-renge-kyo*, supported by another large group – possibly even the majority – who, while they may not practise themselves, will be broadly in agreement with the aims and philosophy of Nichiren Daishonin's Buddhism. Together, these two groups will then have enough power to influence positively the course of world affairs away from war and destructive conflict, despite the lack of cooperation from a third, uncaring group, who will be either directly opposed to, or simply uninterested in, the spread of this Buddhism – or any form of religion, for that matter.

Kosen-rufu is not limited just to eradicating conflict in the international arena, though. Rather, as can be seen in the experiences related earlier, since the practice of this Buddhism gives back to ordinary people an increasing measure of control over their own lives and environment, the effect of a great many people practising in any society will be seen throughout that society: in a lower crime rate, for example, a lower incidence of drug and alcohol abuse, a lower divorce rate, a stronger economy and higher standards of living, generally better health, a greater life expectancy and so on. For just as a climate of fear, apathy, hopelessness and depression can be created by a small but energetic minority – witness the activities of various terrorist groups in Northern Ireland, for example – so an atmosphere of creativity and vitality can be generated by a minority who are inspired and sustained by more positive and humane goals. Moreover, when that minority base their actions on the inexhaustible life-force, courage, wisdom and compassion they draw from their own lives through chanting to the Gohonzon, in time they will quite naturally gain the trust and respect of others around them. The effect of *kosen-rufu* in society is described in poetic terms by Nichiren Daishonin in the following passage:

The time will come when all people,* including those of Learning, Realization and Bodhisattva, will enter on the path to Buddhahood, and the Mystic Law alone will flourish throughout the land. In that time, because all people chant *Nam-myoho-renge-kyo* together, the wind will not beleaguer the branches or boughs, nor will the rain fall hard enough to break a clod. The world will become as it was in the ages of Fu Hsi and Neng Shun† in ancient China. Disasters will be driven from the land and the people will be rid of misfortune. They will also learn the art of living long, fulfilling lives.

This is not merely wishful thinking on the part of Nichiren Daishonin but is, rather, a vision of the future based on a clear and profound understanding of cause and effect, specifically the effect of many people chanting *Nam-myoho-renge-kyo*. It is also worth recalling in this context that, of all the world's major religions, only Nichiren Daishonin's Buddhism foresees the human race developing to a point where it can learn to overcome the many problems which it has created and now confront it, rather than perishing in the flames of some mythical Armageddon.

Buddhism and Culture
Despite the obvious humanity of Buddhism and its traditionally tolerant attitude to other religions and beliefs, some people in the West might still object that it is an alien creed and that, while a few individuals may be able to benefit from it, its adoption on any large scale would be inimical to the indigenous cultures of the various countries into which it is now being introduced. However, as Daisaku Ikeda notes:

Historically, religions or ideologies spread from one country to others. This is true of Christianity, Islam and various Buddhist teachings. It also applies to the arts, literature, music and paintings . . . As one can see from these examples, any aspect of culture tends to spread from its point of origin to other areas . . . The propagation of Buddhism in individual countries does not in any way mean the destruction of a country's culture or the forcing of Japanese religion upon a country.

This is because, like scientific laws, the principles of Nichiren

*Not every one living, but, rather, people in all conditions of life, i.e. the Ten Worlds.
†Legendary kings who reigned over ideal societies in ancient China.

Daishonin's Buddhism transcend time and place. Thus, just as the British, Americans and Japanese make cars which naturally express certain aspects of their respective cultures, yet operate according to the same principles and fulfil the same basic function, so the British, Americans and Japanese who practise Nichiren Daishonin's Buddhism do so in accordance with their own national or local laws, customs and social mores. This is only common sense. For example, Americans are fairly open to new ideas, while the British tend to be more resistant. In the United States, therefore, it is not unknown for Nichiren Shoshu Buddhists to invite perfect strangers to meetings or to talk to people about Buddhism on buses, trains or in the street. To adopt this approach in the United Kingdom would probably cause the listener to recoil in distaste, however, as the British are generally suspicious of unsolicited advances, religious or otherwise. Indeed, most members of NSUK themselves would probably feel highly uncomfortable at working for *kosen-rufu* in this way and so, naturally, find their own ways of teaching others about Buddhism. This is a principle in Buddhism known as *zuiho bini*, literally meaning 'to adapt the precept to the locality'. In short, while everyone shares the same basic practice, Nichiren Shoshu Buddhism considers how each person lives, or each society expresses itself, a matter entirely for the individual or collective wisdom of those concerned.

Buddhism has always held this basic attitude to propagation, as Daisaku Ikeda notes:

> The introduction of Buddhism into any land brings happiness and prosperity to that nation and its people. This is indicated by the fact that the transferral of Buddhism from India, the land of its origin, to China, Korea, Japan, Burma and other parts of southeast Asia produced cultural flowerings but never resulted in subjugation to Indian control.

Indeed, Nichiren Daishonin teaches that *kosen-rufu* can come about only as a result of the enormous diversity of creative talent that is unleashed in society as individuals – indeed, whole races and nations – each learn to express their own uniqueness to the full, while, at the same time, learning to respect the individuality and essentially unique role of others.

Mission

It follows from this that fundamental to the notion of practising for others is the gradual realization in each person who chants that they have a mission. As already explained, Buddhism equates 'mission' with the unique purpose of an individual's life. In other words, because the particular circumstances of our lives are unique to each one of us, no one else can fulfil our particular, individual mission. Of course, someone else may be able to do our job, but the job we do is only a part of our mission, which is the expression or fulfilment of our lives as a whole. In this sense, 'mission' is another way of describing the achievement of our full potential as individuals and members of society.

One woman's potential, for example, might best be expressed as a housewife and a mother, in ensuring her family are well cared for and develop *their* full potential as human beings. In finding and fulfilling her mission as a mother she will, therefore, also find her happiness. Another woman, with different talents, concerns, wants and needs – in short, a different potential – will have a different mission in society: to change attitudes to women at work, for example, or simply to make her own unique contribution to the success of a particular venture in business, administration, the social services or whatever. As her potential is different, so she will eventually discover the way which best expresses it and, in fulfilling *her* mission, will also find *her* true happiness. As each mission is unique to each individual, however, all are worthy of equal respect: the brain surgeon, the businessman and the housewife are all vital to their own unique and specialized environments.

In the deepest sense, though, the most important mission shared by all those who chant *Nam-myoho-renge-kyo*, no matter what their background or circumstances, is that of the Bodhisattvas of the Earth: that is, to help others become enlightened. As Daisaku Ikeda explains:

> Our movement for *kosen-rufu* is on a dimension which differs from the political or economic level, or the level of pursuing one's self-interests. Since the fundamental awakening of mankind lies in the Mystic Law, always and everywhere – whether in the past, present or future, whether on this earth or somewhere else in the universe – we should never forget our primary function of teaching

each other the great Law which penetrates the essence of all life throughout the three existences [of past, present and future].

This does not preclude taking direct action where necessary to relieve suffering arising from poverty, sickness, violence or any other cause; but, just as giving a starving man a fish means he will be able to eat for a day, while giving him a fishing-rod and teaching him how to use it means he will be able to eat for life, so teaching another person how to chant enables them to change their destiny to suffer and experience the greatest happiness for lifetime after lifetime.

Whether or not people start to chant at once, planting the seed of Buddhahood in their life by teaching them about *Nam-myoho-renge-kyo* is a guarantee that, in due course, they will begin to practise – and so become enlightened. This may be difficult to accept unless it is recognized that the state of Buddhahood – the Buddha nature – does exist in every human being and, deep within us, is awakened from latency by even hearing or sensing the vibrations of *Nam-myoho-renge-kyo*. Nevertheless, this is why practice for others constitutes not only the greatest possible act of compassion, but also the greatest source of good fortune and joy for those who carry it out. As Daisaku Ikeda says, 'When we continue our practice for ourselves and others, we can love others and be loved by others. Those around us will say to themselves that there is something attractive about our lives.'

STUDY

The teachings of Nichiren Daishonin are contained in a collection of texts called the *Gosho*. *Go* means 'worthy of the greatest respect' (as in *Go*honzon), and *sho* means 'writings'. Roughly half the *Gosho* comprises personal letters from Nichiren Daishonin to various of his followers, written in an easy style and language and pitched at a level of explanation suitable to each recipient; the other half comprises longer, more difficult and formal doctrinal treatises, written in classical Chinese and with a wider, more learned audience in mind, namely, the scholars and religious and secular authorities of the day. Unlike many major religions, then, the basic texts which explain the doctrines of Nichiren Shoshu

Buddhism have been written by the founder himself and are not interpretations set down later by his followers.

The study of these writings – and various exegeses on them – plays a vital role in Nichiren Daishonin's Buddhism. Study in this context, however, has little in common with academic learning for, although various SGI organizations mount regular courses and lectures on the *Gosho*, at its simplest, study consists of reading a line or phrase of the *Gosho* each day in order gradually to assimilate its profound meaning and further deepen our understanding of the spirit of Buddhist practice. In other words, we do not study Nichiren Daishonin's teachings in order to become Buddhist philosophers, nor simply to amass knowledge about Buddhism, but so that we can understand how the principles of this Buddhism apply directly to life – our lives in particular – and so help us to attain the supreme happiness of Buddhahood. In this Buddhism, as Daisaku Ikeda says, 'Study is the backbone of faith and action.'

This non-academic approach to study is one that has been adopted by Nichiren Shoshu Buddhism from its very beginnings, not simply to make it more accessible to ordinary people – although that is a very good reason in itself – but to avoid the dangers inherent in the worlds of Learning and Realization; arrogance, élitism and a tendency towards self-absorption. To underline the correct attitude towards study, Nichiren Daishonin relates in the *Gosho* the story of Shuddipanthaka, a man so stupid that he was 'unable to memorize even fourteen words in three years, yet he eventually attained enlightenment. On the other hand, Devadatta* mastered 60,000 doctrines but eventually fell into Hell. This represents the way of our own age.' In other words, someone who practises this Buddhism strongly and consistently will definitely make Buddhahood the dominant tendency of his or her life, no matter how little education they may have had; while a person with a brilliant degree from a top university will inevitably 'fall into Hell' – that is, suffer greatly – if they become conceited about their intellect and think that, simply because they can learn Buddhist theory more quickly than others, they are somehow superior. Indeed, mere 'expertise' is no

---

*Historically, Shakyamuni's cousin and one-time disciple who later became his greatest enemy. Figuratively, Devadatta also represents the world of Hell, evil, and fundamental delusion inherent in life.

more a guarantee of personal happiness in Buddhism than it is in law, medicine, or any other field. As Daisaku Ikeda says, 'Faith is like an axle, and practice and study are like the two wheels of a cart. No matter how much you know about Buddhist doctrines, if your practice is weak, your faith can be said to be crippled.'

Bearing this in mind, one could say that study in Nichiren Shoshu Buddhism serves two basic functions, relating to 'practice for oneself' and 'practice for others'. Firstly, study enables us to become personally convinced of the vast scope and depth of Nichiren Shoshu Buddhism and, through putting its principles into practise, to develop a condition of life equally vast and deep. Secondly, it helps each of us to clarify the nature of our unique mission in the world. These two aspects of study are obviously closely related, but let us first discuss it from the former viewpoint.

As there is no such thing as blind faith in Buddhism, great emphasis is placed on understanding what one practises, and why. It may be true that, in the final analysis, comprehension arises from faith – from first practising the teachings and coming truly to understand them as a result of one's own experience – but such understanding must still confirm what is taught, for this, in turn, deepens one's faith in the teachings. In short, actual and theoretical proof must be consistent. In terms of our daily life, then, study helps us develop conviction and therefore courage because, by proving the teachings through practice, we gradually abandon the notion that we are powerless to alter our situation for the better. In particular, through the combination of study and practice, we gain faith in the fact that Buddhahood exists within us. Furthermore, together with practice, study helps us to see the root cause of any difficulty, which is the first step towards taking the correct action to overcome it.

Developing the habit of allying study to practice does not happen overnight and, for many people, even studying 'little but often' represents one of the hardest challenges of their Buddhist practice. Not only is the idea of continual self-improvement probably alien to many of us, but we also take some convincing that we can perfectly analyze even the most seemingly trivial events of our daily lives in the light of something written over 700 years ago, in a different time and an alien culture. The rewards of meeting the challenge of study are immeasurable, however, for as we gradually learn how 'to see with the eyes of the Buddha' – usually by first using them to look at the problems which exist within our own lives – what was previously dark, confused and hopeless suddenly becomes illuminated, and we begin to see a way forward from our suffering which before did not appear to exist.

Moreover, as we see these paths starting to open up in our lives, we gain increasing confidence to turn those eyes outwards to the the society around us. Nichiren Daishonin states, 'When the skies are clear, the ground is illuminated. Similarly, when one knows the Lotus Sutra,* he understands the meaning of all worldly affairs.' In short, when we are eventually able to view everything through the teachings of the 'all-encompassing *myo*' mentioned above, we can perceive the true nature of any event or situation and quickly understand any other teaching. Indeed, the second president of the Soka Gakkai, Josei Toda, once said that, thanks to his mastery of Nichiren Daishonin's Buddhism, he was able to master any other discipline after only three months of concentrated application. This was no idle boast, but simply an indication of the greatly increased power of comprehension produced, quite naturally, through studying and practising the profound and absolutely fundamental principles of life which are explained in the *Gosho*. To give an analogy, if one can jump over a fence six feet high, one can also jump over fences three, four or five feet high.

Nichiren Shoshu Buddhism teaches that the ultimate reason for our self-development is the use of our increased capacities for the sake of other people. This brings us to the second main reason for the importance of study. Daisaku Ikeda comments, 'Without a thorough knowledge of Nichiren Daishonin's teachings, one's practice can easily become self-centred and one may begin interpreting true Buddhism in one's own way. Study will deepen one's confidence in faith and direct one to a correct path towards *kosen-rufu*.' This does not just mean that study helps us to teach others about Nichiren Daishonin's Buddhism (which of course it does), but that the deeper understanding of life which we gain through practice and study and which, inevitably, we express through all our thoughts, words and deeds, enables us in the most natural way to revitalize, and re-orientate along truly humanistic paths, the particular area of society in which we are active. This is

*In this context, 'knowing the Lotus Sutra' means to be enlightened to the Law of *Nam-myoho-renge-kyo*.

possible because, whatever area happens to be our concern and however specialized it may be, it is nevertheless the result of human behaviour and is, therefore, susceptible to the influence of the wisdom and compassion of the Buddha nature at work within us.

Indeed, to this end Daisaku Ikeda himself has held meetings and discussions with a large number of leading figures in many different fields, including the historian, the late Dr Arnold Toynbee; the former US Secretary of State, Dr Henry Kissenger; the French art historian, René Huyghe; the former president of the Club of Rome, the late Aurelio Peccei; a leading sociologist of religion and Fellow of All Souls, Oxford, Dr Bryan Wilson; the US journalist, Norman Cousins; the Japanese astronomer, Masayoshi Kiguchi; and many others. The outcome of some of these discussions have been published in book form and testify to the enormous range of topics to which Daisaku Ikeda can contribute invaluable and humane insights. He would be the first to admit, however, that this facility springs from nowhere other than his practice and study of Nichiren Daishonin's Buddhism, initially conducted under the guidance of his mentor, Josei Toda.

Of course, Nichiren Shoshu Buddhism does not demand that all its practitioners develop the capacity to engage in dialogue with leading intellectuals and politicians, although an increasing number of Nichiren Shoshu Buddhists are already laying the foundations for the movement for *kosen-rufu* in the worlds of medicine, education, business, the law, the arts, economics and so on. Just as important is the capacity to come to a profound understanding of life which can be developed in the housewife, the taxi-driver, the secretary and the shop assistant: in short, in us ordinary people who make up the unseen and unsung mass of any society. For, ultimately, these are the people upon whom the future success of a movement to create a peaceful, happy, yet progressive world depends. This attitude is implicit in the following words of Daisaku Ikeda, which might be said to encapsulate the basic spirit underlying the study and practice of Nichiren Daishonin's Buddhism: 'The philosophy we study must not be one of mere words and ideas. We must all regard this philosophy as alive in the life of each individual. We must do our best to master it to the extent that we can influence contemporary society by discussing our beliefs in words intelligible to everyone.'

5

Soka Gakkai International

In one way or another, most people first hear about Nichiren Daishonin's Buddhism through the activities of members of the Soka Gakkai International (SGI). Founded by Daisaku Ikeda in 1975 and later incorporated as a non-governmental organization of the United Nations, SGI is the name given to the federation of Nichiren Shoshu lay organizations throughout the world. The aims of the SGI are:

- to aim towards the prosperity of society as good citizens respecting the culture, customs and laws of each country;
- to aim at the promotion of humanistic culture and education based on Nichiren Daishonin's Buddhism;
- to join our efforts towards world peace with the United Nations by supporting the spirit of its charter, thus aiming towards the ultimate goal of the abolition of nuclear weapons and the universal renunciation of war.

From this it can be seen that the purpose of the SGI is basically twofold: to aid its members in their individual human revolution by helping them to practise Nichiren Daishonin's Buddhism exactly as the Buddha taught; and, while spearheading the worldwide movement for *kosen-rufu*, to work to create value in all areas of society.

Currently, the SGI comprises some twenty million members in

115 countries around the world, with its headquarters based in Tokyo. Rather like the UN, the authority of the SGI derives solely from the voluntary assent of its members, initially at a national level but, ultimately, at the level of each individual. Unlike the UN, though, the SGI manages to achieve a remarkable degree of unity in its actions and might be said to provide a model for international co-operation. Fundamentally, this unity is possible only because all members of the SGI are able to reveal their highest selves through chanting to the Gohonzon and thus find the ideal balance between the demands of the individual and those of the group. In other words, while closely following the guidance in faith of the sixty-seventh High Priest of Nichiren Shoshu, Nikken Shonin (as expressed through Daisaku Ikeda, to whom he has given the responsibility of lay leader of the worldwide movement for *kosen-rufu*), as members of a federation each national lay organization is able to exercise considerable autonomy in furthering the aims of the SGI in accordance with the culture and laws of their respective countries. As previously mentioned, the UK branch of the SGI is called Nichiren Shoshu of the United Kingdom (NSUK), which is based at Taplow Court in Berkshire and whose motto is 'Trust through Friendship, Peace through Trust'.

The pattern of relationships within the SGI is repeated at all levels throughout the organization of Nichiren Shoshu lay societies in each country. For example, in the UK the basic unit is called a district which, as its name suggests, is the totality of members practising and working for *kosen-rufu* in a particular area or neighbourhood. The size of the area can vary considerably, according to how widely the membership is distributed. In Japan, for example, all the members living in just one or two streets can comprise their equivalent of a district, whereas in a country to which Buddhism is a relative newcomer, the district can consist of the entire national membership. As the number of people practising in any borough, town or county increases, however, districts split and become smaller in area, while retaining roughly the same numerical strength – anywhere from between fifteen to thirty people. A number of districts together comprise a chapter, a number of chapters a headquarters, and the headquarters together make up the national organization. In this way, it can be seen that growth in the organization mimics the growth and division of cells in the natural world, thus keeping the basic size of the organization in any area to a manageable and human scale, no matter how large it becomes overall.

Each district is further divided into two or more groups so that members can quite quickly form friendships with the others in their group and group leaders can easily keep in touch with the half dozen or so members in their charge. This is very important because it highlights the fact that the SGI at all levels exists for the sake of the members, not the other way round. Unfortunately, many organizations which are established to achieve high ideals and social reform do so – if at all – only at the expense of either those outside the organization, or their own members, or both. This is especially true of many revolutionary organizations which preach lofty goals but employ brutal means to reach them and, after eliminating their enemies, often turn on and kill each other. As Buddhism teaches the need for individual human revolution, in which there is no higher value than upholding the dignity of each person, the means of achieving *kosen-rufu* in society must be consistent with the end itself. In other words, to establish a harmonious, creative and happy world, individuals within the SGI must themselves be able to establish harmonious, creative and happy lives through their membership of the organization. To fulfil its *raison d'être*, the SGI must therefore be able to teach its members how to establish such lives. In short, if people usually first learn about chanting from a single individual, it is nevertheless through their association with their fellow members in the organization that they learn how to practise Nichiren Daishonin's Buddhism correctly and so gain the greatest benefit from it. It is the very struggle to respect the differences in others, to seek out the good and great points in each person, which triggers off the process which Josei Toda fittingly named 'the human revolution'.

This is nowhere more apparent than at the monthly district and group discussion meetings which, together with the monthly study meetings, are by far the most important activities each member regularly attends. Indeed, one might go so far as to say that attending the monthly discussion meetings is vital if we are to do our human revolution and work effectively for *kosen-rufu*. One reason for this is that the discussion meeting is the forum for people of all ages, races and widely differing social backgrounds to talk together about their experience of daily life based on the practice of Nichiren Daishonin's Buddhism. For many of us, just the simple experience of regularly mixing in this way with people to whom we might normally never even talk, let alone discuss anything as profound as the meaning of life, is one which gradually expands our tolerance and respect for others. We may not have realized quite how intolerant we are until we are faced with our own reaction to others at these meetings. It is at discussion meetings, in other words, that we first have to learn – not as a theory, but as reality – that all people possess Buddhahood, even though this lesson might involve a great struggle on our part to realize that the Buddha nature exists in someone whom we really do not much like; and that it is those very differences which directly relate to their unique purpose in life.

Moreover, discussion meetings are where we can speak frankly about our fears and doubts, where we can get our questions answered and, most importantly, where we can be inspired by the proof of the power of this Buddhism shown by the experiences of other members of our district – ordinary, everyday people, just like ourselves. As Daisaku Ikeda explains:

> Discussion meetings are not places for doctrinal debates. Nor are they only places to transmit plans and schedules. Discussion meetings have a much more profound meaning. Actually, they are so important that without them there could be no organization. The reason for this is that the discussion meetings, when filled with the sustained brightness of pure faith, will allow every participant to build within himself an inner fortress of faith. Thus he will be inspired to achieve his own reformation and growth. At the discussion meeting one can polish oneself and achieve something which can never be accomplished at school or home through guidance from one's seniors. The result attained at our discussion meetings constitutes the keynote of our social activities.

All in all, then, the monthly discussion meeting functions to deepen our faith, polish and expand our lives, and renew our hope and determination for the future. So refreshed, we can then take the spirit of this Buddhism out into society and use it to create value, each in our own way, in our own unique circumstances and on our own individually chosen paths of life. It is in this light, therefore, that we should remember the encouragement all SGI members are given: to attend their district and group discussion meetings each month – 'no matter what'.

From time to time, members of some SGI organizations also hold meetings based on different groupings – for example, men, women, young men and young women. The idea behind these meetings is to provide an opportunity for members to talk freely and openly amongst themselves about matters that may be especially relevant to that particular group. A young woman who may not want to discuss her difficulties at a district meeting, for instance, may well feel less inhibited when she sees at a young women's meeting that her situation is not so awesome and unique, and that other young women have had to face and overcome similar problems. Other groups within the organization may be formed on the basis of common interests such as education, medicine, ethnic background and so on. NSUK, for example, contains groups as diverse as the Afro-Caribbean group, the Middle East group, the Students' Division, the Lawyers' group, the City Business group, the Arts Division (comprising all those involved in the creative arts), the First Aid group, and many more. Different as they are, though, all these groups have been brought together to discuss ways of using the teachings of Nichiren Daishonin to bring about humanistic reform in those areas of society to which each relates. In other words, like the discussion meetings, they are not merely talking shops but a means by which individuals can come to understand how to take action in the world at large for the sake of *kosen-rufu*.

Even though the organization clearly exists for – and is shaped by – its members, there are sometimes people who, while in broad agreement with what Nichiren Shoshu Buddhism teaches, would prefer to practise on their own, feeling (as Marina Catacuzino did initially) that religious organizations inevitably promote conformity, stifle individuality and limit freedom of thought and expression. Feelings like this are understandable and, indeed, a healthy vigilance over organizations of all kinds is highly desirable. It is also a fact of life, however, that any activity which involves more than one person entails organization to some degree, and the more altruistic the aim of that activity, the greater – and purer – the organization needed to support it. As Daisaku Ikeda explains in terms of the SGI:

The organization is necessary in order for many people to advance together in harmony. Those who practise by themselves tend to become self-righteous and to fall prey to their own narrow views, which Buddhism discourages. All in all, solitary practice does not bring about correct faith, practice and study, or a correct relationship between the individual and society based on the Mystic Law. If you practise alone for a long period of time, you will eventually lose sight of the correct path of faith. If you realize the importance of people encouraging one another to maintain their faith and to live courageously, then you will naturally understand the importance of the organization as a means to practise correctly.

The point I am making here is that our organization exists as a means to guide each individual to happiness and to help each individual improve his or her faith. The purpose of our organization is to make it possible for each member to attain the state of absolute happiness, or Buddhahood.

Of course, being composed of human beings, the SGI is naturally susceptible to the problems inherent in any large organization, such as the tendency towards administrative bureaucracy, authoritarianism, conservatism and so on. Unlike other organizations, however, the SGI does possess a number of unique safeguards against such tendencies.

Itai Doshin
The most important of these is that all the activities of the SGI are based on the principle of *itai doshin*. *Itai doshin* means 'many (*i*) bodies (*tai*), one (*do*) mind (*shin*)', and refers specifically to the unity of purpose many different individuals can achieve when they chant to the Gohonzon for the sake of achieving *kosen-rufu*, through the inner reformation, or 'human revolution, of each person. As Nichiren Daishonin states, 'If *itai doshin* prevails among the people, they will achieve all their goals, whereas in *dotai ishin* [one body, many minds], they can achieve nothing remarkable.'

Essentially, *itai* means each person displaying his or her individual and unique talents and abilities to the full which, in turn, means revealing their Buddhahood, as described by Nichiren Daishonin in the following terms: 'Cherry, plum, peach and damson all have their own qualities and manifest the three properties of the original Buddha without changing their own character.' *Doshin* means that these different individuals are nevertheless united by their faith in the Gohonzon and the goal of attaining *kosen-rufu*. In this sense, then, *itai doshin* implies that a harmonious and creative world can be achieved only through the rich diversity of qualities inherent in each individual human life being fully expressed, yet unified towards the supreme goal of *kosen-rufu*.

To put it another way, *kosen-rufu* could be described as the combined effect of many millions of people revealing, through their practice to the Gohonzon, their full potential as individuals, and thereby fulfilling their unique roles in life, yet never losing sight of the ultimate goal which they all share. Thus, far from implying any sort of conformity, other than in the practice of Buddhism itself, the principle of *itai doshin* stresses the need for enlightened individuality. That is to say, because it is based upon the Buddha nature inherent in each person, *itai doshin* means that it is not just possible, but actually desirable, to achieve one's deepest personal desires while simultaneously contributing to the attainment of *kosen-rufu* and world peace.

This is one reason why the consistent and untiring practice of *gongyo* and chanting *daimoku* to the Gohonzon is essential in Nichiren Daishonin's Buddhism. Not only is it a means of continually refreshing our life-force and our resolve in the face of the obstacles we inevitably meet in the course of our daily lives, but it is also the only way of checking whether our personal desires are truly in accord with *kosen-rufu*. Thus, our highest self, our Buddha nature, always steers us towards *kosen-rufu*, harmony with our environment, and seeing the Buddha nature revealed in other people, no matter what the other, egoistic force in our lives may be telling us. Fundamentally, what unites Nichiren Daishonin's followers is chanting *Nam-myoho-renge-kyo* to the Gohonzon and their desire for *kosen-rufu*, for only this highest and most altruistic of all goals can truly unite people in a way that is lasting, whatever their background. As Nichiren Daishonin explains:

> All disciples and believers of Nichiren should chant *Nam-myoho-renge-kyo* with one mind (*itai doshin*), transcending all differences among themselves to become as inseparable as fish and the water in which they swim. This spiritual bond is the basis for the universal transmission of the ultimate law of life and death. Herein lies the true goal of Nichiren's propagation. When you are

so united, even the great hope for *kosen-rufu* can be fulfilled without fail.

Moreover, as personal membership of the various national Nichiren Shoshu organizations is both free and entirely voluntary, no leader in faith in the SGI at any level has any power or authority in the commonly accepted sense of the words. Rather, in keeping with the spirit and the aims of the SGI as a whole, leaders within the organization are concerned only with taking responsibility for initiating and co-ordinating activities whose aim is the growth in faith and happiness of their fellow members, and the spread of this happiness throughout their respective neighbourhoods, towns, regions, countries and finally the world. For leaders in faith, therefore, this constitutes 'practice for others', which, through cause and effect, brings them benefit in turn, as already described.

It follows from this that there can be no place for externally imposed discipline, commands or orders within the SGI for, even if they wanted to, leaders would be powerless to enforce their will on other members. Instead, the SGI at all levels operates through the freely given consent of the members concerned. Thus, guidance on matters of faith, practice and study, for example, is regularly passed from leaders to members, but then, after first chanting to the Gohonzon, it is up to each individual member to decide how to act on that guidance, or whether to question or even reject it.

Of course, it is part of the function of leaders fully to explain guidance in faith, based on the *Gosho*, and to try to inspire their members to put it into practice, but, in the final analysis, each individual is completely responsible for whether or not he or she does so. Similarly, no leader can force a member to do *gongyo* twice a day, to chant, to study, to attend meetings or to do anything else related to the practice. They can only advise members of the benefit that follows from such actions and, naturally, such advice will be convincing only if leaders themselves can show evidence of having benefited from putting guidance into practice personally.

Thus, although it might seem idealistic in the extreme that any organization can function effectively by relying solely on the goodwill of its members, the effect of this lack of authoritarian power for leaders within the SGI is wholly beneficial, for it means that leaders can inspire their members only by virtue of their

virtues. That is to say, leaders ultimately have to prove themselves to be – above all things – strong in faith, as well as reliable,
sensible, trustworthy, compassionate, courageous, unselfish and
fair. Thanks to the Gohonzon, though, they do indeed develop
these qualities. On the other hand, their lack of power also
underlines the fact that positions of leadership within the SGI
(which are accepted voluntarily and the vast majority unpaid)
are in no way rewards or 'jobs for the boys'. Rather, they are
opportunities for individuals to grow in faith through taking up
the challenge of greater responsibilities for achieving *kosen-rufu* in
a particular area.

Indeed, in this respect the SGI is highly unusual for, whereas
most organizations can be seen as basically pyramidical in
structure, with the boss wielding the most power at the top (while
enjoying the greatest rewards), and supported by each progressively larger layer of personnel beneath him or her, the SGI
rests on its point, like a pyramid in reverse. The president
supports the vice-presidents, who support other senior leaders,
and so on up to the members. In other words, as each leader is
directly responsible for the growth and happiness of those within
his or her charge, the greater the seniority of the leader, the more
people he or she has to support, encourage and nurture.
Moreover, since the principle of *itai doshin* implies the complete
equality of individuals, each of whom possess Buddhahood and a
unique mission for *kosen-rufu*, leaders are considered in no way
superior to members who have no specific responsibility in the
organization. Rather, they simply have a different mission.

This sense of equality is reflected in the fact that every member
has direct access to even the most senior leaders, that ideas and
suggestions are actively canvassed from all the members, and,
most importantly, that the organization is able to respond to
them. Of course, not every idea can be put into effect but, where it
is sincerely based on the Buddha nature, through the chanting of
abundant *daimoku*, it will most likely generate enough interest and
support to become a reality. Indeed, if the SGI were not open in
this way to fresh input from its members, it would soon ossify and
eventually fall apart. Similarly, the SGI as an organization can
keep growing and advancing only because, in the final analysis,
its members are growing and advancing as individuals; in other
words, they are gaining great value, happiness and fulfilment
from their continued practice of Nichiren Daishonin's Buddhism.

Hence, the organization provides the cultivated ground in which many different and beautiful flowers can grow.

In many ways, as a united body of people, the SGI is unprecedented and unique. As an organization founded on *itai doshin*, it is a completely open and tolerant society where everyone can display his or her true character and ability, achieve their human revolution, attain Buddhahood and contribute to world peace. While by no means pretending to be perfect or beyond improvement, through the power of faith and practice alone it has established the Middle Way, a balance between individualism and commonality, freedom and control, initiative and restraint, which could be the envy of many other large institutions. Moreover, it has done so without recourse to any kind of force or persuasion other than the force of logic and common sense, and the persuasion of patient, reasonable dialogue. Indeed, if the SGI is to continue growing as a movement for peace in the future, it can do so only by placing faith first in everything. Daisaku Ikeda explains:

> Various powers in the world – authority, money, brutality – attempt to violate human dignity. The role of Soka Gakkai [International] in society is to employ the spirit that wells from the very depths of life to do battle with such powers. This battle is a starting point for a war of resistance against fascism. In terms of social stability, the value of Soka Gakkai [International], as an organization, is certain to increase. Making intimate appeals to each person with whom one comes in contact seems like modest, slow work; but all great tasks take time to accomplish. Establishing the contacts that enable individual human beings to cultivate and refine the life within them cannot be accomplished overnight. But the result of such an undertaking is the diamond of life, which cannot be destroyed by surrounding circumstances, no matter how severe. The only path left for mankind is the one leading through slow, modest work of the kind I have mentioned. And to anyone who would scoff at my proposal, I can only ask, 'What solution do you suggest?'

Of course many organizations, religious and secular, have been founded to work for peace in the world, yet none have succeeded. To understand why Daisaku Ikeda has such confidence that the Buddhism of Nichiren Daishonin, as propagated by the SGI, will form the basis for world peace, we must finally turn to a consideration of the *Rissho Ankoku Ron*.

6

A Lasting Peace

It is often said that Nichiren Daishonin's Buddhism begins and ends with his *Rissho Ankoku Ron (Treatise on Securing the Peace of the Land through the Propagation of True Buddhism)*. Certainly, the fact that this was the only one of his major writings addressed directly to the ruling authorities of Japan highlights the importance Nichiren Daishonin himself attached to it. Although written over 700 years ago, and dealing with what today might seem a somewhat specialized subject – the relationship between the sufferings of the Japanese people during the thirteenth century and the doctrines and activities of the various Buddhist sects then prominent – the *Rissho Ankoku Ron* is actually a timeless document since the basic issue it discusses – the effect of people's beliefs on their society and natural environment – is fundamental to every age. Indeed, it is primarily in the light of the penetrating insights offered by Nichiren Daishonin in this treatise that the major problems currently facing all humanity can be analysed and a lasting solution discovered.

Before we look at the message of the *Rissho Ankoku Ron* in any detail, it is important to note that it is written in the form of a dialogue between a Guest and his Host. The Guest represents Hojo Tokiyori, then effective ruler of Japan, to whom the treatise was submitted in 1260; and the Host represents Nichiren Daishonin. There are nine questions from the Guest, nine answers from the Host, and a conclusion from the Guest who has been won round to the Host's point of view. In other words, the *Rissho Ankoku Ron* might be described as a partially dramatized, step-by-step refutation by Nichiren Daishonin of the beliefs then prevalent in Japan, as he imagines them being expressed by the most powerful man in the country, Hojo Tokiyori.

Amazing as it may seem, in more recent times a number of commentators have taken some of the Guest's statements out of context and attributed his views to Nichiren Daishonin. For example, at one point the Guest suggests that the issue of state security is more important than any other matter, for only if the security of the state is guaranteed can Buddhism and the people prosper. Such a view might well have been expressed by a man such as Hojo Tokiyori, whose primary concern would naturally be the government of the country, but later critics have cited this passage to support the accusation that Nichiren Daishonin was nationalistic, authoritarian and in favour of state-imposed religion. By failing to explain that the Host – in other words, Nichiren Daishonin himself – goes on to refute all these points in his answer to the Guest, such critics have been responsible for creating the fundamentally distorted picture of Nichiren Daishonin found in many reference books, works on Buddhism and histories of Japan, where he is often described as a militant, right-wing ultranationalist, or words to that effect. Reading the *Rissho Ankoku Ron* correctly, or indeed any of the *Gosho*, quickly dispels this notion.

Given this background of misunderstanding, however, the best way to begin to understand Nichiren Daishonin's reasons for writing this profound treatise, and the great courage and compassion he displayed in so doing, might first be to place it in its proper setting: Japan in the mid-thirteenth century.

THE HISTORICAL BACKGROUND

Although nominally under the rule of the emperor, since the end of the twelfth century Japan had been controlled by what was effectively a military dictator, the *shogun*. Based in Kamakura, a city on the east coast of Japan near modern-day Tokyo, the shogunate was dominated throughout the thirteenth century by just one family, the Hojo, who exercised power by acting as regents to a line of puppet emperors – often young children of royal birth.

Absolute though the Hojo were politically at this time, they appeared helpless in the face of the major problems Japan was experiencing under their rule. Indeed, since around the beginning of the thirteenth century, the country had suffered from a series of disasters unprecedented at any time in its history. Repeated earthquakes, epidemics, unseasonal typhoons, fires, floods, droughts and famines, all seemed to conspire to rob the Japanese people of any sense of security or hope for the future. The general foreboding amongst the populace was further strengthened by the widespread belief that the evil 'Latter Day of the Law' – the age of growing suffering, conflict and confusion predicted by Shakyamuni Buddha some 2000 years previously – had begun in the mid-eleventh century; certainly, the reported sightings, at intervals, of various unusual astrological and metereological phenomena – two suns were said to have appeared in the sky over the imperial city of Kyoto in 1245, for example – were all interpreted as portents of even worse times to come.

Naturally, these continuing crises were deeply worrying to the shogunate, who turned to the country's religious leaders for solutions, ordering the various Buddhist sects to pray for the cessation of disasters. The Buddhist priesthood, however, was in no position to help anyone, racked as it was with bitter and sometimes violent infighting. Moreover, as these disputes were rarely doctrinal in nature, but largely sordid squabbles over property rights and prestige, it is clear that, by and large, Japanese Buddhism had long since forgotten the basic spirit of compassion underpinning all Buddhist teachings, the priesthood preferring instead to concentrate on the material rewards of office. Indeed, the fact that on a number of occassions Buddhist monks even armed themselves to fight monks from rival temples is an indication of the extent to which the various sects had degenerated into mere wealthy élites, concerned above all with guarding their lands rather than 'guarding the precepts', and protecting their status rather than providing spiritual guidance for the people.

The corruption and worldliness then prevalent in Japanese Buddhism in some ways mirrors that of the papacy at about the same period, particularly since, as in Rome, the religious and political spheres had become so closely intertwined. For example, when Hojo Tokiyori retired as regent in 1256, he went to live as a lay priest at a Zen temple; even so, that did not stop him continuing to wield great power and, until his death in 1263, he remained the *de facto* ruler of Japan. (This was one reason why, when Nichiren Daishonin came to present the *Rissho Ankoku Ron* to the government in 1260, he submitted it to Hojo Tokiyori rather than the 'official' regent, Hojo Nagatoki.)

Again, as a number of important temples had been founded by members of the Hojo family, the head priests of these temples, while able to exert influence in political affairs, were also naturally subject to the wishes or pressure of their patrons, no matter what the doctrines of their sect might teach. Not that compromise on doctrinal questions would have elicited much protest: the various sects were so bound up with struggles for power and influence that most monks and priests would have been hard pressed to explain even the sutras on which their own particular sect was based. All in all, it is hardly surprising that neither the religious nor the secular authorities of the day proved capable of offering the Japanese people any wise leadership during this time of continual suffering.

It is an ill wind that blows nobody any good, however, and one Buddhist sect at least did enjoy enormous popular support during this period – the Nembutsu or Jodo (Pure Land) sect. Given the widespread – and growing – feeling of human powerlessness in the face of seemingly unending catastrophes, it is not difficult to understand why this was so. The Nembutsu sect taught that it was impossible for people to change their unhappy state in this impure world but that, by calling on a legendary Buddha named Amida, through his grace one could be reborn after death in a far-off 'pure land' of bliss – the Western Paradise – over which Amida was sovereign. For a suffering and basically ill-educated people, this was obviously a seductive idea. Indeed, at the height of the Nembutsu sect's popularity, the desire to escape from the pain, struggle and uncertainty of thirteenth-century Japan had grown to such an extent that some people even committed suicide to reach the Western Paradise more quickly. Of course, only a small minority went to the extreme of suicide and not everyone in the country practised Nembutsu, but the influence of the teaching was so pervasive that, by the middle of the century, very many Japanese had developed a strong tendency towards passive resignation to whatever fate held in store for them, expecting things to get only worse while they were alive and for happiness to come only after they had died.

As it happens, from 1256 things did get worse – quite considerably so. In August of that year heavy storms caused flooding in Kamakura, destroying the rice stores for the coming winter and, only a month later, an epidemic of a disease resembling smallpox erupted in various parts of the country. 1257 witnessed, amongst other things, a serious drought and in Kamakura alone four major earthquakes, the third of which was especially severe, as a contemporary account describes:

> The twenty-third day [of the eight month, 1257], cyclical sign *kinotomi*, was clear. At the Hour of the Dog [about eight p.m.], a great earthquake struck. There was a roar, and not a single shrine or temple remained standing. Mountains crumbled and dwellings were toppled. Not a roofed mud-wall was left intact. Here and there fissures yawned in the ground and water gushed forth. . .

Needless to say, many were killed, and when the following three years saw an even greater intensification of suffering, with plague and famine in particular exacting a heavy toll amongst the populace, not a few people began to wonder whether the world might actually be coming to an end.

It was against the background of these dramatic and harrowing events that Nichiren Daishonin decided in 1258 to research and write his analysis of the situation, the *Rissho Ankoku Ron*. It took him two years to gather the incontrovertible documentary proof he needed to support his thesis and, finally, on 16 July 1260, he submitted the result of his painstaking efforts to Hojo Tokiyori.

RISSHO ANKOKU RON

The *Rissho Ankoku Ron* opens with a graphic description of the suffering Japan was then experiencing, words spoken 'in sorrow' by the Guest to his Host:

> In recent years, there are unusual disturbances in the heavens, strange occurences on earth, famine and pestilence, all affecting

every corner of the empire and spreading throughout the land. Oxen and horses lie dead in the streets, the bones of the strickened crowd the highways. Over half the population has already been carried off by death, and in every family someone grieves.

Despite the fact that Buddhist temples are offering prayers for the end of these disasters, and the government is doing what it can to help the people, the Guest notes that the situation continues to deteriorate: 'Famine and disease rage more fiercely than ever, beggars are everywhere in sight, and scenes of death fill our eyes. Cadavers pile up in mounds like observation platforms, dead bodies lie side by side like planks on a bridge.'

Clearly at a loss to understand why such things should be happening, the Guest asks his Host for an explanation. The Host's answer is direct and, for the Guest, extremely difficult to accept. 'I have pondered the matter carefully with what limited resources I possess,' he says, 'and have searched rather widely in the scriptures for an answer. The people of today all turn their back on what is right; to a man, they give their allegiance to evil.' The Host goes on to explain in some depth that erroneous – or worse still, slanderous – teachings in the realm of religion inevitably invite disaster in the external world.

For rational westerners, this idea may be hard or even impossible to swallow, and labelled as mere 'mysticism' or superstition. Before dismissing it, though, it might be well to look a little more closely at what Nichiren Daishonin means when he says, 'The people of today . . . give their allegiance to evil.'

Buddhism teaches that the quickest way to create the karma to experience suffering is to 'slander the True Law.' This point occurs in many sutras and might be said to form a cornerstone of Buddhist philosophy. Only the Lotus Sutra, however, makes it clear exactly what 'slandering the True Law' means. In strictly doctrinal terms, at that time it meant to fail to recognize the Lotus Sutra as Shakyamuni's highest teaching, the only sutra which expounds the Law by which all people can attain enlightenment, and to follow instead his earlier, provisional and incomplete teachings, which Shakyamuni himself declared should be ignored: as he states in the *Hoben* (second) chapter of the Lotus Sutra, 'honestly discarding the provisional teachings . . .' This is one reason why Nichiren Daishonin was so critical of the various Buddhist sects of his day. The Nembutsu sect in particular comes in for severe censure in the *Rissho Ankoku Ron*, not only for peddling mere escapism and encouraging apathy at a time when Buddhism should have been fortifying the will of the people to confront and overcome their sufferings through reforming their own lives; but because the sect's founder, a priest called Honen (1133-1212), had actually urged everyone to 'discard, close, ignore and abandon' all Shakyamuni's teachings except those dealing with the Pure Land of Amida Buddha. In other words, in Buddhist terms, Honen had actively encouraged his disciples to 'slander the True Law' – that is, to disregard the Lotus Sutra – even though the very sutras on which he founded his sect contain Amida Buddha's vow to save everyone 'except those who commit the five cardinal sins* or slander the True Law'.

One might be forgiven for thinking that this is all so much arcane doctrinal nit-picking, were it not for the fact that, in a number of other sutras, Shakyamuni describes in some detail the dire consequences of 'slandering the True Law'. These were later summed up as 'the Three Calamities and Seven Disasters'. The Three Calamities are high grain prices (in modern terms, inflation), warfare and pestilence. The Seven Disasters vary slightly according to different sutras, but those most often cited are disease and pestilence amongst the populace; invasion and plunder from foreign lands; revolt within one's own domain; irregularities and strange occurences amongst the stars and constellations; solar and lunar eclipses; unseasonable wind and rain; and unseasonable droughts. We shall look at these in more detail shortly.

Quoting passages from the sutras in which the Three Calamities and Seven Disasters are outlined, Nichiren Daishonin explains in the *Rissho Ankoku Ron* that the prediction of such catastrophes befalling a nation which 'slanders the True Law' is in no way metaphorical, but is a clear description of the strict law of cause and effect. That is to say, when the true teachings of Buddhism are obscured or disregarded, resulting in the life-force of the people being sapped through apathy and resignation to their fate (cause), the Three Calamities and Seven Disasters *must* appear (effect), since the people are no longer 'feeding' the protective forces of the universe with the power of their positive

---

*The five most serious offences in Buddhism. Explanations vary according to different sources, but the most well-known version is (i) killing one's father; (ii) killing one's mother; (iii) killing an *arhat*, or near-Buddha; (iv) injuring a Buddha; (v) causing disunity amongst the Buddha's disciples.

impulses. Indeed, not only are these the very calamities and disasters Japan has been experiencing for years, he argues, but those not yet to have occurred – internal revolt and foreign invasion – definitely would appear in due course if such 'slander of the True Law' in Japan continued unchecked. In purely historical terms, then, the *Rissho Ankoku Ron* represents Nichiren Daishonin's warning to Hojo Tokiyori that, unless the secular authorities stopped supporting sects based on teachings other than the Lotus Sutra, Japan would face civil war and invasion by a foreign power.

It is important to note here that Nichiren Daishonin did not demand that the Kamakura shogunate make his Buddhism the religion of the state, but simply that official sanction should be withdrawn from those sects which misled the people about the true nature of Buddhism. The people would then be able to choose freely on the basis of what each sect taught. The implication of this is that *kosen-rufu* will come about not because of the action of the state, but because many millions of people freely decide to practise Nichiren Daishonin's Buddhism. Neither does the Soka Gakkai International wish that Nichiren Shoshu Buddhism should be the religion of any state but, rather, upholds the right of all people to be entirely free in their choice of which religion to practise.

Hojo Tokiyori never replied to the *Rissho Ankoku Ron*, but its presentation to the government marked the beginning of a lifetime's persecution for Nichiren Daishonin, persecution which abated to some degree only as his predictions began to come true: of internal revolt in 1272, when there was an attempted coup within the Hojo clan and serious fighting broke out in Kyoto and Kamakura; and the prediction of foreign invasion when the Mongols under Kublai Khan attacked Japan, once in 1274 and again in 1281.

It might be objected that since the Mongols were not successful in their invasion attempts, and neither was the conspiracy to unseat the regent in 1272, Nichiren Daishonin's predictions in reality proved false. This is to view them from too short a perspective, though. The Kamakura shogunate was eventually forcibly unseated in 1333, and thereafter Japan suffered periodic bouts of bloody and bitter civil war.

The fulfilment of the predictions of foreign invasion had to wait somewhat longer, until the occupation of Japan by the Allied forces following its defeat in the Second World War, but it is not insignificant that this defeat followed what, in Buddhism terms, constituted extreme 'slander of the Law' – the attempt by the military authorities to amalgamate all Buddhist sects in Japan and incorporate in their doctrines a form of Shinto-based emperor worship. As Nichiren Daishonin commented when the Mongols were threatening Japan almost 700 years earlier:

> An invasion would be deplorable – it would mean the ruin of our country – but if it does not happen, the Japanese people will slander the Lotus Sutra more than ever and all of them will fall into the hell of incessant suffering. The nation may be devastated by the superior strength of the Mongols, but slander of Buddhism will cease almost entirely. Defeat would be like moxa cautery which cures disease or acupuncture which relieves pain. Both are painful at the moment but bring happiness later.

Seen in the light of these words, it also appears not insignificant that the spread of Nichiren Daishonin's Buddhism throughout Japan, and later the world, finally became possible after 1945 as a direct result of the establishment, at the insistence of the occupying forces, of a new constitution which included a guarantee of the freedom of religious worship for the first time in Japan's history.

What is one to make of the fundamental message of the *Rissho Ankoku Ron*, that all Japan's suffering stemmed from following the wrong religion, and how does this relate to our times? After all, history shows that every country has had its ups and downs, and that calamities and disasters have occurred in all ages in all parts of the world, regardless of what religion people might practise. In other words, are not catastrophes an unwelcome but inevitable aspect of life and, as such, something that will naturally occur from time to time, whatever one believes? How can one's beliefs affect the physical world? Moreover, how can one 'slander the True Law' if one has never read the sutras – indeed, if one is not even a Buddhist? All things considered, would it not be much easier to simply dismiss as irrational the whole idea that any link exists between so-called 'religious errors' and the events of the physical world? These are good questions and to understand the answers is not that easy. In order to do so, however, we need to dig more deeply into the concept of the Three Calamities and Seven Disasters.

The Three Calamities and Seven Disasters

As stated above, the Three Calamities and Seven Disasters overlap to a certain degree. Strictly speaking, astronomical irregularities are not disasters in themselves, but were probably classed as such because they were traditionally viewed as harbingers of bad times and therefore caused anxiety amongst the people. Given the close correspondence between these two groupings (once the disasters relating to the heavens are put to one side) let us concentrate for a moment solely on the Three Calamities.

On close examination, it soon becomes clear that the calamities of high grain prices, warfare and pestilence are sufferings occurring, respectively, in the three realms of the natural environment, living beings and the Five Components (see pp. 139-145). That is to say, Buddhism teaches that the Three Calamities are the result of disharmony in the realms of nature, human society and the self and, in effect, represent all the catastrophes that threaten the very basis of human survival. Yasuji Kirimura explains:

> First, we have the sphere of nature. From the natural environment, we draw the sustenance we need to survive. If that sustenance becomes unobtainable, our survival is imperilled. The basic material necessities that we obtain from the environment are the constituents of food, clothing and shelter. Of these, food is perhaps the most directly related to survival, and the most important food group is grains. When grains become difficult enough to obtain, we have the 'calamity of high grain prices'.
>
> Secondly, we have the sphere of society, which is composed of human beings. We human beings exist only within the context of our relationship to other human beings. This interaction should be based upon harmony and mutual assistance. However, should the basis of our interaction become one of mutual antagonism and destruction, we are faced with a grave calamity indeed. Expressed in its extreme form, it becomes the 'calamity of warfare'.
>
> Third, there is the sphere of the self. A sound body and mind are essential to fulfilment and happiness. If either body or mind should cease to function in a healthy manner, the individual will be troubled and tormented. The self cannot find fulfilment or, in extreme cases, even be sustained. This disruption or damage to the body or mind is represented as the 'calamity of pestilence'.

Indeed, it is not unusual to see the Three Calamities stalking the land at one and the same time. For example, although various parts of the African continent have always experienced periodic drought, in times of peace the people have usually been able to make provision for this lack of rainfall, storing food against expected shortages and supporting one another in a variety of ways. To put it another way, when the people are living in harmony with each other they can also live in harmony with the natural environment, as they are able to adjust to its occasional vagaries. In times of warfare, however, when the harmony amongst the people is destroyed, so is their harmony with the natural world. People are uprooted from their land, what food is available cannot be moved easily to where it is needed – if at all – and neither can plans be laid for the future when the drought will end and food production can begin again. Examples of this can be seen in Ethiopia and Mozambique, where millions of people have died through starvation and diseases which they could probably have survived if not already weakened through malnutrition, all of which ultimately stems from the wars being fought in those countries. Clearly, the Three Calamities tend to compound one another.

This is no accident, for not only do the Three Calamities correspond to the Three Realms, but also to the three poisons of greed, anger and stupidity, arising from the worlds of Hunger, Anger and Animality respectively. As Yasuji Kirimura comments, 'High grain prices, warfare and pestilence . . . occur as the outward expression of the darkness within human life.' Thus, the calamity of 'high grain prices' is caused by greed; that is to say, when the state of Hunger is strong in any society it creates fundamental distortions in the economy, driving up the material desires of the people – and with them prices – until they eventually reach a level which, for one reason or another, cannot be satisfied, at which point there is usually a crash or economic slump. If the basic cause of the slump, the inherent greed of the people, is not rectified, the whole cycle will start again as the conditions once more become favourable for economic growth.

Warfare is ultimately caused by the dominance in society of the state of Anger, the belief that one's side alone is in the right. Moreover, just as war inevitably leads to hunger, so hunger (or greed) in its extreme form can lead to war, as Jacob Bronowski notes:

It is tempting to close one's eyes to history, and instead to speculate about the roots of war in some possible animal instinct: as if, like the tiger, we still had to kill to live, or, like the robin redbreast, to defend a nesting territory. But war, organized war, is not a human instinct. It is a highly planned and cooperative form of theft.

Viewed in Buddhist terms, Bronowski understands that, although men may express the bestial aspects of their natures in war, the world of Animality is not warfare's prime motivating force, but rather greed coupled with contempt for others. The sixteenth-century Italian historian, Luigi da Porto, makes the point rather more elegantly: 'I have always heard it said that peace brings riches; riches bring pride; pride brings anger; anger brings war; war brings poverty; poverty brings humanity; humanity brings peace; peace, as I have said, brings riches, and so the world's affairs go round.'

According to Buddhism, the calamity of pestilence arises out of the stupidity or ignorance associated with Animality; in other words, because people do not know how to live correctly they naturally become ill. While this may appear quite obvious in some parts of the world – those with a poor knowledge of sanitation, for example – living 'correctly' basically means leading a balanced life, in which one is adequately nourished, not only physically but spiritually, so that one is able to exercise the good judgement that will perpetuate one's general well-being. This idea relates to the principle of *shikishin funi*, or the inseparability of mind and body.

Whatever the specific reasons for people living 'incorrectly', when this happens on a large scale the calamity of pestilence appears, even if we might not recognize it in quite those terms. For example, the single largest cause of death in the West is heart disease, which has been shown to be intimately linked both to poor diet and stress – in other words, to a failure to live correctly. Similarly, increasing alcoholism and drug addiction are calamities of pestilence arising from mental and spiritual causes. All in all, then, the net result of the three poisons of greed, anger and stupidity becoming rampant in any society is the emergence and subsequent dominance in that land of the world of Hell.

While this may not be too hard accept as an analysis of the causes of suffering over which human beings clearly have some control, more difficult to see is the relationship between human beings and natural disasters such as earthquakes. The highest teachings of Buddhism, however, perceive a connection between human activity and even these apparently random events. For example, the principle of *ichinen sanzen* discussed earlier teaches that the Ten Factors of life are common not only to the Ten Worlds, but also to the Three Realms. This means that just as the environment possesses physical appearance and unseen but equally real 'spiritual' qualities (such as perceived by poets like Wordsworth and Hardy), so it is subject to the law of cause and effect. The implication of this, in short, is that even the inanimate, objective world – the 'land' – possesses karma. The concept of *esho funi* – the inseparability of life and its environment – literally means that, at root, the karma of an individual life is identical to that of its physical environment.

We can understand this more clearly if we look again at the terms *shoho* (living self) and *eho* (its environment). One thing we notice is that both contain the word *ho*. *Ho* means the manifest effect of one's actions, or karmic reward. Its presence in both these terms means that effects of our prior actions appear both in our selves and our external circumstances. We might think of our environment as a screen upon which the effects of our karma are projected. From this viewpoint one is born into particular circumstances as a result of causes one has made in the past; the formation of one's environment thus coincides with one's emergence into the world.

In the light of the concept of *esho funi*, then, natural disasters are not punishments from on high for sinful acts, but rather the external manifestation of bad karma existing within the lives of all the individuals concerned, karma that may have been accumulating over many lifetimes. It is important to remember, however, that while we ourselves create the karma to suffer under the domination of the three poisons of greed, anger and stupidity, we can also alleviate the effects of our bad karma by resolving to make the right causes from this moment on.

Thus, when the Host – Nichiren Daishonin – states in the *Rissho Ankoku Ron* that 'The people of today all turn their backs on what is right; to a man, they give their allegiance to evil', he is trying to awaken the people of thirteenth-century Japan to an understanding that they are basing their actions on incomplete teachings which, because they fail to explain fully the workings of life, not only have no power to enable ordinary people to overcome the influence of the three poisons in their own lives, but actually exacerbate their effects. To give an analogy, if the diagnosis of an illness is wrong, the medicine prescribed to treat it may not prove simply ineffective but can cause great suffering. This can be seen, for example, in the idea that repressive force is the best way to deal with expressions of discontent in society; since it does not take into account the law of cause and effect it fails to recognize that, inevitably, repression must finally prove counter-productive.

In the broadest sense, the message of the *Rissho Ankoku Ron* is that 'wrong religions' – or shallow and incomplete philosophies of life (what Nichiren Daisonin calls 'provisional' or 'heretical' teachings) – inevitably lead to suffering of one kind or another. And when many people in society base their lives on 'provisional teachings', such suffering increases and intensifies on a rising scale. To 'slander the True Law', then, does not nowadays mean to disregard the teachings of the Lotus Sutra, but to believe that anything other than the development of one's own Buddhahood can lead to lasting and secure happiness. As Nichiren Daishonin states:

> Now in the Latter Day of the Law, neither the Lotus Sutra nor the other sutras lead to enlightenment. Only *Nam-myoho-renge-kyo* can do so. And this is not merely my own opinion. Shakyamuni, Taho and all the other Buddhas of the ten directions have so determined. To mix other practices with *Nam-myoho-renge-kyo* is a grave error.

In short, Nichiren Daishonin teaches that valuing anything above the inherent dignity of all life, as encapsulated in the Gohonzon, ultimately leads to unhappiness for individuals, injustices in society (usually stemming from bad government), and disharmony in nature.

In this context, Arnold Toynbee's comment that 'human nature abhors a religious vacuum,' appears highly significant, especially as he considers the vacuum created in the West by the recession of the traditionally established religions to have been filled 'by the rise of three other religions: the belief in the inevitibility of progress through the systematic application of science to technology; nationalism and communism.' Although blind faith in the beneficent power of science has been profoundly shaken by the destructive use of atomic power, he argues that nationalism, 'the worship of the collective power of a local human community', is today 'perhaps ninety per cent of the religion of perhaps ninety per cent of mankind.' Communism, he notes, is simply 'a Christian heresy', stressing a need for social justice more strongly than the Christian establishment, but borrowing 'Jewish and Christian mythology translated into a non-theistic vocabulary.'

While the extent to which these three forces can be defined as religions may be open to debate, there is no doubt that, as ideas which in various combinations have gripped the minds of people throughout the world, they are exerting a dominant influence on the future course of humanity. The question that needs to be asked, though, is whether these 'provisional teachings' are capable of solving the grave crisis now facing mankind or whether, indeed, they are largely responsible for creating them. For, as Daisaku Ikeda remarks in reply to Toynbee's comments above, 'Whereas the older religions [of Christianity, Buddhism and Islam] strove to control and suppress human greed, the newer ones seem to have originated – or at least to be employed – for the sake of the liberation and fulfilment of that greed. I consider this to be the basic nature of the new religions and in that nature I see the fundamental problem facing all three of them.'

In the light of the profound analysis offered by these two men, the concept of the Three Calamities and Seven Disasters, when viewed from a global perspective, seems clearly applicable to the condition in which humanity currently finds itself. Quite apart from an apparently ever-increasing toll worldwide of natural and man-made disasters – floods, droughts, fires, plane crashes, traffic accidents and so on – the calamity of 'high grain prices' could be a fitting description of a world economy which is increasingly unable to meet even the most basic demands of a vast number of the people it is ultimately supposed to serve. To the list of diseases which currently prey on human beings, the new and deadly pestilence of AIDS must now be added; while the calamity of warfare, perhaps the most unequivocal example of the continuing slander of the inherent dignity of life, certainly shows no signs of abating, with or without the presence of nuclear weapons, which in themselves threaten us with the greatest calamity of all – total destruction.

The steady growth of Nichiren Shoshu Buddhism around the world is a direct response to this seemingly inexorable decline, for those who chant *Nam-myoho-renge-kyo* have taken to heart

Nichiren Daishonin's warnings in another writing that, 'In the final analysis, unless we demonstrate that this teaching is supreme, these disasters will continue unabated.' The greatness of this Buddhism, however, lies in the knowledge that ordinary people can, indeed, demonstrate this teaching to be supreme, since it places in their hands the power necessary to start fundamentally changing themselves and their world for the better, whoever they are, wherever they are, and whatever their situation.

Rissho of *Rissho Ankoku Ron* literally means 'to establish what is true'; this means that, by basing our lives on this practice, as individuals we can begin to learn how to live 'correctly', in rhythm with the ultimate truth of life, *Nam-myoho-renge-kyo*, thus transforming the three poisons of greed, anger and stupidity in our lives into the great qualities of compassion, courage, wisdom and joy. As more and more people come to reveal their Buddha nature in this way, so *ankoku*, the peace of the land, will be secured. As we have seen from the experiences related in this book, *ankoku* is secured first in our own immediate environments – in our families and our work – but then it gradually moves out, like a series of small, overlapping ripples in a pond, to encompass an ever-widening circle of people until, finally, it embraces our world.

Of course, this process will take time and great efforts will still have to be made to achieve social, political and economic reforms. When those efforts are based on Buddhahood, though, the highest possible aspect of the human being, they will eventually lead to a time, not of no problems, but when the people, in Nichiren Daishonin's words, will have learnt 'the art of living long, fulfilling lives'. In short, they will lead to a lasting peace – and the process has already begun.

Ultimately, however, the practice of Nichiren Shoshu Buddhism is up to us alone, whilst the growth of our faith ultimately derives from the proof which we see in terms of the benefits it brings to the lives of ourselves and others. In this context, it seems fitting to end with the following words of Nichiren Daishonin:

> Therefore, I say to you, my disciples, try practising as the Lotus Sutra teaches, exerting yourselves without begrudging your lives! Test the truth of Buddhism! *Nam-myoho-renge-kyo*! *Nam-myoho-renge-kyo*!

CHRONOLOGICAL HISTORY OF THE
LIFE OF NICHIREN DAISHONIN

YEAR	Age*	EVENTS IN NICHIREN DAISHONIN'S LIFE
1222	1	February 16, born in the province of Awa and named Zennichimaro.
1233	12	Spring, enters Seicho-ji temple to study Buddhism as a disciple of Dozen-bo
1237	16†	Renamed Zesho-bo Rencho upon entering the priesthood.
1239	18	Spring, leaves for Kamakura to study Buddhism for three years.
1242	21	Spring, returns to Seicho-ji temple from Kamakura. Then leaves for Enryaku-ji temple on Mt. Hioi where he continues his studies for four years.
1246	25	Leaves Enryaku-ji temple for further study in nearby provinces.
1252	31	After studying at Onjo-ji temple, he leaves for Seicho-ji temple.
1253	32	April 28, declares the establishment of true Buddhism at Seicho-ji temple, chanting *Nam-myoho-renge-kyo* for the first time, and renames himself Nichiren.
1260	39	July 16, the first remonstration with the Kamakura government: *Rissho Ankoku Ron (On Securing the Peace of the Land through the Propagation of True Buddhism)* is submitted to Hojo Tokiyori. August 27, cottage in Matsubagayatsu is attacked by Nembutsu fanatics.
1261	40	May 12, exiled to Izu Peninsula.
1263	42	February 22, pardoned from exile, he returns to Kamakura.

*Nichiren Daishonin's age is given according to the lunar calendar.
†Some sources say eighteen.

1264	43	November 11, Komatsubara Persecution: attacked by swordsmen led by Tojo Kagenobu.
1268	47	Returns to Kamakura. October 11, writes eleven letters to government officials and high-ranking priests.
1271	50	September 10, second remonstration with Hei no Saemon. September 12, Tatsunokuchi Persecution: government tries to execute him, but fails. October 10, exiled for a second time, to Sado Island.
1274	53	February, pardoned by the government. March 13, leaves Sado for Kamakura. March 26, arrives in Kamakura. April 8, third remonstration: with Hei no Saemon. May 12 leaves Kamakura to live at the foot of Mt. Minobu.
1279	58	October 12, inscribes the Dai-Gohonzon, fulfilling his ultimate purpose in this world.
1282	61	September, writes *Document for Entrusting the Law which Nichiren Propagated throughout His Life* to Nikko. This certifies Nikko as his successor and the leader of the propagation of true Buddhism. September 8, leaves Mt. Minobu. September 18, arrives at Ikegami. October 13, dies at Ikegami.

Index